'This timely volume traces the asymmetric development of devolution in key public policy areas. An important text for students and scholars of political science and public policy.'

–*Colin Knox*, *Nazarbayev University*

'The perfect combination of clarity and detail, this book does a masterful job of covering the fundamentals of the post-devolution UK political system, its institutions and administration.'

–*David Moon*, *University of Bath*

'An excellent, informed and well-rounded comparative consideration of devolution in Scotland, Northern Ireland and Wales. This text will provide any reader with all they need to know about the contemporary situation in the devolved areas.'

–*Murray Leith*, *University of the West of Scotland*

'The devolved UK has changed markedly since 1999. Birrell, Carmichael, and Heenan have done a wonderful job in helping researchers to understand what a contemporary multi-level UK looks like.'

–*Paul Cairney*, *University of Stirling*

'This is an indispensable book for anyone interested in devolution. Comprehensive and authoritative, the volume covers the politics, parliaments and processes associated with a fundamental reshaping of the UK. A triumph.'

–*Jon Tonge*, *University of Liverpool*

'This text is brilliantly comprehensive in its analysis of the big political trends that have shaped UK devolution as well as analysing the minutiae of policy outcomes. A must-read for devolution scholars and practitioners.'

–*Sarah Ayres*, *University of Bristol*

'As someone who works within and across all four nations of the UK I consider this essential reading for understanding how we got to where we are now, and where's next.'

–*Jon Glasby*, *University of Birmingham*

Devolution in the UK

Politics, Powers and Policies

Derek Birrell, Paul Carmichael &
Deirdre Heenan

BLOOMSBURY ACADEMIC
LONDON • NEW YORK • OXFORD • NEW DELHI • SYDNEY

BLOOMSBURY ACADEMIC
Bloomsbury Publishing Plc
50 Bedford Square, London, WC1B 3DP, UK
1385 Broadway, New York, NY 10018, USA
29 Earlsfort Terrace, Dublin 2, Ireland

BLOOMSBURY, BLOOMSBURY ACADEMIC and the Diana logo
are trademarks of Bloomsbury Publishing Plc

First published in Great Britain 2023

Cover design: Eleanor Rose
Cover image © Getty Images

A catalogue record for this book is available from the British Library.

A catalog record for this book is available from the Library of Congress.

ISBN: HB: 978-1-3503-5845-4
         PB: 978-1-3503-5841-6
       ePDF: 978-1-3503-5842-3
      eBook: 978-1-3503-5843-0

Typeset by Integra Software Services Pvt. Ltd.
Printed and bound in Great Britain

To find out more about our authors and books visit www.bloomsbury.com
and sign up for our newsletters.

BRIEF CONTENTS

CONTENTS

FIGURES

TABLES

MAPS

BOXES

ACKNOWLEDGEMENTS

We would like to thank everyone who helped and supported us in writing this book. Special thanks are due to several colleagues who made comments on various chapters and to our colleagues and students on whom we tested out some of our ideas. Our appreciation goes to Rob Helm in the Welsh Government for assistance in providing local government maps and to the Institute for Government for permission to use their work in the preparation of tables and charts relating to the civil service. Particular thanks to Liz McNeill at Ulster University and especially to Colin Harper for their assistance in preparing the final manuscript. As authors, however, we must take responsibility for any errors or omissions.

ABBREVIATIONS

AME	Annually Managed Expenditure
BIC	British–Irish Council
CAP	Common Agricultural Policy
CCT	Compulsory Competitive Tendering
COBRA	Cabinet Office Briefing Rooms[A]
COSLA	Convention of Scottish Local Authorities
CPP	Community Planning Partnership
DEFRA	Department for Environment, Food and Rural Affairs
DEL	Department Expenditure Limits
DWP	Department for Work and Pensions
EU	European Union
GLA	Greater London Authority
HMRC	Her Majesty's Revenue and Customs
IBW	International Business Wales
IGS	International Government Services
IMGs	International Ministerial Groups
JEC	Joint Exchequer Committee
JMC	Joint Ministerial Committee
JMC [EU]	Joint Ministerial Committee [European Negotiations]
LAA	Local Area Agreement
LSP	Local Strategic Partnership
NDPB	Non-Departmental Public Board
NIO	Northern Ireland Office
NIAC	Northern Ireland Affairs Committee

NILGA	Northern Ireland Local Government Association
OFMDFM	Office of First Minister and Deputy First Minister
OIM	Office for the Integrated Market
ONS	Office for National Statistics
OSSS	Office of Secretary of State for Scotland
PCfW	Partnership Council for Wales
PSB	Public Service Board
Quango	Quasi-Autonomous Non-Governmental Organisation
RDA	Regional Development Agency
SCS	Sustainable Community Strategy
SNP	Scottish National Party
SRIT	Scottish Rate of Income Tax
STV	Single Transferable Vote
UK	United Kingdom
WLGA	Welsh Local Government Association

1

Introduction and preface

Over two decades have passed since the enactment of legislation setting up devolution for Scotland, Wales and Northern Ireland. New forms of governance for Scotland and Wales and the return of a form of devolution for Northern Ireland have been in operation from 1999. Devolution meant a significant shift in the overall government of the UK towards multi-level governance and away from the previous more centralized form of unitary state. The establishment of devolution did not involve a totally new blueprint for governance, and a number of historical influences shaped its planning. The UK had well-established forms of territorial decentralized administration on which to build new political institutions. Devolution legislation in 1998 was also not the first legislation at Westminster introduced to establish devolution, there having been previous Scotland and Wales Bills over a lengthy time period and different legislation and proposals addressing devolution in Northern Ireland. Important in the pathway to the 1998 legislation were the attitudes and policies of successive UK governments and the political parties involved and also the views of the respective populations, electorates and campaigning groups.

The term 'devolution' has been used with a largely settled meaning in UK discourses, but it has at times been used in a more flexible way. Devolution in the UK can be described as having four main attributes: firstly, it involves a delegation or devolution of powers from the central UK Parliament and government, particularly of legislative and executive powers. Thus, full legislative powers over government functions are transferred from the national UK government to devolved government level. Secondly, devolution is recognized as distinct from federalism, with the devolved governments subordinate in power to the UK government. Thirdly, devolution has largely developed in the context of a form of government for the three nations in the UK outside England and is thus related to the boundaries and distinct populations of Scotland, Wales and Northern Ireland. Fourthly, devolution has normally been distinct from local government, although the concept of city devolution has now appeared, used in the UK local government context.

In an examination of the scope of the term devolution, a distinction can also be drawn between three dimensions of devolution: legislative devolution, executive devolution and administrative devolution. The legislation of 1998 was to create legislative devolution for Scotland and Northern Ireland embracing all three dimensions. Originally, Wales was not given full legislative devolution but a form of executive and administrative devolution. With comprehensive legislative devolution, Scotland and Northern Ireland also encompassed extensive executive devolution. All three nations put into operation an extensive system of administrative devolution.

Support for devolution

Referendums held in 1997 and 1998 indicated public support for the devolution proposals, with a large majority in favour in Scotland, a slim majority in Wales, which was to increase in the following years, and a large majority in Northern Ireland in favour of the Good Friday Agreement, leading to the arrangements to restore devolution. The proportions supporting devolution in Scotland and Wales a few years later were mirrored by a similar proportion of people in England approving of devolution for Scotland and Wales. The introduction and implementation of devolution was facilitated by this degree of public support and by the support of the majority of political parties across the UK as a whole. This meant a high level of acceptance of the case for devolution (see Box 1.1). The main general rationales can be listed, but some would have more applicability to individual nations than others.

BOX 1.1 THE CASE FOR DEVOLUTION

- reflects local preferences in wide area of policy, giving better government
- provides capacity to be largely self-governing and invokes popular sovereignty
- improves democratic accountability
- decentralizes power and decision-making, giving access to policymaking
- improves efficiency and innovation
- original use of Barnett funding formula gives local control over wide area of expenditure
- facilitates coordination of service delivery and administration
- increases local democratic participation
- devolved governments can act as major lobbying force with UK government
- helps devolved nations' status as a political entity

- helps Scottish and Welsh identity each as a nation state
- gives legitimacy to government, particularly in Scotland, in a context where UK government may often neglect Scottish interests or be perceived to do so
- alters government of the three nations by replacing in part a UK government that does not represent them politically
- opens up new possibilities for representation, policymaking and governance
- facilitates developing relationships with foreign countries

The first ten years of devolution in each nation saw a process of establishing the institutions of devolution and making adaptations to the role of devolution in overall governance. This covered the functioning of the Scottish Parliament, Welsh Assembly Government and the Northern Ireland Assembly, the detailed work of the legislative and committee systems, the implementation of decisions by the structure of central administrations, the linkage with local government and public bodies, developing relationships with the UK government and funding arrangements with the Treasury. To an extent, a process of the routinization of devolved government took place (Bradbury and Mitchell 2005). A House of Commons report on a decade of devolution described its main focus as seeking to improve the practice of government and facilitate the efficient and effective functioning of government (House of Commons Justice Committee 2009). In each of the three nations, differences arose because of the political contexts, as the formation of coalition governments had to be negotiated in Scotland and Wales and a power-sharing system engaged with in Northern Ireland. The devolved administrations could also turn their attention to policy initiatives and a programme for government. A number of problems and potential difficulties with the smooth operation of devolution did emerge, some anticipated, some unexpected. The question of the extension of devolved powers became an area of interest and lobbying, particularly in Wales, with a desire to move to full legislative devolution and more equity in status with Scotland and Northern Ireland. This was accompanied by negotiations on the devolution of justice and policing to Northern Ireland and deliberations starting on greater fiscal and other powers for Scotland. The growth of the Scottish National Party (SNP) and its success in achieving an overall majority led to some threat to two of the tacit assumptions underlying the enactment of devolution in Scotland and Wales, namely, that it was unlikely that there could be one-party majority rule and also that devolution would dissipate the significance of nationalist demands for greater independence. Expected problems related to concerns about dealing with the West

Lothian question and the handling of England-only matters in the House of Commons and the general impact on Westminster business. Less anticipated were difficulties in producing effective mechanisms for intergovernmental relations, promoting collaboration, and an increasing focus on functions and disputes with devolved UK governments.

Approaching the second decade of devolution, it could be argued that devolution was on a linear pathway of change and adaptation, with progress made and likely to continue on the enhancement of devolved powers, and renewed efforts to sort out problem areas, particularly more effective intergovernmental cooperation. The further embedding of devolution and gradual expansion of devolved powers was not a prediction universally held; indeed, Jeffrey (2009) had referred to devolution having a trajectory that was open, the endpoint of which being unclear. In practice, a series of political and economic developments roughly over the last ten years of devolution were to have a disruptive influence on its development and stability. These major challenges can be identified as:

- The rise of the SNP leading to the referendum on Scottish independence, with the size of the vote indicating a high degree of dissatisfaction with the achievements delivered by devolution. The referendum outcome was to generate much speculation concerning the future nature and direction of devolution and the options for another future referendum presented by the SNP.
- The impact of the economic crisis and austerity agendas initiated by the coalition government and then the Conservative government's major programme of welfare reform and public expenditure cuts, leading to tensions between the devolved administrations and the UK government.
- The continuing political volatility in Northern Ireland, leading to the collapse of the Executive and Assembly for periods.
- The impact of Brexit, relating to the EU referendum and the voting patterns in Scotland, Northern Ireland and Wales; the emergence of major disputes between the Scottish and Welsh Governments and the UK government over the repatriation of powers from the EU and the impact of withdrawal from the EU; the salience of Northern Ireland issues in the Brexit negotiations and following the Protocol agreed by the UK and the EU; and tackling Covid-19 increased the awareness of the importance of devolved powers and the nature of collaboration between the UK and the devolved governments.

The study of devolution

This study of devolution aims to provide an understanding of devolution, placed in its historical, territorial, political administrative, and policy context. It covers the evolution of the devolved settlement and over the last decade the development of devolved powers, changes in party politics, the growth of fiscal devolution and also the devolved response to the crises over austerity, Brexit, Covid-19 and the cost of living.

The study of devolution has generated a number of different approaches and the use of a range of concepts (see Box 1.2). These are explained below and all are used to varying degrees in this study.

BOX 1.2 APPROACHES TO DEVOLUTION

Comparative
Asymmetrical/symmetrical
Multi-level governance
Convergence/divergence
Inter-governmental relations

In devolution, there is a strong element of analysis relating to comparative government, politics and policy studies. Comparative studies of devolved government focus not only on forms of executive government and legislative processes and systems but also on wider governance through devolved central administrations, local government, quangos and partnerships. Comparative politics tends to focus on political parties, ideologies and electoral systems while comparative policy focus has an emphasis on the policymaking process, and social and economic policy.

Evaluations and descriptions of devolution in the UK have often made a basic declaration that a key feature of devolution is its asymmetrical nature. This concept flags up the differences within the UK, especially the fact that England does not have devolution and there are differences between the systems in Scotland, Wales and Northern Ireland. This view had special salience when Wales originally had a different form of devolution. The assertions of asymmetry were widely held, and examples of such early evaluations were that 'one of the most important features of the current devolution settlement is that it is asymmetrical' (Curtice 2001: 232) and that devolution has been asymmetrical in that the nature and degree of devolution has been different in different parts of the UK (Oliver 2003). This view continued as devolution developed, for example, 'the UK's devolution development is highly asymmetrical' (Hazel and Rawlings 2005: 1) and 'the devolved government arrangements are markedly asymmetrical' (Jeffery and Wincott 2006: 3). A number of factors contributed to the durability of this perspective, including a focus on the party-political differences in each of the devolved nations, and the fact that most studies have taken a one-country approach, with relatively few detailed comparative studies. It has been argued that there was a tendency to underestimate the extent of similarities in the institutions, processes and operation of devolution (Birrell 2012). A broad view of the main institutions, structures and processes of the operation of devolution suggests a degree of similarity. This would cover: Parliament and assemblies; the legislative process, scrutiny committees, the forms of executive-led government; the use of programmes of government; the form of central administration and civil service structure; the relationship with quangos and local government; financial procedures and the Barnett formula; concordats with UK departments; the role of Secretaries of State and the territorial offices; and intergovernmental bodies and relationships. A detailed comparative analysis is necessary to establish the actual nature of similarities and differences.

The concept of multi-level governance has been used in more recent analysis as a perspective or lens through which to examine the operation of devolution. Multi-level governance refers to the different levels of government, specifically including those outside national government, at federal, devolved, regional and local levels, with a division of powers and usually geographically organized (Hooghe and Marks 2010). The EU can also be considered as a further level of governance. Scotland and Wales have functioned with four levels of government while Northern Ireland has had a fifth level of North–South cross-border bodies. The multi-level lens draws attention to the legal basis of governments, the allocation of different functions and the intergovernmental relations. An analysis of governance in Northern Ireland using the multi-level governance lens has been produced (Birrell and Gormley-Heenan 2015). Cole and Stafford (2015) draw on the frame of multi-level governance to analyse the development of Welsh devolution. The year 2017 also interprets Scotland as operating within a system of multi-level governance in contrast to the Westminster model, although in a relatively ordered system in which each level's responsibilities are relatively clear. Analysis using the multi-level governance framework also identifies what is described as MLG 2, in which decision-making and service delivery is diffused among a range of organizations (Hooghe and Marks 2010), each with a degree of autonomy in exercising governance functions. Type 2 bodies may include quangos, agencies, boards, partnerships, voluntary and private sector bodies. The multi-level governance framework has been seen as useful in studying government policy and provision, which does not easily fit into each distinct level of government. The relationship between the devolved governments and the UK government has become more important, but also more difficult and uncertain.

The position of England has continued to impact on the operation of devolution, with England having no elected form of government; therefore, Westminster acts in a double role, as the UK government and also as having responsibility, in England, for all functions devolved to Scotland, Wales and Northern Ireland. While the main focus of the book is on devolution in Scotland, Wales and Northern Ireland, most of the approaches to the study outlined earlier at times required reference to England whether for comparison, as a benchmark or as the centre of UK decision-making.

One of the earliest frameworks for the analysis of devolution to be established related to the policy outcomes and the use of a divergence–convergence spectrum. Devolution offered scope for policy innovation and differentiation. The basis for the comparison of divergence in policy is usually UK-wide or England, but comparisons can also be made between the three devolved systems. It has to be noted that some policy differences existed before devolution and could be continued or developed further. Some of the early analysis noted factors promoting convergence: the core principles of the NHS; uniform social security policy; financial influences; the UK economy; 'the EU'; the attraction of following the example of England (Keating 2002). This led to views that divergence was not as significant as expected (Mooney and Scott 2012). Overall, the devolution of much of social policy encouraged distinctive, unique policies and provision to appear (Birrell 2009). Over time, devolution did produce significant differences in public policy across the UK (Curtice 2010). Factors encouraging divergence were: party ideologies becoming dominant in devolved administrations; opposition to UK austerity agendas; the development of devolved policymaking capacity; the impact of Brexit; and addressing Covid-19. Also associated with the divergence–convergence spectrum was the role of policy copying and transfer, the role of policy networks, the development of policy communities and the emergence of distinctive policy styles.

A more recent perspective for the analysis of devolution has come through intergovernmental relations. This perspective reflects the development of the devolved governments as full governmental entities, and the need for an intergovernmental relationship with the UK government. Collaboration, overlapping powers, disputes, financial allocations, Brexit and Covid all produced a need for intergovernmental forums. Mechanisms were created for joint meetings with a varying degree of success. Cooperation between governments, departments and parliaments continued but some aspects were weakly developed and left a question concerning the most effective form of cooperation, as well as raising issues about the role of UK sovereignty under devolution, addressing Brexit and Covid has produced tensions and strains between the devolved systems and the UK government (Hunt and Minto 2017; McEwen 2017).

Structure of the book

This introductory chapter sets out the aims of the book and the conceptual frameworks used. It notes the changing political and economic context in the UK, describes the content of the book and comments on the sources used. Chapter 2 discusses the definitions of devolution and related systems and rationale for devolution and the principles used in the arrangements for devolution in the UK. This is followed by a summary of the origins of devolution and the impact of the legacy of the pre-1999 systems of governance in Scotland, Wales and Northern Ireland. In describing the background to the enactment of devolved legislation, comment is made on the levels of party-political and public support. The main elements of the devolved systems established in 1999 are set out and compared. Chapter 3 examines the key aspects of devolved powers and the principles adopted for the allocation of powers. The pressures for the enhancement and change in powers leading to a process of increased devolved powers in each nation are analysed. Particular attention is paid to the development of full legislative devolution in Wales vis-à-vis the more incremental changes to legislative devolution in Scotland and Northern Ireland. The demand for a more radical development of devolved powers for Scotland is described, leading to developments in fiscal devolution and welfare devolution. Similar proposals for fiscal devolution were to emerge in Wales. A further development was an increasing recognition of overlapping powers and areas of conflict between devolved and non-devolved matters. A political crisis was to develop over devolved powers connected to the EU Withdrawal Bill, the repatriation of EU powers and the assertion of UK sovereignty.

Chapter 4 describes the financing of devolution and related issues. The basis of Treasury funding has remained the Barnett formula, which determines the overall allocation of funding but allows devolved decision-making on the details of public expenditure. Criticisms of the formula by the devolved administration and others are examined. An account is given of the campaign for greater fiscal devolution for Scotland leading to a Scottish income tax and of the similar campaign in Wales. The nature of special funding for Northern Ireland is also noted. An analysis is made of the extent of financial subsidies to the devolved administrations and a comparison made of expenditure per capita between the four nations of the UK. The likely impact of Brexit, including the loss of EU funding, is also analysed.

Chapter 5 deals with the political parties and political systems in the devolved nations, including party support, political representation and electoral systems, participation in government and changing trends in electoral outcomes. The ideology of the political parties in the three nations is examined and in particular the salience of national identities, symbols, languages, flags and culture. The growth of nationalist parties and the impact of the forms of nationalism is examined, including the impact on the UK-wide political parties operating in Scotland and Wales. The threats to devolution from Scottish independence campaigns, deep political divisions in Northern Ireland and the emergence of England-only agendas are discussed. The formation of executive governments is analysed in terms of configurations including coalitions, forms of power-sharing and majority and minority governments. The governing principles for devolved executive government are noted, compared with each other and with the Westminster model.

Chapter 6 makes a comparison of the operation of the Scottish Parliament and the two assemblies and departures from the Westminster model. Particular attention is paid to the legislative and scrutiny procedures. This covers the legislative process, private members' bills, delegated legislation, legislative consent motions, and committee initiatives. The scrutiny role has operated through subject committees, public accounts committees and specialist committees, and their effectiveness is important in evaluating devolution. Also noted is evidence of strong commitment to participative democracy, for example, through public petitions. There is also a public significance attached to the Scottish Parliament and the assemblies in Wales and Northern Ireland.

Chapter 7 addresses the policy outcomes of devolution largely using the divergence–convergence spectrum. This involves the identification of major examples of divergence drawn from the devolved areas of health and social care, education, children's services, higher education, treatment of offenders, housing and planning, agriculture and rural policy, the environment and aspects of social security. Degrees of difference between the devolved administrations and differences with England are categorized across policies and administration structures. Discussion of the impact of the use of devolved powers is made through comparisons of programmes of government and key strategies between the four nations. Attention is also drawn to the use of performance indicators and outcome measures by the devolved administrations.

Chapter 8 examines the models of public administration that were developed to accommodate devolution. New forms of central administration developed in each administration differ in certain ways from the Whitehall model. However, the influence of UK civil service practices remained strong. The role of senior civil servants remained significant, as did the role of political advisors. Ideas discussed include: the concept of a devolved civil service, as existing in Northern Ireland; a unified public service; and joined-up public service delivery. The devolved administrations took over a large area of delegated governance operated by quangos/public bodies, which generated a major debate over the number, accountability and role of quangos. Strategies were launched, with limited success, in each jurisdiction to merge or abolish quangos. The development of devolution was marked by some major reports into public service delivery and also the promotion of participation and co-production.

Chapter 9 examines another aspect of the new relationships demanded by devolution at the more local level involving local government and partnership working. The devolved administrations inherited a highly developed, extensive system of local government in both Scotland and Wales and a more limited system in Northern Ireland. The question arose of what new form of relationship was required, and major developments took place in relation to localism through outcome service agreements, partnership working and community planning. Proposals and action on local government reform took place in all three administrations covering structures, powers, financing and performance. A major development occurred after the emergence of a City and Growth Deals strategy in England with its application to city areas in Scotland, Wales and Northern Ireland, raising some tensions with devolved governments.

Chapter 10 examines intergovernmental relationships between the devolved administrations and the UK government as an area of growing importance. A range of institutional formats exist including: the three territorial offices and the Secretaries of State; the Joint Ministerial Council (JMC) and its committees; the British–Irish Council; as well as contacts developed through quadrilateral ministerial meetings. A set of concordats and guidance covered relations in the areas of departmental cooperation, funding allocations, foreign relations and EU business. Bilateral arrangements continued more informally but joint exchequer committees developed more formally. Developments related to overlapping powers, new powers and disputes, while Brexit and Covid-19 have raised issues about the nature of intergovernmental relations.

This chapter also covers relations with the Westminster Parliament, the role of the three territorial select committees, representation on other committees, legislative consent motions and the controversial establishment of English votes for English laws (EVEL), with England-only legislation. The emergence of mechanisms for inter-parliamentary cooperation and contact are noted and assessed.

The concluding chapter analyses the performance of devolution, outlining the major differences between Scotland, Wales and Northern Ireland. Differences are noted in terms of political developments, party support, public support and sustainability. The impact of enhanced powers is assessed, as is the performance of the devolved institutions. An evaluation is made of the degrees of policy divergence and convergence and the policy achievements of devolution. Comment is made on the impact of devolution on the politics of the UK, the stability of the Union, the recognition of England-only governance and the need for sustainable intergovernmental structures. An assessment is made of the degree of threat to devolution posed by Brexit, Scottish independence, the breakdown of arrangements in Northern Ireland and more assertive actions by the UK government.

Sources of material

The main sources for this book are drawn from academic literature and from publications by government and public bodies. The academic analysis is based on books, articles in academic journals, research reports and policy analysis. A number of think tanks, research institutes and voluntary trusts, for example, the Institute for Government, have also produced significant reports. Often, this literature is specific to one nation and only a limited amount is cross-nation or comparative. The second major source is the large output of material from the devolved governments and the UK government. This category includes: government and departmental reports and strategies; official commissioned reports and inquiries; devolved administrations' programmes for government: the reports of devolved government departments; the work of subject and scrutiny committees in the Scottish Parliament and the assemblies, including public accounts/audit reports and inquiries. Also significant have been reports from UK parliamentary committees, particularly the Public Administration and Constitutional Affairs Committee, the Select Committee on the Constitution and the three territorial select committees for Scotland, Wales and Northern Ireland. The devolved institutions all have research and information units producing a range of relevant material. Probably the most important documents are major reports on inquiries into the operation of devolution or aspects of devolution, commissioned by the devolved administrations from independent sources. Relevant work has also been produced by other public bodies and local councils and representative bodies, and by voluntary organizations and private sector bodies, especially in the area of service delivery.

Terminology

The use of certain terms in discussing devolution and government in the UK can be contested as reflecting political opinions and there may be differences in usage. For purposes of clarity in this book, the following can be noted. The term 'UK' refers to England, Scotland, Wales and Northern Ireland, and the term 'UK government' is used in preference to British government or national government. The term 'Great Britain' refers to England, Scotland and Wales. The terms 'Northern Ireland' and 'the Republic of Ireland' are used except where a direct quote with other words is used. The book also uses the terms Scottish governance, Welsh governance, Northern Ireland Executive and, at times, the Irish government. The term 'nations' is usually used to refer to Scotland, Wales and Northern Ireland. The terms 'devolved governments' and 'devolved administrations' cover all three nations. The term 'devolved Parliament and assemblies' is sometimes used historically to refer to the Scottish Parliament, the National Assembly for Wales and the Northern Ireland Assembly. In May 2020 the National Assembly for Wales was renamed Senedd Cymru, when section 2 of the Senedd and Elections (Wales) Act 2020 came into force.

2

The meaning and foundation
of devolution

Introduction

This chapter examines the meaning of devolution mainly within the UK context and its historical uses within Scotland, Wales and Northern Ireland. Attention is drawn to the distinction between devolution and federalism in the wider conceptual context. The development of devolution as a concept of governance in the UK led to the identification of differences between legislative, executive and administrative devolution. These differences became important as proposals emerged for devolution in Scotland and Wales and reforming devolution in Northern Ireland. Debates on devolution involved considerations of the scope and nature of territorial and regional decentralization, including in England. Defining devolution also raised issues relating to the development of increased powers for local government as existed in the UK and the language of city devolution and devolution deals. Scotland also produced a particular debate on differences between greater devolution or devolution max and forms of independence. The move to devolution for Scotland and Wales marked a radical departure from the historical pattern of a highly centralized and unitary British state. Devolution, however, developed from key backward factors: a historical model of devolution in Northern Ireland since 1921; established patterns of devolved administrative arrangements: the acknowledgement of the composition if the UK from distinct (Burnham and Horton 2013) and also increasing demands from political parties and the public for devolution.

The move to devolution for England and Wales marked a radical departure from the historical pattern of a highly centralized and unitary British state. Devolution developed against a background of key factors, including: an existing Northern Ireland model of devolution established in 1921; an existing pattern of devolved administrative arrangements acknowledging the composition of the UK from distinct nations and provinces (Burnham and Horton 2013); and also increasing demands from political parties and the public for devolution.

The meaning of devolution

Devolution has no internationally agreed definition or meaning in political science in the way that federalism has. Devolution is often seen as having some similarities to federalism and both indicate forms of governance occupying the space between national government and local government. Thus, international literature may refer to regional government or sub-state government rather than devolved government. The term devolution has developed in the UK since the 1960s with particular application to Northern Ireland, Scotland and Wales, and with a fairly clear meaning. Bogdanor (2001: 2) expresses this meaning as 'the transfer to a subordinate elected body, on a geographical basis, of functions at present exercised by ministers and parliament'. This emphasizes a key characteristic of devolved institutions as subordinate in position to UK central government and created by parliament through ordinary legislation. Overall, the supremacy of parliament has remained intact, and it is constitutionally empowered to legislate on any matter for Scotland, Wales and Northern Ireland. This power is constrained by the adoption of certain political conventions but led to debate on how devolution has implications for the exercise of UK sovereignty. A convention was originally established that UK government would not legislate on devolved matters without the consent of the devolved governments. However, this was to be formalized in the Sewel Convention through which the devolved governments could consent to Westminster legislation. While this has proved useful it had the potential to weaken devolution and give rise to future difficulties. Questions arose, particularly in Scotland, concerning the sovereign right of the people of Scotland to determine their form of government. The Scotland Act 2016 put in statute the permanence of the Scottish Parliament and Government and a clause that it could not be abolished without a referendum of the people of Scotland. Similarly, the Wales Act 2017 had a clause stating that the Welsh Government and Assembly were a permanent part of the UK constitutional arrangements and could not be abolished except on the basis of a referendum. This does give rise to a question of the compatibility of these provisions with UK parliamentary sovereignty.

Devolution is most often contrasted with federalism as a form of sub-state government based on recognizable territorial differences. Federal states are often defined as having the characteristics of operating in very large countries with clear geographical boundaries, for example, Australia and Canada, and/or reflecting or accommodating ethnic or linguistic divisions, for example, Switzerland (Requejo 2005). As with devolution, there is in federalism a division of powers between the national government and the federal states or provinces. A distinction with devolution is often made in that, in a federal system, sovereignty is shared so that the sub-states are seen as coordinate in power with the national government; thus, the constituent levels are not subordinate to each other. In the UK, supreme law-making power lies in the hands of the central legislature, emphasizing the subordinate position of devolved states and marking how devolution differs from federalism (Tierney 2009). Federal systems also usually have a written constitution, which makes their federal status more rigid and difficult to alter, in contrast with the ease with which UK devolution can be altered by an ordinary Act of Parliament. Over time, this distinction based on coordinate status in federal systems became less sustainable with the growth in national government powers and political realities. Attention turned more to patterns of intervention and control of resources and the interplay and relationship between tiers of government (Enderlein et al. 2010). A clear distinction between devolution and federalism and other forms of regional government became more unsustainable. Alternative ways of measuring the scope of regional autonomy have been suggested, for example, through measuring a number of dimensions related to the degree of self-rule, policy scope, capacity to tax, independence of an executive and legislature (Hooghe and Marks 2010). Thus, it has been suggested that both devolution and federalism have been replaced by more interactive and interdependent models (McHarg and Mitchell 2017) as part of systems of multi-level governance.

As proposals for devolution developed through the 1970s to the 1990s, a distinction was made between three forms of devolution. This distinction between legislative devolution, executive devolution and administrative devolution was discussed in detail in the Kilbrandon Royal Commission on the Constitution (1973). Legislative devolution was the most advanced form of devolution, in which extensive powers for primary legislation with resources and administrative machinery is transferred to a devolved government and legislature. Executive devolution meant that the central government would be responsible for the framework of legislation but, for major areas of policy, would transfer to elected assemblies powers within the framework to execute and amend the policies, administer and fund them. The third form is administrative devolution, which has been usually interpreted as meaning the carrying out of central government functions in a distinct geographical setting and ascribed to the operation of the Scottish and Welsh Offices pre-1998. In the event of legislative or executive devolution, there is also administrative devolution, that is, the administration of devolved functions transferred from central government. In one sense, a model of administrative devolution only would suggest a devolved assembly or executive with powers only over administration. The relevance of differences in forms of devolution was to become apparent in the 1998 legislation that conferred legislative devolution on Scotland

and Northern Ireland but only a form of executive devolution on Wales. With legislative devolution, Scotland and Northern Ireland would also have devolved extensive executive functions. The weaker form of devolution for Wales was later to be reformed and enhanced and brought more into line with the models in Scotland and Northern Ireland.

Local decentralization or devolution?

Decentralization has been used in UK governance mainly to refer to administrative decentralization from the UK central government in London and, in its simplest form, to local offices of Whitehall departments delivering services. Decentralization has also been associated with the growth of regional forms of governance and administration in England. In 1994, the Conservative government set up Government Offices (GOs) for the regions to integrate several government functions being implemented in each region, and they were expanded to include coordination of government policy across departments. This was followed by a decision by a Labour government to establish eight Regional Development Agencies (RDAs) to carry out economic development, seen as perhaps the most significant devolution in regional governance in England (Smith and Wistrich 2014). Their functions were extended to cover tourism, transport and rural development. The performance of GOs and RDAs was seen as patchy (Tomaney 2000). New Labour continued with a form of more devolved regional decentralization to promote policy integration and strategic planning. An element of fiscal decentralization was added through Regional Funding Allocations to better coordinate investment at the sub-national level. Ayres and Stafford (2014) identified a differential pattern of responses across Whitehall departments to decentralization, despite these more flexible allocations exerting a positive influence.

The development of regional decentralization had no strong regional political or elected dimension with the exception of the Labour government exploring the idea of elected assemblies for the regions (Ayres and Stafford 2014: 48). This would be a form of regional devolution based on RDAs and voluntary local assemblies with very little power. In England, the idea of a directly elected assembly was put to a referendum in 2004 for the North-East of England, but only 22 per cent of the vote favoured the proposal, and planning for elected assemblies stopped. This seemed to rule out any future form of devolution for England. Moves towards elected regional assemblies for England progressed at a snail's pace (Sandford and Hetherington 2005). Proposals for regional government in England were not comparable to the devolution of political power in the UK and the coalition of government 2010 marked the end of such propositions (Smith and Wistrich 2014: 102). The localism agenda was to lead to the UK government adopting a new policy of City Deals or devolution deals in city regions, many not dissimilar to the metropolitan county councils abolished in 1986. This was based on an earlier idea of allowing local councils to form a combined authority to promote planning, transport and the environment. In a radical approach, the coalition government elected in 2010 announced plans to dismantle the regional administrative tier in England including the RDAs and regional GOs and leave in place more localist approaches. This was part of the coalition's emphasis on a deregulatory approach (Bochel and Powell 2016).

In 2014, the Chancellor of the Exchequer signalled the start of a new devolution programme aimed at devolving powers and budgets to cities in the north of England (Randall and Casebourne 2016). The use of the term devolution was continued in an enabling bill, the Cities and Local Government Devolution Bill 2016. The strategy was seen as a devolution revolution, transferring powers and opportunities to local government through a series of bespoke devolution deals (House of Commons Communities and Local Government Committee 2016). The first City Deals were in the eight largest cities in England, followed by negotiations with some twenty others (Ward 2020). The first area outside England was Glasgow and Clyde Valley, involving eight local authorities, followed by other Scottish and Welsh examples, plus two in Northern Ireland in 2019 and 2020. In the devolved administrations, the City Deals meant funding by the Treasury, by the devolved governments, funding and borrowing by the local authorities and the anticipated contribution of private finance. City devolution related to contracted projects in transport, skills and innovation, road schemes, housing, business, apprenticeships and higher education. The term 'devolution for England' has been widely used to describe the new arrangements for City Deals in government publications and other bodies (Hammond 2015). A House of Commons Communities and Local Government Committee report on City Deals was entitled *Devolution: The Next Five Years and Beyond*.

The Local Government Association (2015) referred to all the nations of the UK being at different points on the path towards devolution, including England. English devolution has been seen as giving sub-regional areas substantial responsibilities and powers. These governance arrangements, however, differ considerably from the legislative devolution enacted for Scotland, Wales and Northern Ireland in terms of primary legislative powers, parliamentary systems, a civil service, financial procedures and control over public bodies and local councils. It is more appropriate to define City Deal arrangements or devolution deals as forms of partnerships led by councils. A study by Ayres et al. (2018) concluded that a devolution revolution had not occurred in England and a central autonomy model remains the dominant mode of statecraft. It can be misleading to frame City Deals in the language of devolution.

The UK also has an example of a more unique form of decentralized city governance through the operation of the Greater London Authority (GLA) with a directly elected mayor and elected scrutiny assembly. Set up as a Tony Blair initiative, the post of mayor originally had only strategic powers over transport, the police and fire services, but after 2007, additional powers were added relating to waste, planning, culture, housing and land-holding. The twenty-five-member assembly holds public question times and can conduct its own inquiries. The GLA structure is separate from the London boroughs, which deliver most local government services. There have been some doubts about the model, relating to limited policy powers, little control over finance and the effectiveness of scrutiny (House of Commons Communities and Local Government Committee 2016); nonetheless, it can be viewed as England's only elected regional body.

To complete an examination of the meaning of devolution in relation to other forms of governance in the UK context it is useful to note the status of Guernsey, Jersey and the Isle of Man. The islands are constitutionally Crown Dependencies with their own parliaments and governments and fiscal autonomy. They are self-governing and not part of the UK, but the UK is responsible for their external relations and provides for their defence. In comparison to the devolved governments and the UK government, their governance arrangements are unique and do not fall within the usual meaning of federalism, devolution or decentralization. The status of these unique jurisdictions was given a boost by their full membership of the British–Irish Council established after the Good Friday Agreement.

Legacy of territorial administration

When the architecture of devolution was created there was a pre-existing basis of decentralized administration in place in Scotland, Wales and Northern Ireland on which to develop new devolved political institutions. It is therefore important to appreciate the continuities from the pre-devolution arrangements (Mitchell 2009). Territorial administration took the form, eventually, of a Scottish Office, Welsh Office and Northern Ireland Office with Secretaries of State as ministerial posts.

The Scottish Office dates back to 1885 and the Secretary of State to 1926. The underlying principle was that it brought together a range of UK government services in the Scottish Office. The functions were to increase substantially with the creation of the post-war welfare state. By the 1960s, the Scottish Office had five main departments – agriculture, education, health, development and a Scottish home department. Policy discretion was limited, and political, financial and administrative pressures meant Whitehall priorities were closely followed (Bogdanor 1999: 114). The Scottish Office and its ministers remained accountable solely to Westminster and Whitehall.

The Welsh Office, in contrast, dates from 1964 and was the result of a long process of pressure for creating Welsh administrative machinery (Mitchell 2009: 54). The original responsibilities covered functions in housing, planning and local government, which were followed by health and tourism and, in 1970, by education and childcare, with a steady accumulation of functions continuing into the 1980s. The increase in functions of the UK state in the twentieth century had seen, as in Scotland, the emergence of a distinctive form of devolved territorial administration in Wales. (NB This refers to pre-1999. In 1999 powers were transferred to the National Assembly for Wales and the Office for the Secretary of State for Scotland.)

Northern Ireland differed in having a legacy of political devolution that existed between 1921 and 1972, with its own parliament and cabinet and structure of central government departments. Significantly, since the foundation of the state, it had its own civil service independent of the UK (Home) Civil Service. The Home Office in London was responsible for Northern Ireland matters in the UK government but it was the imposition of direct rule from Westminster in 1972 that led directly to the establishment of a new Northern Ireland Office and the post of Secretary of State for Northern Ireland, modelled on the existing Scottish and Welsh offices (Birrell 2009). The Northern Ireland departments, modelled closely on Whitehall, continued to function during direct rule and by 1998 there were six departments: finance, economic development, agriculture, education, health and social services and the environment, plus a central secretariat. These were directly accountable to the Secretary of State and headed by ministers from the Northern Ireland Office, located in Belfast and London. A central administration was thus in place for a new devolved executive to fit into. Unlike their Scottish and Welsh counterparts, the Northern Ireland Office continued after 1999.

Views of UK government and political parties on devolution

The establishment of devolution reflected, in the end, decisions by the UK government in office and thus by the political parties. It was the development of a more positive response by UK governments and parties to devolution, especially for Scotland, in the late 1960s that led to change. The Labour Party under Harold Wilson moved towards a position of exploring further commitment to Scotland and Wales. This was in part a response to the growing electoral threat to Labour in Scotland from the Scottish National Party from 1967 onwards – to the issue of Scottish oil revenues (Mitchell 2009: 28) contributing to a new Scottish question becoming central in UK politics (Devine 2017). The Labour Party remained divided, with devolution regarded by a section of the party as presenting an obstacle to achieving socialism throughout Britain. The Conservative Party had also made a response by setting up a Scottish constitutional commission. The outcome, in 1964, was a decision made by Labour and continued by the Conservative government: the setting up of a Royal Commission to consider the whole issue of unitary government and federalism. The Kilbrandon Commission published majority and minority reports in 1973, including a number of options for dealing with Scotland and Wales (Kilbrandon 1973). A form of legislative devolution was proposed for Scotland, although it recommended that only prescribed functions would be transferred. With the Labour Party in power in 1974, the government committed to Scottish devolution. It was suggested, however, that this was symbolically expedient, with little thought given to its public policy implications (Mitchell 2009: 118).

Kilbrandon's main proposal for Wales, supported by just six members, was for a legislative assembly with fewer powers than Scotland, more akin to the powers of the Welsh Office. Kilbrandon took evidence on what lessons could be learned from Northern Ireland's experience of devolution but, given the ongoing discussions on constitutional change, he did not formulate recommendations for the region. With somewhat unclear messages from Kilbrandon, the UK government published a Devolution Bill in 1976. There was originally a single bill, but this 'shaky devolution alliance' had fallen over a guillotine motion, and all progress came to an end (Deacon 2006). With the Callaghan government in a minority position, it was a Liberal–Labour Party pact that led to an agreement to introduce a new devolution measure. There were separate bills for Scotland and Wales, and the requirement for a referendum was a concession to anti-devolutionists. An amendment by an anti-devolution MP George Cunningham, a Labour backbencher, was passed that stipulated that, if a 'yes' vote of less than 40 per cent of the electorate happened, then a motion to repeal the devolution bill had to be laid. The referendum vote in Scotland in March 1979 did not reach this. The 51.6 per cent yes vote represented just 32.9 per cent of the electorate (Deacon 2006: 80). A government attempt to vote down the repeal motion failed, leading to a vote of no confidence and the resignation of James Callaghan. With the incoming prime minister, Margaret Thatcher, a strong opponent of devolution, the prospects for devolution seemed bleak.

Public opinion

The growth of electoral support for the SNP and Plaid Cymru in the 1960s and 1970s was taken as indicating a growth in favour of some form of devolution, or at least for political institutions to give expression to nationalist ambitions. In Scotland, there was a view that the Scottish Office had not used its opportunities to increase expenditure on services for which it was responsible, although it was also suggested that many people were unaware of the role of the Scottish Office. The treatment of Wales by Westminster was also the subject of much criticism. The Kilbrandon Report had not produced a wide debate in either nation. It is doubtful whether devolution would have assumed as prominent a place on the political agenda of the UK without the

TABLE 2.1 *SNP and General Elections 1974–9*

Date	Vote %	MPs
28.2.74	21.9	7
10.10.74	30.4	11
3.5.79	17.3	2

Source: Cairney (2011: 25).

growing electoral success of the nationalist parties. In the October general election of 1974, the SNP won eleven seats (see Table 2.1). Yet the referendum results in 1979 showed limited appeal for the devolution agenda. In Scotland, 51.6 per cent voted 'yes' and 48.4 per cent 'no'. In Scotland, the referendum campaign was influenced by deep inter-party and intra-party divisions (Lynch 2001: 10), particularly in the Labour Party (Devine 2017: 132), exacerbated by the confused Kilbrandon message. In Wales, the 'no' vote was 80 per cent and the 'yes' vote only 20 per cent, and no county in Wales voted 'yes'. As Deacon (2006: 81) notes, the issue of devolution in Wales seemed truly dead, and the Wales Act was repealed in the House of Commons. Following the 1979 election devolution fell down the political agenda, until the UK's modern system emerged in the 1990s (Cairney 2011: 21).

Legacy of legislation

The detailed proposals in the Scotland and Wales Acts provided a legacy that was to have a major influence when new devolution legislation was being prepared for 1998. These included the principle of an elected assembly, a division of powers between transferred and non-transferred matters, funding arrangements and the retention of Westminster sovereignty. The basic mechanics of the system of legislative devolution for Scotland were broadly similar to the Northern Ireland system, originally drawn up in the Government of Ireland Act 1920 but revised and updated in the Northern Ireland Constitution Act 1973, drawn up to provide a basis for restoring devolution after the introduction of direct rule. It has been argued that the Scotland and Wales Acts, in some proposals, overlooked some of the relevant lessons from the Northern Ireland experience (Birrell 1978). Some of the 1978 legislative proposals were to be changed by 1998 Acts, including the 'first past the post' electoral system, the powers of the Secretary of State and the delineation of the powers of the Scottish Assembly. Another very significant legacy of the 1978 proposals was the principle of different schemes for Scotland and Wales. The legislation for Wales was less comprehensive than for Scotland, setting out a scheme for devolution focused on executive powers rather than legislative powers.

Revitalizing devolution

The year 1979 appeared to mark the end of progress towards devolution, yet less than twenty years later three major Acts were passed introducing devolution in Scotland, Wales and Northern Ireland. Deacon (2006: 84) states that when Margaret Thatcher arrived in Downing Street in 1979, it appeared as though devolution for Scotland was dead and that the possibility of devolution was buried for ever in Wales. In Northern Ireland, attempts to create a form of devolved government acceptable to the political parties were still unsuccessful. What happened to produce a major change? In Scotland, a series of influences came together (Cameron 2008: 136). Conservative fortunes in Scotland faded badly, with hostile reaction to what was widely perceived as unfair treatment of Scotland with the closure of mines, shipbuilding and steel works, the continuing issue of ownership of North Sea oil, and the decision to experiment with the poll tax first in Scotland in 1989. Devine (2017: 170) suggests that Thatcher undermined the balanced partnership between Scotland and England within the Union and the hostility her policy engendered guaranteed the creation of a Scottish Parliament (Devine 2017: 182).

The question of legitimacy of government was important in Scotland in the years of Conservative rule, with the low level of support in Scotland leading to questions about the lack of a mandate and consent in Scotland. The SNP made ground with its alternative separatist agenda, leaving the Labour Party to work out its position on devolution after 1979. By 1983, it had committed itself to supporting the idea of a Scottish Assembly or Parliament, including one with revenue-raising powers (Mitchell 2009: 124). In the 1990s, a change also occurred with the Labour leaders John Smith and Gordon Brown giving strong support to devolution. Pro-devolution lobbying groups had also mobilized, leading to the establishment of a Scottish Constitutional Convention in 1989 representing groups, churches, trade unions, local authorities and politicians, although the SNP and Conservatives did not take part. The Constitutional Convention gave a role to civil society in advancing devolution (Keating 2005: 15) and pressed for a 129-member Scottish Parliament elected in part on a proportional representation (PR) basis. The Constitutional Convention was seen as playing a significant role in giving a legitimizing role to the pro-devolution lobby and establishing a nascent 'yes' campaign (Lynch 2001: 12). The work of the Convention was viewed as making it difficult for a future Labour government to deny devolution (Devine 2017: 195).

In Wales, two rather similar factors were in operation during the same period. The Conservative government became intensely unpopular against the backdrop of a decline in mining and steel production and the miners' strike, with accusations of de-industrialization and lack of investment. The Labour Party leadership was initially reluctant to give priority to a form of devolution. Plaid Cymru had limited support, and the close institutional links between Wales and England did not lead to the same popular expression of support for devolution as in Scotland. It was not until 1992 that devolution appeared as a Labour Party goal; the following year, the party produced a report, *The Welsh Assembly: The Way Forward*, with the promise of legislation if in office. The 1997 general election resulted in a Labour landslide and Tony Blair took office with the promise of action to introduce devolution. The Blair government decided that it would seek pre-legislation mandates from Scotland and Wales with a simple majority required. Blair's role in bringing about devolution is often overlooked, but at the time his devolutionary programme aligned with New Labour commitments to challenging the centralist state and promoting ideas of a more participative and stakeholder democracy (Driver and Martell 2002).

Constitutional proposals for a new form of devolved governance for Northern Ireland appeared not long after the imposition of direct rule. The Northern Ireland Assembly Act 1973 simply provided for the election of a seventy-eight-member assembly, but the Northern Ireland Constitution Act 1973 was more complex. The proposed division of powers was similar to the 1920s Government of Ireland Act, except that justice and policing were reserved to the UK government and the 1973 Act was to become very similar to the 1998 Act for Northern Ireland. The new and controversial clauses in 1973 related to the requirement that the devolution of legislative and executive power could only take place if a Northern Ireland Executive had widespread acceptance throughout the community. Apart from a devolved elected Assembly, from this point on, any settlement would have to have an Irish dimension and a British–Irish arrangement (Tonge 2005). This planned Assembly and Executive never got off the ground due to the hostility of a loyalist coalition to power-sharing and the idea of a Council of Ireland, and the constitutional provisions were suspended. The UK government set about planning a new initiative to restore devolution while direct rule continued but with the devolved administrative structure of Northern Ireland departments remaining in operation. The outcome was an Act of 1982 setting out a process of devolution by gradual stages. The Act provided for a seventy-eight-member assembly whose main task was to report on forming a new devolved administration (Birrell 2009: 11). This Assembly did make a report; however, the unionist parties withdrew in protest at the Anglo-Irish Agreement drawn up by the British and Irish governments in 1985 and in 1986, the Assembly was dissolved.

In this period, both the Conservative and Labour parties were in agreement about continuing to give primacy to finding a workable devolution strategy (Cunningham 2001). Also in this period, the Anglo-Irish Agreement led to the closer involvement of the Irish government. A major political initiative came with the Downing Street Declaration of 1993, which stated that both governments undertook to create comprehensive structures that would return power to the people of Northern Ireland on an agreed basis. A Joint Framework document set out the three key themes of internal political institutions. Assisted by paramilitary ceasefires, this led directly to negotiations with the two governments and the political parties except for the Democratic Unionist Party (DUP). The negotiations led to a formal agreement, the Good Friday or Belfast Agreement. The Agreement covered a constitutional guarantee, North–South cooperation and British–Irish coordination and other issues. However, the main focus was on strand one, new devolved arrangements for Northern Ireland, to be enacted through a Northern Ireland Act 1998 and ending over a quarter of a century of suspended devolution. In practice, the 1998 Act was completely moulded by the 1973 Northern Ireland Constitution Act (Hadfield 2001).

The devolved legislation 1998

Thus, in 1998, the three Acts – the Scotland Act, the Government of Wales Act and the Northern Ireland Act – established new forms of devolved government in a historic constitutional change. Public referendums were held in each nation to provide legitimacy for the government in bringing forward legislation. Scotland displayed very strong support for devolution, with 74.3 per cent voting 'yes' with the SNP and Labour Party working together. In Scotland, 63.5 per cent also voted for the Scottish parliament having tax-raising powers. The vote for a more limited form of devolution in Wales, with 50.3 per cent voting 'yes' on a turn-out of only 50.1 per cent, reflected less support for nationalist principles and fears of the costs and extra bureaucracy. In Northern Ireland, there was strong support for the Good Friday Agreement, with 71.1 per cent in favour on a high turn-out of 81.1 per cent, which gave a clear mandate for a power-sharing devolved government (see Table 2.2). Devolution had arrived in all three nations at a similar starting date after a lengthy political process and pathway. At this time, the units of devolution were clearly seen as subordinate and financially dependent on UK central government (McEwan 2017). The immediate focus of analysis at this time was on the asymmetrical nature of devolution, including not only differences on governance between Scotland, Wales and Northern Ireland but also with England; also seen as significant were the inter-party differences in devolved systems. Less

TABLE 2.2 *Devolution Referendum 1997–8*

Country	Date	Yes	No	Turn-out %
Scotland	1997	74.3	25.7	60.1
Wales	1997	50.3	49.7	50.1
N. Ireland	1998	71.3	28.9	81.1

attention was paid to the impact of devolution on the UK government and Parliament on inter-governmental relations, and a lack of a vision for the future direction and development of devolution within the Union. Having accomplished the establishment of devolution, it was suggested a UK government view was to leave them to get on with it, unless forced to react to any problems (House of Commons Justice Committee 2009: para. 7).

The forms of devolution implemented in 1999 had a configuration of legislative, executive and administrative processes. Devolution was set up and defined by Westminster legislation and any major change would require Westminster legislation. Devolution would exist within the UK national government and as a tier of governance between the UK government and the extensive system of local government. While this represented an innovation in governance, it still drew on existing foundations, the Stormont system of devolution, and territorial decentralization in Scotland and Wales. At the same time, the emergence of devolution contributed to a shift in the UK in the direction of multi-level governance. It was accepted that the forms of devolution, although having similar aspects, created an overall asymmetric system. This applied most clearly to the position of England. The original debates on devolution prior to the 1998 legislation did not pay much attention to relationships with England. The constitutional developments took place in a context of political party positioning on devolution at UK level and within each nation. Also important was the degree of public support expressed in various elections. Finally critical was the outcome of UK government acceptance of the electorate's views and an early supportive attitude of letting devolution work.

3

The growth of devolved powers

Introduction

At the time of the drawing up of the devolution legislation of 1998, there was a surprising lack of analysis of the principles to be used to determine what criteria should be adopted to identify what would be devolved and what not devolved. In relation to the 1998 provision for each nation, historical and territorial office functions had a significant role in influencing what was devolved. In the case of Northern Ireland, it was the legacy from the 1920 legislation, as amended in 1973. For Scotland and Wales, the range of devolved matters reflected closely the functions of the Scottish and Welsh Offices pre-1968.

The existence of devolution has been marked by a largely continuous debate over the extension of devolved powers and a continuous process of expansion, which, at intervals, required legislative intervention from the UK Parliament. The pathway for an increase in devolved powers differed between the three nations. In Scotland, an originally more gradual progression towards more powers became much accelerated after the referendum on independence and the development of ambitions of maximum devolution, popularly referred to as devo-max. In Wales, the process was dramatic, with a pathway from originally no primary legislative power to an enhanced scheme and subsequently towards more comprehensive legislative devolution, through a process involving a convention, a referendum and major UK legislation. In Northern Ireland, where devolution recommenced in 1999 with the greatest range of devolved powers, there was a more limited focus on additional potential powers.

It is possible to describe the process in each nation in relation to the development of devolved powers in its political, policy and legislative context and then subsequently discuss the main issues that arose, covering not only the reserved versus conferred models question and the basis for determining what should be devolved but other issues. These included jagged edges and disputes over powers between the devolved and UK governments;

overlapping powers and cooperation; the use of legislative consent motions; the use of judicial review; and growing controversy especially post-Brexit over UK government interventions on devolved matters.

Reserved and conferred models

The models used for the allocation of powers have been either the reserved model or the conferred model. The reserved model has applied to both Scotland and Northern Ireland since the 1998 Acts, under which all matters not explicitly reserved to Westminster are within the competence of the devolved body. Northern Ireland had two categories of non-devolved matters, excepted and reserved, while Scotland had only the reserved list. The major post-devolution debate and change occurred in Wales, which had, since 1998, a conferred powers model that limited devolved competences to those specified in statute. It took twenty years for the move to a reserved model to be completed in Wales. Welsh governments found it difficult to draft a reserved powers model simply by inferring it from what is devolved in the conferred model. While Wales had the reserved models from Scotland and Northern Ireland to follow, this was not a complete guide as Wales did not move to a separate legal system akin to Scotland and Northern Ireland. A reserved model seemed simpler to implement with a distinct and separate legal jurisdiction. Apart from the political will, the well-established historical and wide-ranging integration of laws covering England and Wales presented an obstacle to a comprehensive reserved model. The separate legal jurisdictions in Scotland and Northern Ireland, however, had not thrown up any fundamental barrier to the operation of the reserved model. Using the reserved model was believed to be easier to understand, more workable in practice, and more robust. The number of referrals to the Supreme Court related to interpretations of the Welsh Assembly powers suggested that judicial review was more likely under the conferred model. The reserved model created more certainty about what is devolved, less confusion over matters that were not listed, and improved accountability. There was a suggestion that the reserved model was more appropriate to devolution as it involved not just treating devolved powers as exceptions to an English-driven norm (Wyn Jones and Hazell 2015). The UK government had to justify why matters were reserved, not why subjects should be devolved. A reserved powers model appeared to offer more certainty at the margin.

Two principles are of key importance in analysing devolved powers. Firstly, the model for the statutory distribution of powers between the devolved administration and the UK government. For Scotland and Northern Ireland, a reserved powers model was used in which the powers reserved to the devolved governments were set out in the legislation and everything else is assumed to be a devolved matter. While Scotland had a single list of reserved matters (Table 3.1), the Northern Ireland Act had

TABLE 3.1 *1998 Act, reserved model allocation of powers – Scotland*

Main reserved powers	Main excepted powers	Main devolved powers
Constitution, Crown	Constitution, Crown	Health
Foreign relations	Foreign relations	Education
Defence	Defence	Social care
Civil Service	Immigration, nationality	Housing and asylum
Fiscal, economic and	Elections	Higher education monetary policy
Employment, industry	National security	Skills and training related
Social security (non-devolved)	Nuclear energy	Planning
Financial services	UK-wide taxation	Policing
Currency	Currency	Fire and rescue
Misuse of drugs	National insurance	Civil and criminal law
Health and safety	Intellectual property	Environment
Data protection		Agriculture, forestry and fisheries
Immigration and nationality		Transport
Intellectual property		Economic development
National security, emergency powers		Sport
Betting gaming and lotteries		Arts
Trade and industry		Income tax variation
Import and export control		Prisons
Consumer protection		Tourism and heritage
Equal opportunities		
Product standards, safety and liability		
Telecommunications broadcasting		
Postal services		
Electricity, oil and gas, coal, nuclear		
energy, energy conservation		
Road transport, rail, marine, air transport		
Abortion, genetics, surrogacy		

two categories, reserved and excepted matters. The distinction allowed reserved powers to be devolved in future by an Order in Council whereas excepted powers could not be devolved, although the distinction actually goes back to the political context of the 1920s Government of Ireland Act. In Wales, a different model was used, the conferred model, in which the legislation set out a list of devolved powers with all other matters reserved to the UK government. Thus, the Government of Wales Act (1998) sets out the subjects devolved to the Assembly along with exceptions within these powers for which the UK government was still responsible.

The second important principle in analysing devolved powers is the basis for distinguishing between devolved and non-devolved matters. The original basis for the decisions in the 1998 Acts did not appear to be determined by any major analysis or discussion on what should and should not be devolved. The principles originally recommended by the Kilbrandon Commission (1973: 337) were largely those used. The matters transferred to the Scottish and Welsh Assemblies were described as those for which the Secretaries of State for Scotland and Wales had responsibility. Devolved matters for Northern Ireland largely simply followed the historical precedents of the 1920 Act and the 1973 Northern Ireland Constitution Act, and overall were not dissimilar to the Scottish scheme.

The growth in Scotland's powers

In the Scotland Act 1998, the powers of the Scottish Parliament were delineated using the reserved powers or exclusion principle. Listed as reserved were the powers that remained the responsibility of the UK government and were not devolved (Table 3.1). This meant, consequently, that everything not listed as reserved was devolved, implying that any 'new' area of government intervention that arose was considered devolved unless action was taken to prevent devolution. This situation could arise, for example, in matters associated with climate change.

The main powers originally devolved are listed in Table 3.1. The list of non-devolved matters for Scotland was larger than that for Northern Ireland and this mainly reflected the exclusion of matters that had not been within the remit of the Scottish Office. Demonstrated by the list is the core focus on areas of social policy, the environment, infrastructure, community protection and cultural matters with a limited economic focus. The Scotland Act was sufficiently flexible to allow for an increase or decrease in devolved competences. Schedules 4 and 5 of the Act can be amended to give the Scottish Parliament legislative competence over matters previously reserved. A reserved matter could become a devolved matter by way of primary legislation or delegated Orders in Council. Also under the Act, executive powers could be transferred from UK government ministers to

Scottish ministers. The first six to seven years of devolution had seen small alterations in competences on an ad-hoc basis; for example, in 2004 the Scottish Parliament obtained the power to allocate rail transport functions to Scottish ministers. Scottish ministers had a range of mainly regulatory functions transferred, for example, in relation to food safety and standards and to fire authority pensions. During and after the 2007 election for the Scottish Parliament, more attention was paid by the political parties to the extension of devolution through a reallocation of powers.

The most significant influence on the development of devolved powers came with the work of a Commission on Scottish Devolution established in 2008 by the Scottish Parliament and UK government, although not supported by the SNP. The final report focused on four main aspects: an increase in devolved financial powers (see below); strengthening intergovernmental cooperation; strengthening the operation of parliament; and strengthening the devolution settlement through devolving certain powers and through managing areas of joint responsibility better (Commission on Scottish Devolution 2009). The Calman Commission suggested that some reserved powers should be devolved, including Scottish parliamentary elections, animal health, licensing of controlled substances, regulations on drunk driving, national speed limits, regulation of air guns and elements of the Social Fund. An adjustment of devolved boundaries was recommended in other areas: health and safety, local immigration policy, housing benefit and funding of research institutions. There was also a recommendation that some matters could be returned to reserved status, for example, regulation of health professionals and definition of charities.

The SNP had launched a separate national conversation exercise in 2007, not supported by the other parties on options for the future of the nation, including independence for Scotland but also extending the responsibilities of the Scottish Parliament and Government (Scottish Executive 2007). The final report on the National Conversation (Scottish Government 2009), while supporting a referendum on independence, suggested in the meantime a more extensive devolution including responsibility for oil and gas, competition law, the civil service, employment and trade union law, health and safety, and consumer protection, plus greater devolution in aspects of pensions, energy, transport and the Post Office. The UK government accepted a need to set out a plan for the next stage of devolution, although the report published by the Scotland Office took the format of a response to the Calman Commission (Scotland Office 2009) see Figure 3.1. This response concentrated on supporting the idea of greater financial accountability for the Scottish Parliament (see below) but did announce some new powers to be devolved. These proposals were specific and limited, covering the regulation of air weapons, setting an alcohol limit for driving, determining the national speed limit, and a number of

1998	Scotland Act
2007	*Choosing Scotland's Future: A National Conversation* (Scottish Government)
2009	Commission on Scottish Devolution (Calman Commission) Scottish Parliament
2009	*Your Scotland Your Voice – A National Conversation* (Scottish Government)
2009	*Scotland's Future in the United Kingdom* (White Paper – HM Government)
2012	Scotland Act
2014	Smith Commission Agreement
2015	*Scotland in the United Kingdom: An Enduring Settlement* (HM Government)
2016	Scotland Act
2018	Social Security Act
2020	Coronavirus Act

FIGURE 3.1 *Timeline for the development of devolved powers in Scotland*

public appointments. A promise was made to consider further Scottish Parliament elections, licensing arrangements for drugs and regulations for charities. Some Calman recommendations were rejected, for example, on air passenger duty. There was little direct reference to alternative or even similar recommendations from the Scottish Executive's National Conversation, with the exception that the UK government gave a strong commitment against the idea of a separate civil service for Scotland.

The proposed devolution of further powers required UK legislation and the UK Labour government envisaged introducing legislation quickly in the next parliament, legislation that would require the consent of the Scottish Parliament. The main parties in Scotland demonstrated less commitment in taking the matters forward (Cairney 2011: 236). In practice, the task of delivering the legislation fell to a new UK government elected in 2010. This Conservative/Liberal Democrat coalition did move quickly to implement election commitments and published a Scotland Bill accompanied by the paper *Strengthening Scotland's Future* (Scotland Office 2010). This paper again had a focus on new financial powers (see below) and the Bill largely implemented the recommendations of the Calman Commission. Changes during the Bill's passage through Parliament removed clauses reserving the regulation of health professions and insolvency (Bowers 2012). Listed in the boxes below are the non-finance powers devolved, which were largely similar to those proposed in the Labour government White Paper *Scotland's Future in the UK*.

BOX 3.1 NEW DEVOLVED FUNCTIONS (SCOTLAND ACT 2012)

- Scottish rate of income tax
- Stamp duty and income tax
- Tax on land transactions
- Powers relating to drink driving
- Speed limits
- Air weapons
- Creation of new devolved taxation
- More capital borrowing powers

BOX 3.2 NEW DEVOLVED FUNCTIONS (SCOTLAND ACT 2016)

- Elections for Scottish Parliament
- Income tax (powers to set rates and bands)
- Air passenger duty, aggregates levy
- Universal Credit aspects
- Frequency of payment, household payments arrangements, paying landlords directly, varying housing costs
- Assignment of VAT revenues
- Benefits for carers, disabled and carers allowance, some social security powers
- Regularity social fund, cold weather payments, winter fuel, funeral payments and Sure Start maternity grant
- Discretionary housing payments
- Some employment services
- Tribunals
- Consumer advocacy and advice
- Additional powers over equal opportunities
- Crown Estate
- Roads: speed limits, parking, traffic signs

- Gaming machines
- Abortion
- Broadcasting appointments
- Licences to explore onshore oil and gas resources
- Policing of railways
- Designing schemes relating to energy efficiency and fuel poverty.

The outcome of the election for the Scottish Parliament in 2011 was an SNP majority government, which meant it cast a more critical eye on the perceived lack of a more significant extension of powers, including the devolution of broadcasting (Foley 2013). Any possibility of blocking the Bill was removed by negotiations, and the UK coalition government was committed to taking it forward only with the consent of the Scottish Parliament. The period 2008–12 marked a stage in the development of devolution with a modest extension of Scottish competences outside the more significant financial initiatives. While the SNP agreed to accept the legislation, the whole context of developing devolved powers was changing as the Scottish Government turned its attention to address the issue of independence and the legislation to permit a referendum.

The wording of the referendum had only a single question on independence and did not include a second question on the future powers for a devolved Scottish Parliament, as had been suggested (Page 2016). Before the referendum, the leaders of the Labour, Conservative and Liberal Democrat parties had issued a joint statement supporting a further strengthening of the Scottish Parliament's powers in the immediate run up to the referendum vote. On what became known as 'the Vow', the three largest UK parties pledged to deliver change for Scotland through devolution with extensive new powers, in the event of the rejection of independence (Political and Constitutional Reform Committee 2015). This proved highly significant as on the day after the referendum, 19 September 2014, the prime minister invited Lord Smith to set up a cross-party commission to produce recommendations for the devolution of future powers, with the process to be informed by a command paper. The Smith Commission consisted of eleven members, Lord Smith and two representatives from each of the five main parties. The report of the Commission, known as the Smith Commission Agreement, reflecting the inter-party negotiations, appeared fairly quickly, on 14 November 2014. There were four main themes in the proposals:

1   increased powers over taxation and spend;
2   a power to create new benefits and make discretionary payments in areas of welfare;

3   the Scottish Parliament and Government to be made permanent; and

4   the voting age for Scottish elections to be lowered to sixteen
    (Smith 2014).

Lord Smith had invited the political parties to set out their views on which further powers should be devolved to the Scottish Parliament. The further powers agreed by the Smith Commission were arranged under heads of agreement according to three pillars (Smith 2014: 12). Pillar 1 related to the constitutional settlement including the permanency of institutions, voting age, elections and intergovernmental relations. Pillar 2 related mainly to social security, some powers over benefits outside Universal Credit, some administrative aspects of Universal Credit and the powers to create new benefits. Pillar 3 covered strengthening the financial responsibility of the Scottish Parliament over shared income tax, assignment of VAT and air passenger duty and aggregates levy and a fiscal framework. It was accepted that the Agreement was the outcome of compromises by the political parties, but the next steps in implementing the Smith Agreement would pass on to the UK government and the Scottish Government.

The Smith Commission report did not explain the rationale for the particular package of social security powers recommended for devolution and neither did the UK government's response (Mullen 2016). Welfare devolution had not featured strongly but this began to change with a growing campaign in Scotland (Lodge and Trench 2014). This was caused by a number of factors – the public support for the welfare state and the importance given to welfare and social justice in Scotland and the close links between the existing areas of devolved social policy and welfare benefits. A view had also emerged during the debate that some aspects of welfare should not be devolved, meaning those closely linked to the perceived UK social union and single market (Lodge and Trench 2014: 9). Following the initiation of the UK welfare reform programme, some aspects of welfare support had been devolved to Scotland. In 2013, the Social Fund community care grants and crisis loans were abolished and funding was made available to the devolved administrations to provide this assistance and create their own administrative format. The statutory cap on expenditure on housing benefit was devolved to Scotland. Complementing this was the abolition of council tax benefit and its replacement by localized/devolved support (Kennedy 2015).

The Scotland Act 2016 was enacted quickly over a period of eighteen months after the declaration of 'the Vow' and consequently did not reflect a lengthy deliberation on the increase in powers (McTavish 2016: 259). In the period since 2011, the focus on increased powers had been on fiscal powers, with the 2016 Act also including welfare powers (Box 3.2). To a large extent, the 2016 Act did fulfil the recommendations of the Smith Commission, although a dispute arose over requirements for consultations between the

Scottish Government and the UK government in twelve areas covering welfare, Universal Credit and fuel poverty, which could be seen as imposing restrictions or a veto (Scottish Affairs Committee 2015: 16). The Act has also been seen as moving the Scottish Parliament and Government closer to the ambitions of the SNP as expressed in 2007 (Keating 2017). However, it was clear that the Scotland Act 2016 did not bring to a conclusion the demands for further extensive devolution or devo-max.

Of significance for the continuing development of devolved powers were two clauses in the Scotland Act 2016. One clause affirmed the permanence of the Scottish Parliament with the declaration that it could not be abolished except following a referendum in Scotland (Political and Constitutional Reform Committee 2015). Another clause gave statutory recognition to the Sewel Convention stating that Westminster will not normally legislate on devolved matters without the consent of the Scottish Parliament. This clause did not, however, make it a legal requirement. These provisions can be interpreted as strengthening the constitutional position of the devolved Parliament as a basis for the further devolution of powers. Progress continued on the implementation of powers under the Scotland Act 2016, delayed also by Covid-19, so the potential of the 2016 Act has only slowly been realized. The Coronavirus (Scotland) Act 2020 gave powers to government to respond to the pandemic, to slow the spread of the virus within the remit of the Scottish administration. It also conferred new powers on devolved ministers to restrict gatherings or close access to premises, or to close schools. Scotland was able to pass its own Coronavirus Act 2020 to complement and supplement the UK Act.

Changing the legislative powers for Wales

In Wales, the nature of legislative powers was to become a dominant issue during the whole period of Welsh devolution. The Government of Wales Act 1998 conferred only executive powers, i.e. decision-making powers, on the National Assembly for Wales, which were in practice exercised by Assembly ministers. The fields for executive action were specified in the Act and numbered eighteen (see Table 3.1). After 1999, the executive powers could develop outside these fields only through a transfer of functions order at Westminster or a section of a UK Act of Parliament. Criticism of this limited transfer of powers and its impact on a lack of coherence in Welsh Assembly government policymaking led to the setting up of a commission of inquiry into powers as well as electoral arrangements (Richard 2004).

The Richard Commission made recommendations for the separation of executive and legislative functions and the transfer of primary legislative powers (see Figure 3.2). The UK government responded by making a commitment to enhance the Assembly's powers over legislation and was complex. The Government of Wales Act 2006 introduced a procedure for the

1998	Government of Wales Act
2004	Richard Commission
2006	Government of Wales Act
2011	All Wales Convention, Report and Referendum
2011	Commencement order for section of 2006 Act
2014	The Wales Act
2014	Silk Commission, Part 2
2015	*Powers for a Purpose: Towards a Lasting Devolution Settlement* (Cm 9020)
2017	The Wales Act
2020	Coronavirus (UK) Act

FIGURE 3.2 *Timeline for development of devolved powers in Wales*

Assembly as a legislature to have a new power to make laws, to be known as measures. Twenty fields were listed for the application of measures, largely similar to fields in the 1998 Act (Box 3.2). The period from 2004 to 2006 has been referred to as marking Welsh devolution moving beyond the end of the beginning and developing on a more solid edifice (Wyn Jones and Scully 2008). The process for the passage of measures required an Order in Council called a Legislative Competence Order (LCO) to be approved by the Assembly and both Houses of Parliament. Measures also required a suitable Westminster Bill to be included in order to add to the Assembly's powers. They had the same effect as Acts of Parliament and, despite their piecemeal nature, did bring Wales closer to the legislative powers in Scotland and Northern Ireland. In practice, however, the LCO process proved complex, lengthy and cumbersome, involving Westminster cooperation, and allowing intensive scrutiny by Parliament. It was suggested (Shortridge 2010) that the whole process was flawed through giving a role to the UK government. Significantly, the number of measures enacted was small.

The Government of Wales Act 2006 provided a facility for a future direct devolution of primary legislative powers in all the prescribed twenty fields following a referendum. In pursuing this option, the Welsh Assembly government established an All Wales Convention to report on the level of public support for primary law-making powers. The report concluded that the transfer of full legislative powers would produce greater clarity, be more consistent with democratic traditions, would reflect the maturity of the Welsh Assembly, would reduce dependency on Westminster and remove the unfavourable comparison with Scotland and Northern Ireland. There was an extensive engagement with stakeholders and the public. The report came to a judgement that a 'yes' vote in a referendum was obtainable (All Wales Convention 2009). The Assembly voted in favour of a referendum which produced a vote of 63.49 per cent in favour of strengthening the legislative powers of the National Assembly for Wales. Following this, in accordance with the 2006 Act, the Assembly made a commencement order to allow the introduction of part 4 of the Act and this was passed in March 2011. The restriction of devolved legislative powers to the twenty fields meant that Welsh devolution was still based on a conferral or inclusive model, rather than the reserved model used for Scotland and Northern Ireland (Moon and Evans 2017: 334). The list of matters attributable to Westminster reflected a close historical integration with matters dealt with on an England and Wales basis. Some confusion did exist over where legislative competence lay and over shared or concurrent powers.

In practice, the UK coalition government made a broader commitment to further devolution and established a body similar to the independent Calman Commission reviewing devolution in Scotland, which would engage with the public, business and politicians. In 2011, an all-party commission on devolution was set up, chaired by Paul Silk, to review both the case for the devolution of fiscal powers and the powers of the National Assembly for Wales and the wider constitutional settlement. There were two Silk reports, with the first report on taxation and borrowing powers in 2012. The Commission on Devolution in Wales (2012) which followed the earlier Holtham Report on funding (Holtham 2009). Most of a series of recommendations were accepted by the UK government and led to a Wales Bill and the Wales Act 2014 (discussed below). The second Silk report was based on terms of reference that were quite broad: 'to review the powers of the National Assembly for Wales in the light of experience and to recommend modifications to the present constitutional arrangements that would enable the UK Parliament and the National Assembly for Wales to better serve the people of Wales' (Commission on Devolution in Wales 2014). A specific remit of the Silk Commission was to consider the boundary between what is devolved and non-devolved, and make recommendations to modify the boundary (Thomas 2011b). Part 2 of the Silk Commission's report was published in March 2014, containing a number of recommendations that challenged the UK coalition government view that the Welsh system was working well and radical change was unnecessary. The Silk Commission recommended replacing the conferred powers model mirroring Scotland with the reserved powers model, which it saw as being more certain, stable and coherent. It would remove the confusion caused by the referral model, which had already led to Supreme Court proceedings. The main recommendations included policing and youth justice, which would bring Wales into line with Scotland and Northern Ireland. The report did not, however, call for an immediate separate criminal justice system. Other functions recommended included powers over energy projects and water supply, regulatory powers in relation to rail franchising, ports, bus and taxi regulation, speed limits and drink driving. There was no recommendation regarding the devolution of welfare/benefits and no recommendation to transfer any existing Welsh powers back to Westminster.

Following the Silk 2 report, the Secretary of State for Wales led a process with the four main political parties to identify which of the Silk recommendations commanded a cross-party consensus. The UK government accepted that the existing Welsh devolution settlement was not fit for purpose and especially did not provide a clear boundary between devolved and non-devolved powers. The outcome of this process became known as the St David's Day Agreement, with the Conservative Party committed to implementation in full (Cairns 2016). The UK government built on Silk 2, relevant sections of the Smith Commission in Scotland and parts of the Wales Act 2014 to produce a command paper *Powers for a Purpose* as a blueprint for a lasting devolution settlement in Wales (HM Government 2015a). The most significant Silk recommendation accepted was that the existing conferred powers model should be replaced by a reserved model to provide a more coherent, stable and better functioning devolution. This meant that a specific list of matters was excluded from devolved competences and reserved to Westminster. The exceptions to the conferred matters were never designed to be a complete list of what is not devolved. Thus, it was not always clear what the Assembly and the UK Parliament were responsible for (HM Government 2015a: 14).

Silk's recommendations were also accepted relating to responsibility for Assembly elections, ending the direct involvement of the Secretary of State for Wales in Assembly proceedings. An agreed list of new powers to be devolved was set out, including: energy planning; speed limits; marine licences and conservation; aspects of water supply; sewerage; port development; building regulations; the size of the National Assembly; and the power of the Assembly to change its name, i.e. to Parliament.

A draft Wales Bill was published in July 2015 with the main aim of providing greater clarity on where the devolution boundary lies and ending the continuous discussion and dispute over what is and is not devolved (Welsh Affairs Committee 2016: para. 9). Moving from a conferred basis to a new model was not a straightforward process. Welsh politicians acted to produce very critical comments with, initially, the House of Commons Welsh Affairs Committee suggesting the draft Bill with a list of 200 reservations went further than the non-devolved subjects in the existing model and many silent subjects would be classified as reserved. The UK government did not set out principles underpinning the delineation boundary. The Welsh Affairs Committee also criticized the 'necessity test' to be applied if devolved law modified criminal or private law and the requirement of the draft Bill to maintain the unified legal jurisdiction of England and Wales. The Committee asked the Secretary of State to reflect on issues in the draft Bill: the list of reservations, the necessity tests and the matter of ministerial consent (Welsh Affairs Committee 2016: para. 28).

Controversy continued with the Welsh Government drawing up its alternative version of a draft Bill – the Government and Laws in Wales Bill – aimed at moving away from simply amending the existing conferred powers model based on the legacy of executive devolution. This proposal sought to give full effect to the Silk recommendations. It provided for the immediate creation of a distinct Welsh legal jurisdiction, the immediate change to a reserved powers model on the basis of principles about a vision for Wales within the Union. The alternative Bill also proposed those deferred matters – policing, the administration of justice, criminal and family law – to be devolved at a future date.

The revised Wales Bill 2016 was published in June 2016 and reflected the UK government's attempts to address concerns. The Bill's approach was judged to retain the central thrust of the draft Bill. Its approach was more permissive in giving the Welsh Assembly power to make law on any matter not expressly reserved to the UK government, although with certain restrictions (Bowers 2016: 12). One declaratory clause stated that the Assembly and the Welsh Government are a permanent part of the UK's constitutional arrangements. There was recognition in the Bill of a distinct body of Welsh law, but this is not the same as the creation of a separate legal jurisdiction. The Bill also created a new arrangement, based on one introduced in Scotland, whereby the Assembly gained power over some sensitive subjects, but could pass laws on them only by a special majority of two-thirds.

The list of new powers covered: road transport, speed limits, traffic regulations, taxi licensing; harbours and ports; electricity generating stations; developments of national significance; equal opportunities; a socio-economic duty; marine licensing and conservation; sewerage; and coal-mining licensing. Responses to the new Bill were still not totally positive. The Assembly's Constitutional and Legislative Affairs Committee published a report that welcomed the move to the conferred model, the permanence of the Assembly and the additional powers and the greater freedom to legislate. However, it voiced criticism that the settlement had not produced greater parity, if not absolute symmetry, with the devolved settlement in Scotland and Northern Ireland. The statutory provisions were still seen as over-complicated, with the retention of a single England and Wales jurisdiction and the complex way in which the Assembly's legislative competence is described. The Constitutional and Legislative Affairs Committee argued that the list of reservations did not create more space for legislative competence and proposed that further powers, for example, policing and the sale of alcohol, should be added (National Assembly for Wales 2016).

The Government of Wales Act 2006 had not been based on a reappraisal of devolved matters, and the new legislative power applied to twenty areas where executive powers were already devolved. The main discussion over the boundary of devolved powers became part of the deliberations of the Silk Commission on Welsh devolution (2014). Part 1 of Silk focused on an increase on financial powers and Part 2 identified a list of powers that it recommended for devolution. The Silk Commission did briefly discuss principles, in the broad sense of raising the question of what should be the powers of the UK Parliament within the devolved Union. It identified macro-economic policies, constitutional matters, defence, foreign affairs and immigration as reserved matters necessary to avoid undermining the interests of the Union or related to fundamental standards and rights that should be enjoyed by citizens across the UK (Commission on Devolution in Wales, 2014: para. 4.8.2). A number of very general principles were produced to guide the delineation in devolved matters but expressed in concepts such as accountability, clarity, coherence and efficiency. There was no comprehensive list of non-devolved powers. In line with the recommendation for a change to the reserved model, Silk examined a range of key areas and selected aspects for devolution recommendation. The main areas examined were: transport, the economy, natural resources, broadcasting, police and justice, health, the Welsh language, equal opportunities, teachers' pay and higher education. Thus, for example, under the umbrella heading 'transport' were port developments, rail franchises, bus and taxi regulation and speed limits. The recommendation that attracted most attention related to the devolution of policing, community safety and crime prevention.

The opportunities presented in formulating the division of powers for the Wales Act 2017 were not used for detailed analysis. The St David's Day process on reaching inter-party agreement was not underpinned by a discussion of principles but by a political negotiation between the parties (Wyn Jones and Hazell 2015: 15). Another influence on detail was that Whitehall departments were asked to identify where they thought the devolved boundaries should lie in their respective departments (Welsh Affairs Committee 2016: para. 18). It was suggested that the Whitehall departments tended to draw up their list of reservations by simply mapping the existing legislative competence (Welsh Affairs Committee 2016) and the Wales Office was not able to take a lead role. It seemed that the division of powers in Wales reflected the pre-existing arrangements under the conferred powers model. The outcome was a proposed lengthy list of reserved matters, described by Rawlings (2015: 487) as reflecting Wales' long dependence on its larger neighbour. The number of reservations in the draft Bill was around 200 but it was likely that this list was not exhaustive and the division was not set in stone. One reason for the length was the attempt to address the issue of 'silent subjects' which were not reserved but were never intended to be devolved to the Assembly. There also still remained the potential for grey areas or uncertainty as some matters appeared very wide-ranging, such as 'prevention of crime'. The main areas accepted by the UK government for devolution, i.e. not reserved, would relate to: natural resources, transport, health, employment and skills, justice, the Welsh language, and equalities (HM Government 2015a: Chapter 2). The final Act retained the central trust of the draft Bill and did give the Welsh Assembly power to make law on any matter not expressly reserved to the UK Parliament, although restrictions on not straying into reserved areas might at times lack clarity, with possible ambiguity over the use of terms such as 'relates to reserved matters' (Bowers 2016: 20). An analysis of matters proposed for reservation in Wales identified thirty matters that were not subject to reservation in Scotland and Northern Ireland (Wyn Jones and Hazell 2015: 15). While some of these were seen as reflecting high-level political decisions about policing and justice, others would seem more appropriately devolved, such as teachers' pay and alcohol licensing. A Welsh perspective remained that there is an inappropriate lengthy set of matters reserved to Westminster and an incoherent set of functions lying with the Welsh devolved institutions (Welsh Government 2021b).

The Wales Act 2017 received royal assent in 2017, and its provision came into effect in two stages, in March 2017 and April 2018. New powers included taxation and borrowing, speed limits, roads, harbours, petroleum licensing, water and sewerage and equal opportunities and can be seen as increasing devolved capacity in Wales (see Table 3.2). Legislation was introduced in 2020 by the government, which distributed new powers to Wales to allow Wales emergency powers to the Coronavirus Act, allowing action to strengthen quarantine and mass gathering powers, employing staff and closing schools and modifying mental health and capacity legislation. Pressure to devolve justice and policing has continued alongside the growing body of Welsh law. A Commission on Justice in Wales (2019) called for justice to be devolved in line with Scotland and Northern Ireland, with a new justice department along with a Welsh high court and court of appeal. The Welsh Government has argued that a legislature should always be accompanied by alignment with a corresponding legal jurisdiction (Welsh Government, 2021d). It emphasized that it was necessary that control of policing, the criminal and civil law, the administration of justice and social behaviour should be devolved to complete legislative devolution.

TABLE 3.2 *Growth of devolved powers for Wales*

1998 Executive fields	Govt of Wales Act 2006	Wales Act 2011
Agriculture, fisheries, forests	Agriculture, fisheries, forests	Primary law-making powers
Ancient monuments, powers devolved	Ancient monuments, historic buildings	
Culture	Culture	
Economic development	Economic development	**Wales Act 2014**
Education and training	Education and training	Devolved taxes
Environment	Environment	– land transactions
		– disposals of landfill
Health and health services	Health and health services	

Housing	Housing	Welsh rate of income tax
Local government	Local government	
Social services	Social welfare	Extension of borrowing powers
Sport and recreation	Sport and recreation	
Tourism	Tourism	
Town and country planning	Town and country planning	**Wales Act 2017**
Water and flood defence	Water and flood defence	– taxation and borrowing
Welsh language	Welsh language	– onshore petroleum licences
Industry	Food	– speed limits, roads, traffic signs
Highways	Fire and rescue	– taxis and buses
Transport	Highways and transport	– equal opportunities
	National Assembly for Wales	– harbours
	Public administration	– planning electricity stations
		– water and sewerage
		– marine licensing and conservation

Limited change in Northern Ireland powers

The reserved or exclusive principle was used in Northern Ireland to delineate the powers of the Northern Ireland Executive and Assembly in the 1998 legislation. The Act specified the powers that would not be devolved but differed from the Scotland Act in having two categories of matters that were not transferred (see Figure 3.3). 'Excepted matters' was the term used for a list of matters of national, constitutional and international importance that would remain the responsibility of the UK government (see Table 3.3). Reserved matters were also dealt with at a UK level but were matters that could become devolved at a future date. The Assembly could legislate on

1998	Northern Ireland Act
2002–7	Direct rule imposed
2006	St Andrews Agreement and Northern Ireland Act 2006
2009	Northern Ireland Act processing devolution of policing and justice
2010	Hillsborough Castle Agreement, complete devolution of policing
2014	Stormont House Agreement
2015	Fresh Start Agreement
2015	Corporation Tax (Northern Ireland) Act, Welfare reform
2017	Collapse of Executive and Assembly
2018	Northern Ireland (Exercise of Functions) Act
2020	New Decade, New Approach, Executive and Assembly restored
2022	Collapse of the Executive and the Assembly

FIGURE 3.3 *Timeline for increase in devolved powers in Northern Ireland*

TABLE 3.3 *Northern Ireland Excepted and Reserved Powers 1998 Act*

Main excepted powers	Main reserved powers
Constitution, Crown	Policing
Foreign relations	Criminal law
Defence	Firearms
Immigration, nationality and asylum	Supreme Court
	Civil defence
National security	Financial services
UK-wide taxation	National minimum wage
National insurance	Civil aviation
Currency, coinage	Navigation
Appointment of judges	Post office and telecommunications
Intellectual property	Data protection
Nuclear energy	International trade and export controls
Foreshore	Consumer safety
	Environmental protection
	Genetics

a reserved matter but only with the consent of the Secretary of State and, in certain circumstances, with the approval of the Westminster Parliament (Hadfield 2001). All other matters not specified were devolved. This principle had been used historically, in the Government of Ireland Act 1920, creating the Northern Ireland Government, and in the Northern Ireland Constitution Act 1973. The scope of devolved matters in 1998 therefore reflected what had been previously devolved and remained, even during direct rule, functions of the Northern Ireland departments at Stormont (Birrell 2009). In the time since 1921, the scope of devolved matters had greatly increased, particularly to include social policy areas.

Excepted and reserved powers

The division of non-transferable matters into excepted and reserved had its origins historically in the Home Rule debates, when the category of reserved matters could have been the responsibility of an all-Ireland Parliament in a three-tier system of government. In practice, since the devolution legislation of 1998, the list of both excepted and reserved matters is similar (Figure 3.1) to the single reserved list for Scotland (see Table 3.1). The retention of the distinction for Northern Ireland meant that changes in status between the three categories of excepted, reserved and transferred where possible were delivered through legislation, usually Orders in Council. Excepted matters have been changed to reserved status, usually to align cognate powers (Birrell and Gormley-Heenan 2015: 27). Legislation in 2014 changed the subjects of Civil Service Commissioners and Human Rights Commissioners from excepted to reserved matters, aligning with the status of the Equality Commissioners. The subject of local government election boundaries was also moved from an excepted to a reserved matter, to align with other local government election matters. The size of the Assembly became a reserved matter too. In terms of significance, changes from reserved to devolved status are more important, constitutionally and politically.

Northern Ireland differs from Scotland and Wales in that there has not been, over the twenty years of devolution, a major political debate over a general increase in devolved powers, and no investigative body was ever established to investigate, report on or make recommendations for increasing powers. At the same time, none of the political parties campaigned for a major increase in functions. The actual extension in devolved power was limited and closely related to key political developments. The major development in devolved powers related to one important policy area, the devolution of policing and justice powers see Table 3.4.

There was some concern when the new Wales Bill appeared in 2016/17 that the extensive list of reserved matters, greater than in Scotland, might

TABLE 3.4 *Powers devolved to Northern Ireland in 1998 and subsequently*

Main powers devolved to Northern Ireland	Powers devolved post-1998 in the 1998 Act
Health	Justice and policing
Social care	Prisons
Social security	Corporation tax
Education	Aspects of welfare reform
Housing	Civil Service Commissioners
Planning	Human Rights Commission
Agriculture and fisheries	Local electoral areas
Employment and skills	
Economic development	
Higher education	
Transport	
Fire and rescue	
Environment	
Electricity, oil and gas	
Forestry	
Culture and sport	
Local government	
Civil service and public administration	
Equal opportunities	
Industrial relations	
Health and safety	
Irish language and Ulster-Scots	

actually reduce the space for legislation (Jones et al. 2016) and many of the reservations were general and expansive (Moon and Evans 2017: 354). Also, if proposed legislation has a loose relation with a reserved subject, it is outside devolved competence. The Act appeared to roll back Welsh legislative competence.

Policy implementation and expansion of devolved activity

While it is important to draw attention to major constitutional and political developments having an impact on the growth of devolved activities, there was a fairly continuous process of expansion in the scale and scope of devolved activities and competences. This activity took place within the broad areas of devolved matters, for example, housing, health, education and planning. Detailed policy developments in these areas could be promoted by the devolved governments and parliamentary bodies, but also reflect lobbying groups or policy-copying or petitions. The mechanisms for detailed policy innovation and implementation could come from public consultations, legislation reviews, government reports, research reports and public inquiries. The outcomes of these processes are legislation, regulations, plans, strategies, programmes for government, new institutions and administrative formats. The devolved area of health demonstrates a wide expansion into many sub-areas of devolved activity including mental health, dementia, public health event, community partnerships. Housing is another example of a process of enhanced activity, on homelessness, affordable housing, home buying, allocation of social housing, islands housing.

Disputes over powers

The most serious development arising from uncertainty or conflict over powers is the use of judicial arbitration. The UK Supreme Court has a specific jurisdiction regarding devolution as well as being the final court of legal appeal; the most significant forms of judicial involvement have concerned the legal competence of the devolved administrations. In 2012, the Attorney General referred a Welsh Assembly bill to the Supreme Court, which was the first time a devolved bill had been questioned since 1999. In fact, the case arose from the first use of new primary powers in Wales. The matter referred to the Supreme Court was the Local Government Byelaws (Wales) Bill 2012 over the impact it would have on the powers of UK ministers to approve Welsh by-laws. The Supreme Court ruled that the Bill was within the competence of the National Assembly of Wales. This led to criticism of the Welsh Secretary of State for initiating the procedure despite his assertion that he was seeking clarification of the legal position. More controversy surrounded the Agricultural Sector (Wales) Bill in 2014. The UK government challenged the Bill, which retained a system of agriculture in Wales, on the grounds that it went beyond devolved powers. Agriculture was a devolved matter according to the Assembly, while the Attorney General asserted that the real purpose and effect of the Bill related to employment and industrial matters, which were not devolved. The Supreme Court found in favour of the Welsh Government, stating that exceptions to this devolved matter were not listed in legislation and it did not matter that in principle it might be capable of relating to a subject that had not been devolved (Welsh Affairs Committee 2016: para. 39). Thus, a matter is devolved if it fairly and realistically relates to a subject of devolved competence (Rawlings 2015: 486). This decision was seen as broadening the competence of the Assembly to include 'silent subjects' whose status was questionable.

Judicial interpretations and decisions have not always been consistent or demonstrated judicial agreement. In 2014, in what is known as the 'asbestos diseases' case, an innovative Welsh Government scheme for the recovery from employers/insurers of the costs of NHS treatment was referred by the Counsel General for Wales to the Supreme Court. The Court divided three to two against the Welsh Assembly on several grounds. Rawlings (2015: 483) particularly notes one majority view implying greater respect for primary legislation of the UK Parliament, i.e. legislation for England compared with devolved legislation. A contrary minority view found that there was no logical justification for treating the views of one body differently. Thus, there was early evidence of different approaches to the constitutional significance of devolved powers.

Conflicts between powers could produce tensions that were more difficult to resolve. The reserved powers over Crown Estates led to conflict with the devolved areas of renewable energy and the marine environment. A major conflict arose in Scotland over the treatment of the children of asylum seekers living in an immigration detention centre. The conflict arose because immigration was a reserved matter while childcare, public well-being (Commission on Scottish Devolution 2009) and education were devolved matters. The Fresh Talent Initiative to help grow Scotland's population clashed with Home Office requirements on immigration rules. Political and policy differences could sometimes be pursued by reference to prioritizing conflicting powers, for example, the use of devolved planning powers to frustrate UK policy on building nuclear power stations. Such conflicts over powers required a degree of political flexibility to resolve – or referral to judicial review and the courts as the final arbitrator.

As devolution settled in, it became clear that it was not always easy to have a clear separation of powers and the use of more general categories meant that a note had to be added referring to 'in part devolved' or 'mainly devolved' or 'exceptionally devolved'. This could apply particularly to lists of conferred or reserved powers. It indicated the existence of many cognate or closely linked powers, but also of what could be termed overlapping powers. Overall, a scenario developed that inevitably produced some element of conflict between the devolved governments and central UK government, which, on occasions, involved referral for a judicial determination. The complex nature of the configuration of devolved and non-devolved matters for Wales under the original conferred principle was analysed in detail by the Wales Office for the Silk Review (Wales Office 2012).

The complexity of cognate powers is demonstrated in agriculture policy, where the implementation of CAP payments is devolved but negotiations on the reform of CAP was reserved. Legislative competence in relation to inshore fishing was devolved but non-devolved for offshore fisheries. Economic development was also an area of cognate powers, with some, such as foreign direct investment, described as concurrent powers. Science and research policy was also complex, with key elements non-devolved but some cognate areas devolved. Concordats between a UK government department and its devolved counterparts often acknowledged the sharing of common aims, for example, in employment and training.

In Wales, grey areas of uncertainty included the scope of Welsh ministers' power to license Welsh ships fishing beyond the Welsh zone. Although consumer protection is non-devolved in Wales two areas, consumer law enforcement and representation of consumer interests were described as areas in which the devolution boundary is not clear (Wales Office 2012: 26). In some areas, the devolved administration requested that a devolved service be undertaken by a UK government body, for example, plant health. In relation to some matters, boundaries in Wales appeared more arbitrary and reflected political influences; for example, while education is mainly devolved, the matter of schoolteachers' pay and conditions was reserved. Other boundary lines appeared unhelpful; for example, the prevention of collection and disposal of waste is devolved but the transboundary movement of waste is not devolved. Promoting fire safety in Wales is devolved but the power to prohibit and regulate in the context of fire safety is non-devolved.

The length of the list of reserved matters in the new Welsh legislation reflects the nature of overlapping and cognate powers along with the identification of the significant exceptions. In Scotland, the Scottish Parliament was to successfully utilize its devolved competence for planning powers, which conflicted with the UK government's powers to build nuclear power stations in Scotland (Harvey 2020: 381). Keating (2017 16) describes the Scotland Act 2016 as enhancing the area of shared competences and also highlighting the remaining grey areas in which some matters could be lost with neither government taking responsibility, or where there was still a complex mixture of responsibilities. In Scotland, equal opportunities were described as one of the most challenging grey areas (McTavish 2016. The configuration produced a need for coordination at key overlaps and intersections. Crises could produce incentives for coordination, for example, at the time of action needed on swine fever, but in other areas there could be a lack of attempts at more integrated relationships. This could affect efficient delivery, for example, in health and safety, which was reserved but was implemented through devolved agencies. Inevitably, this could produce disputes and confusion in accountability. Some arrangements seemed only to require some rational reorganization; for example, animal health was a devolved matter but the funding arrangements were looked after by the Whitehall department, and the Scotland Act reserved the matter of firearms although powers over the sale of weapons were devolved. There could be pragmatic arrangements and responses to resolve problems by allowing ministers to carry out functions outside the devolved requirements, for example, on minor cross-border criminal justice issues. While foreign relations were reserved, a formal agreement was reached to allow the devolved governments to carry out international aid and the promotion of economic activities. The implementation of international agreements made by the UK government could sometimes be more readily undertaken by the devolved government.

In October 2021, the Supreme Court made a ruling, based on a unanimous interpretation of the Scotland Act, requiring two SNP government bills passed in March – on children's rights and on local government – to be referred back to the Scottish Parliament for 'reconsideration'. The Court found that six provisions within these bills fell outside the parliament's competence. The five judges involved

> also criticised the way the children's rights Bill would rely on the courts to clarify its extent through litigation, instead of being clear about its extent upfront. That approach would force courts to take on functions well beyond interpreting the law as currently understood, circumvent established pre-legislative checks, and make it harder to rely on what Holyrood Bills said in future.
>
> (Gordon 2021)

The Secretary of State for Scotland had flagged up concerns about these bills before March but had been ignored; some reportage suggested that the SNP had been using the bills' wording to deliberately test or stretch the limits of devolution by leaving legal holes that Scottish courts would have to rule on, thus allowing the potential for expanding the extent of devolution through a back door. Delivering the Supreme Court's ruling, Lord Reed stated that the drafting would make legal uncertainty inevitable, as it effectively obliged the courts 'to sort out the problems on a case-by-case basis'. Lord Reed went on to say, 'In most liberal democracies one expects the law of the land to be publicly available and accessible. Whereas this technique of drafting guarantees that the one thing you can be sure of is that the terms of the statute do not represent the law' (ibid.). One firm implication of this ruling is that the SNP's stated intention of unilaterally passing a Referendum Bill, should a second independence referendum not be granted by Westminster, would now have a legal precedent, almost certain to nip its legitimacy in the bud.

Overriding devolved powers

The convention that the UK Parliament would not normally legislate in relation to devolved matters without the consent of the devolved legislatures proved controversial. A ruling by the Supreme Court that the convention was political and not justiciable meant that the UK government could readily legislate on devolved matters, ignoring the convention. Parliamentary sovereignty had been used in relation to Northern Ireland, where the UK sovereignty has been exercised to override what were considered to be devolved matters. This arose when, with a deadlock at Stormont over gay marriage and abortion, the House of Commons voted to change the law in Northern Ireland with UK government support. In 2021, with deadlock over action in the Assembly to legislate to support the Irish language, as set out in the Agreement to restore devolution, the Secretary of State declared his intention to legislate at Westminster.

The Withdrawal Bill introduced in 2018 proposed converting EU laws into UK law, called retained EU law. Clause 11 of the Bill proposed to amend the Scotland Act 1998, the Northern Ireland Act 1998 and the Wales Act 2006, which would impose a restriction not to modify retained EU law. It had been assumed that, on exit from the EU, powers related to agriculture, fisheries, environmental protection and economic development would go to the devolved administrations, but the Withdrawal Bill meant that in the first instance the powers would be repatriated to London. The UK government wished to ensure a common framework for a functioning single market but suggested that most of these powers would later become the responsibility of the devolved administrations. The plan was to pass the powers down a few at a time to the devolved institutions.

These proposals produced much concern in Scotland and Wales. A list was produced of 111 areas that would be affected by the likely restrictions, with two areas dominating, judicial cooperation and the environment, followed by agriculture. The list for Wales was smaller, consisting of sixty-four areas, while the list for Northern Ireland was the largest at 141, including employment, social security, energy and cross-border matters (House of Lords Select Committee on the Constitution 2018). A study (Page 2016) mapped the reserved matters of the Scotland Act 1998 to EU competences and found twenty-eight shared competences. The Scottish Government saw clause 11 as undermining the principles of the devolution settlement, and that represented a power grab to take powers that should be devolved (Public Law for Everyone 2017). The Welsh Government stated that the proposals represented a significant attack on the founding principles of the Assembly (Welsh Government 2017).

There had been no consultation with the devolved governments before the Bill was published (Moss and Jones 2017) on what could be a permanent change in the devolved settlement. The Scottish and Welsh Governments took action to block consent through legislation. In March 2018, the UK government tabled amendments to clauses in the Bill to replace the blanket reservation with a commitment that some twelve powers had to be controlled at UK level with some twenty-four powers shared. These arrangements were judged to be still short of what was needed to obtain the consent of the Scottish and Welsh Governments and the matter was referred to the Supreme Court for a ruling on the validity of the blocking legislation in the Scottish Parliament and the Welsh Assembly, and to give legal clarity to the devolved administrations taking the EU powers in devolved areas.

The Welsh Government was to break the stalemate by accepting changes made to the Withdrawal Bill on the basis of a sunset clause whereby any regulations made by the UK government on policy areas they were temporarily holding would expire after five years, after which the Assembly would be free to legislate. However, in Scotland, the matter was the subject of court adjudication, which ruled that the European Union (Legal Continuity) (Scotland) Bill was, as a whole, not outside the competence of Holyrood except for one section that was ruled outside the Scottish Parliament's powers as it would have the effect of making UK law conditional on the consent of Scottish ministers.

Direct intervention by the UK government in devolved matters has continued, particularly on financing in the areas of levelling-up projects and EU replacement funding (see Chapter 4). The impact of Brexit on devolved powers continued with the UK Internal Market Act 2020. This legislation sought to ensure that there were no barriers to trade within the UK following Brexit. New powers were conferred on UK ministers to unilaterally take decisions on devolved matters relating to trade, ignore devolved legislation, for example, on food standards and made state aid a reserved matter and spend money on devolved matters. This created a collision course between the UK Governments and Scottish and Welsh governments (Sargeant and Jack 2021). Many devolved policies, for example, minimum alcohol unit pricing, had implications for trade. The market access principle could clash with the wishes of the devolved governments. The main areas of likely conflict could arise in a range of areas (see Box 3.3).

BOX 3.3 AREAS OF DISPUTE ARISING FROM INTERNAL MARKET ACT

- Environment
- Transport
- Water supply
- Energy
- Agriculture
- Food and drink
- Health
- Social care
- Animal welfare
- Safety matters

The Scottish Government took the view that the potential transfer of devolved powers to UK ministers undermined a central plank of devolution (Scottish Government 2021c) based on the clear division of powers. The Welsh Government saw the legislation as a form of aggressive unilateralism and the biggest attack on devolved powers in twenty years (Welsh Government 2021a). Several *Senedd* committees stated that the Internal Market Act would remove devolved powers, reduce the impact of Welsh laws and impose England's will on Wales (Senedd Wales 2020). The outcome was a stand-off as the Scottish and Welsh governments refusing consent to the measure (Torrance 2020) and an appeal to the Supreme Court by the Scottish Government. To date the case has not been adjudicated on, but it is clear the Internal Market Act represented a new regime, and not a restoration or continuation of existing trading relationships. The position of Northern Ireland parties did not reflect the concerns articulated by the Scottish and Welsh governments, due to a focus on the contentious Northern Ireland Protocol. The DUP argued strongly for Northern Ireland as part of the internal market, ignoring the other issues around devolved powers.

Conclusions

The trend in the operation of devolution has been towards an enhancement in devolved powers and devolution has operated in the context of continuing constitutional change. The major area of development lies in the area of the increased devolution of fiscal activities. Evidence of the potential barriers to progression to the enhancement of devolved powers has been growing intervention on devolved matters by the UK government. It is an approach that the Welsh Government has seen as indicative of a lack of respect for devolution. The policy areas of significant development included social security in Scotland and in justice and policing in Northern Ireland. The process of giving Wales full legislative devolution has been completed to allow Wales to develop further devolved powers. The overall result has still fallen short of producing more symmetric devolution of powers. Scotland has moved ahead with fiscal and welfare devolution but has still not overtaken Northern Ireland formally in the scope of devolution, with differences in terms of, for example, employment. The later years of devolution, however, saw the emergence of obstacles to further enhancement, through the focus in Scotland on independence as an alternative to enhanced devolved powers; the repatriation of powers from the EU to London rather than to the devolved administrations, and the volatility and collapse of the Assembly and Executive in Northern Ireland. Evidence of a potential barrier to progress with a greater enhancement of devolved powers has been growing intervention on devolved matters by the UK government.

The process of devolving further powers has also reflected the work of inquiries set up in the devolved administrations, which involved detailed investigations and considered deliberations, particularly the Calman and Silk reports. The devolution of new powers has necessitated that their implementation must be a priority issue. The more recent period of devolution has seen the clearer recognition of concurrent powers alongside the growth of devolved functions. This has increased the need for more intergovernmental cooperation and alignment of powers to deal with Covid-19. Other consequences have arisen in the production of more jagged edges between functional areas and more conflict over boundaries, although there has not been a sharp increase in turning to judicial review.

The process of the devolution of further powers has been strongly influenced by political developments and priorities in each nation, disputes over Brexit, the Scottish referendum, implementing political agreements in Northern Ireland and support for stronger devolution for Wales. The pathway towards enhanced devolution has been destabilized by the UK Conservative government asserting the Union and Westminster sovereignty over a range of devolved activities, interfering with or removing powers without consent.

4

Fiscal devolution

Introduction

The arrangements for the funding of devolution after 1999 displayed little change from the arrangements prior to devolution for the Treasury financing of major services delivered in Scotland, Wales and Northern Ireland. The main category of UK funding for the devolved administrations was in a block grant for each administration. This block grant funding allocated to each devolved administration was determined by the Barnett formula. This had been introduced for Scotland, Wales and Northern Ireland between 1978 and 1980 through the Treasury and the relevant UK territorial departments, and continued to be applied after the introduction of devolution in 1999.

Devolution did make a difference in that the Barnett formula became a mechanism for allocating money between different levels of government, not as previously within a single government (Heald and McLeod 2005). Funding for the devolved administrations was not determined solely by grants from the UK Parliament but also by local taxation, EU grants, other revenue-raising powers, borrowing and devolved taxation. In 1999, only Scotland was given the power to vary the basic rate of income tax, by three pence in the pound, but this was never to be used. A crucial feature of the funding arrangements meant that despite the lack of revenue-raising power, once the overall budgets had been determined, the three devolved administrations were able to make their own spending decisions on devolved matters. The UK Treasury set out a formal statement of funding policy for the Scottish Parliament, the National Assembly for Wales and the Northern Ireland Assembly, which came to be updated regularly to reflect changes (HM Treasury 2021b). In practice, the funding of devolution and related issues became the subject of intense debate and discussion. Criticisms of the existing arrangements and a growing interest in greater fiscal devolution were to lead to a number of major inquiries, reports and resulting initiatives.

The Barnett formula

The Barnett formula has played a key role in the funding arrangements for devolution and determining changes to the block grant allocation. Three factors determine the change: the quantity of the change in planned spending in UK government departments; the extent to which the UK departments' expenditure is comparable with the service carried out by each devolved administration; and each country's population proportion.

Barnett formula – changes in planned spending on programmes by department by comparability percentage by population proportion

The funding policy sets out the methodology for determining a comparability percentage. The percentage is set at 100 per cent if the programme refers to services that are the responsibility of the devolved administration, weighted by its spending in the base year. The detailed comparability factor is published as an annex to the Treasury statement on funding policy. The population proportions use the mid-year estimates by the Office for National Statistics (ONS) and reflect the coverage of the UK departmental programme to which they apply. In the majority of cases, the departmental programmes cover England only and the proportion of England's population is applied. Thus, in 2018, Scotland as a proportion of England is 9.71 per cent, Wales 5.66 per cent and Northern Ireland 3.36 per cent (HM Treasury 2020).

Block grant funding through Barnett relates to devolved departments spending within what is known as Departmental Expenditure Limits (DEL) set out over three years. The UK government also provides funding for other responsibilities as Annually Managed Expenditure (AME), which is reviewed and set annually. Programmes are funded in AME if they are not only demand-led but also may be volatile in a way that could not be adequately controlled by the devolved administrations, such as welfare payments (HM Treasury 2015: 13), see Table 4.1.

Apart from the Barnett formula channelling funding into the block grant and AME funding, the only other sources of funding for the devolved

TABLE 4.1 *Examples of annually managed expenditure programmes*

Scotland	Wales	Northern Ireland
NHS pensions	Fire service pensions	NHS pensions
Teachers' pensions	Student loans	Police pensions
Student loans	Other pension schemes	Student loans
Most welfare payments		Regional rates

Source: HM Treasury (2015).

TABLE 4.2 *UK expenditure £ per capita by country*

	2004/5	2007/8	2011/12	2013/14	2015/16	2017/18	2019/20
Scotland	7,458	9,179	10,601	10,394	10,536	10,881	11,566
Wales	7,315	8,577	10,326	9,954	9,996	10,397	10,929
Northern Ireland	8,294	9,789	11,203	11,139	10,983	11,190	11,987
England	6,442	7,790	8,929	8,729	8,816	9,080	9,604

Source: HM Treasury, Country and Regional Analysis (2021a).

administration were through local council taxation and business rates, special EU funding, charges for services and limited borrowing powers. The Scottish Parliament was reluctant to use the flexibility given by the Scottish variable rate of income tax. A major benefit for the devolved administrations was the virtually complete freedom over expenditure, with the only constraint on the split between capital and current expenditure imposed to help the UK manage macro-economic targets. After devolution, the Barnett formula continued with substantial support helped by the first ten years of devolution producing growing budgets. Table 4.2 indicates the degree of growth and equity in spending by year for the devolved administrations under the Barnett-led arrangements. For 2018/19, spending per person was highest in Northern Ireland and lowest in England (Keep 2020).

The outcome of the Barnett allocations produced a higher per capita expenditure for Scotland, Wales and Northern Ireland compared to the UK average, reflecting mainly that the costs of providing public services were higher. It appeared that Scotland and Northern Ireland received more than they needed through the formula, whilst Wales received less. Devolved spending has been calculated as 29 per cent higher per person in Scotland and Northern Ireland and 23 per cent higher in Wales compared to England (Paun et al. 2021), but the share of independent spending for each country has remained broadly unchanged over the last decade. Northern Ireland has seen the highest level of spending per head; England has seen the lowest.

The endurability and survival of the Barnett formula has been ascribed to the determination of the Treasury to maintain its use. Arguments in support of the reliance on Barnett can be listed:

- the formula is very simple to apply, can be applied largely automatically and is publicly available;
- it removes the need for a detailed annual negotiation between the Treasury and the devolved administrations;
- it has proved to be a robust mechanism for funding allocations over forty years;

- it has delivered largely stable and predictable allocations with no wild fluctuations in financial provision;
- it has minimized conflict between the four nations over total allocations and spending levels;
- it was seen as removing many of the problems associated with revenue raising from the devolved administrations.

Growing criticisms of the formula

The new devolved administrations continued to operate with the familiar Barnett formula determining most of the available funding. Only a small number of disputes arose, mainly in two areas. After devolution, there were significant increases in funding for the devolved administrations outside the application of the formula. The term 'formula bypass' came to be used to describe this process. There was evidence that Scotland and Northern Ireland were more successful than Wales in obtaining favourable treatment from the Treasury in allocations of public money outside the formula (House of Lords 2009: para. 35). More politically controversial were a number of Treasury decisions on the Barnett consequentials. When spending on a project in England, the Treasury had to decide whether the expenditure was England-only or UK-wide. The decision to categorize spending in England as England-only triggered a consequential payment through the formula to the devolved administrations, in contrast to UK-wide expenditure. This led to disputes, for example, over the 2012 London Olympics spending, which was classified as UK-wide, thus meaning no consequential payments. The Treasury, however, classified Crossrail expenditure as England-only, triggering consequential payments. The Olympics case led to a protracted conflict until a new disputes resolution process led to a settlement of a reduced payment to the devolved countries. This principle remained inconsistent and produced a major row over the confidence-and-supply agreement in 2017 between the Conservative Party and the Democratic Unionist Party, which resulted in extra funding for the Northern Ireland Executive of some £1 billion. The governments of Scotland and Wales strongly criticized this decision on the grounds that the funding was to be spent on devolved matters and should have given rise to consequential payments, estimated at £2.9 billion for Scotland and £1.67 billion for Wales. A formal disputes resolution process was invoked by the Scottish and Welsh Governments over their right to receive consequential funding (Birrell and Heenan 2020). The Treasury Statement of Funding Policy did include a disputes procedure, with an appeal finally to the intergovernmental Joint Ministerial Committee. Such disputes did produce criticisms that the Treasury was in a position to act as the judge in the matter.

There was a growing trend towards a questioning of the value of the methodology and practical application of the Barnett formula, strongly expressed originally by two parliamentary committees. A House of Lords select committee, after examining the evidence, concluded that the formula was no longer an appropriate mechanism to determine annual increases in the block grant for the devolved administrations. It accepted that the advantages of the Barnett formula of simplicity, stability and no ring-fencing were important and should be retained. The Lords report, however, found the argument that devolution funding should be based on relevant need to be a compelling one (House of Lords 2009: para. 49). A House of Commons committee had also concluded that the formula was overdue for reform and lacked any basis in equity and logic, lacked transparency in the decision-making process and created concern in the constituent parts of the UK (House of Commons Justice Committee 2009: para. 257). Concern in the devolved administrations was particularly directed at the desirability of the incorporation of need into the formula, but the attention of the devolved administrations turned as well to questions of devolved funding and fiscal responsibility. The Calman Commission on devolution in Scotland reviewed the existing arrangements for taxing and spending and considered the future option of the devolution of some revenue raising. It adopted the view that the Barnett formula should continue to be used to determine the grant element of the Scottish budget until such time as a needs assessment is conducted (Commission on Scottish Devolution 2009: 9).

Political dissatisfaction with the formula was more pronounced in Wales, leading to the establishment of an independent commission on funding and finance for Wales. The Holtham Commission was to look at the pros and cons of the existing formula-based approach to the distribution of public expenditure in Wales and identify alternatives. The Commission discussed the failure of the Barnett formula to take real account of needs, and took the view that all allocations generated by Barnett were bound to be detached from needs. The concluding belief was that the Barnett formula must ultimately be superseded by a needs-based formula (Independent Commission on Funding and Finance for Wales 2009: 13). A report from the Northern Ireland Assembly had been more cautious about a change to a needs-based principle, and recommendations in 2015 had been confined to more procedural matters. It suggested that the Treasury publish the data upon which Barnett consequentials are based and that the Statement of Funding Policy be subject to approval by the devolved administrations (Northern Ireland Assembly Committee for Finance and Personnel 2015). It was accepted, however, that potential changes to funding in both Scotland and Wales would necessitate change for Northern Ireland. In Scotland, the debate on Barnett was less focused on need. There was in practice little agreement on what could replace Barnett. Heald (2020) also suggests that Barnett has served most political interests involved, even surviving in a more complex form as part of the new Scottish fiscal framework. The

Scottish debate on change was to focus on increasing fiscal devolution. How the levels of public spending, 20 per cent above the UK average, can be justified by any needs-based formula is a question that has also been asked (Gallagher 2016).

Increasing fiscal autonomy for Scotland

Increasing support for the SNP in Scotland brought to the fore the political future of Scotland, and, in a discussion paper *Choosing Scotland's Future*, the SNP, as the governing party, raised the question of greater fiscal authority for Scotland (Scottish Executive 2007). A separate exercise by the other political parties in the Scottish Parliament led to the establishment of a Commission on Scottish Devolution charged with making recommendations to improve the financial responsibility of the Scottish Parliament. The Commission viewed income tax as a prime candidate for tax devolution (Commission on Scottish Devolution 2009: 93). A key proposal that emerged suggested that a greater share of the Scottish Parliament's budget should come from devolved taxation determined by the Scottish Parliament. While noting that the Union required the pooling of some taxation and redistribution across the UK, the Calman Commission adopted the principle of substituting income from devolved taxation for some of the block grant (Commission on Scottish Devolution 2008: 87). A precise proposal was made that the basic and higher rates of tax should be reduced by 10 pence and the block grant for Scotland would be reduced by an equivalent amount. The Scottish Parliament would supplement the block grant by setting Scotland's income tax. The SNP government, after its National Conversation exercise, reported support for a clearer link between taxation decided in the country and the levels of public expenditure. While the SNP government's preference was for full fiscal autonomy for an independent Scotland, it put forward in the meantime a case for maximum policy discretion in relation to fiscal power (Scottish Government 2009). The official UK government response placed an emphasis on ending the absence of accountability with no existing obligation on the Scottish Parliament to make a tax decision. There was general agreement on the desirability of reducing the dependency on UK grants. The government proposal was along the lines suggested by the Calman Commission that the UK government would replace the Scottish Variable Rate in the 1998 legislation with a new Scottish rate of income tax set by the Scottish Parliament (Scotland Office 2009). This would mean that all income tax rates would be reduced by 10 pence with a corresponding reduction in the block grant, to be augmented by the Scottish rate of income tax. HM Revenue and Customs (HMRC) and the UK departments would implement and administer the Scottish scheme on behalf of the Scottish minister.

The Scotland Act (2012) implemented the recommendation, meaning that, from 2016, the Scottish Parliament would set a Scottish rate of income tax (SRIT). The tax would be charged on the income of those defined as Scottish taxpayers, an issue that had caused some controversy. The three main rates of income tax band would be reduced by 10 percentage points for Scottish taxpayers, who would then pay this reduced UK rate and the Scottish rate.

This means that if the Scottish Parliament sets a Scottish rate of income tax of 10 per cent, then Scottish taxpayers will pay the same overall rate as in the rest of the UK, but any change from 10 per cent will mean a higher or lower tax rate in Scotland. HMRC would continue to collect, administer and manage the SRIT as part of the UK system.

Before the introduction of the SRIT, a further analysis and proposals had been made by the Smith Commission, set up after the referendum on independence and the 'Vow' by the the main UK parties to strengthen devolution. The Commission was asked to make recommendations including on financial and taxation powers. On tax powers, the Smith Commission agreed that the Scottish Parliament should have the power to set the rates and thresholds of income tax on non-savings and non-dividend income (Smith 2014: 23). As the recommendations represented the views of the Scottish political parties, this persuaded the UK government to publish a White Paper with a commitment to quickly translate the recommendations into law at the beginning of the next parliament. This development was seen as another significant milestone in Scotland's devolution journey

TABLE 4.3 *Scottish income tax*

Band	UK rates	UK rates in Scotland
Basic	20%	10%
Higher	40%	30%
Additional	45%	35%

Source: HM Treasury (2015: 27).

TABLE 4.4 *Scottish income tax rates and bands 2019/20*

Band	Band name	Rate
Over £11,850 to £13,850	Starter rate	19%
Over £13,850 to £24,000	Basic rate	20%
Over £24,000 to £43,430	Intermediate rate	21%
Over £43,430 to £150,000	Higher rate	41%
Over £150,000	Top rate	46%

Source: Scottish Government (2020).

(HM Government 2016) and strengthened the income tax powers already devolved in the Scotland Act 2012. The new legislation was enacted as the Scotland Act 2016, one of the main purposes of which was to increase the financial accountability of the Scottish Parliament through the devolution of the rates and bands of income tax and the assignment of other taxes. After the first year, adjustments to the block grant would be indexed to reflect the dynamic nature of tax revenues and ensure that neither the UK nor Scottish Government was worse off simply from the devolution of tax (Sandford 2015). The devolution of this power led the Scottish Parliament to set income tax rates and bands for 2018 to 2019 (see Tables 4.3 and 4.4).

The receipts from the SRIT would be collected by HMRC and paid via the Treasury to the Scottish Government (National Audit Office 2021). The Scottish Government has now assessed the income tax as the most fair and progressive in the UK, protecting lower- and middle-income groups. It notes that the majority of people in Scotland will pay less tax than they would have if they lived elsewhere in the UK (Scottish Government 2021a). The Calman Commission had, as well as a Scottish income tax, recommended the devolution of a number of minor taxes: air passenger duty, stamp duty land tax, landfill tax and aggregates levy. These taxes, along with income tax, would have given the Scottish Government the capacity to fund a substantial proportion of the Scottish Parliament's budget from taxation. Subsequently, the UK government agreed to devolve two taxes – but not air passenger duty and aggregates, because of rules on state aid. From 2015, UK stamp duty land tax and the landfill tax ceased to apply in Scotland. Parliament became responsible for taxes on land and building transactions and waste disposal from landfill. The legislation in 2012 also provided powers for new taxes to be created in Scotland and for additional taxes to be devolved. In the UK government's Vow after the referendum on greater devolution it was clearly stated that the Barnett formula should be kept in a new devolution settlement (Hallwood and McDonald 2016). The Smith Commission contended that the air passenger duty tax be devolved by 2018 and also that the power to charge tax on the commercial exploitation of aggregate be devolved to the Scottish Parliament on demand (Smith 2014: 24). In the case of minor taxes, the block grant would be adjusted. The possible devolution of VAT had been discussed by the Calman Commission, which concluded that devolution of the tax was not possible but that some form of tax assignment would be possible. The Smith Commission suggested that the first 10 percentage points at the standard rate of VAT would be assigned to the Scottish budget, with a corresponding adjustment to the block grant. The UK government went further and proposed additionally assigning the first 2.5 percentage points of the revenue from the reduced rate (Sandford 2015: 12). This was incorporated into the Scotland Act 2016 with the VAT assignment to be implemented in 2019/20. The Scottish Government was pushing for full control of VAT. A further tax was considered for devolution, corporation tax, but this received little support from either the commissions or the political parties (Seely and Keep 2016). Among the negative consequences referred to were the creation of economic inefficiencies as firms reacted to tax considerations rather than commercial factors.

Following the implementation of most of the financial recommendations of the Smith Commission, an agreement was reached between the UK and Scottish Governments on setting out a fiscal framework (UK Government/Scottish Government 2016). This covered the principles for funding the Scottish budget, the block grant adjustments for tax and welfare, dates for the commencement of the arrangements, the sharing of costs, the principle of the no-detriment provision, and rules for capital and resource borrowing. While Landfill Tax and Land and Buildings Transactions Tax came into operation, Air Passenger Duty and Aggregates Tax were delayed. A process for dispute resolution was included in the fiscal framework with referral levels to the Joint Exchequer Committee and ministers. These arrangements represented the largest ever transfer of financial power from Westminster to Scotland. Provisions in the Scotland Act 2012 saw the Scottish Government raise in the region of 21 per cent of the expenditure; with the 2016 Act, this would rise to around 50 per cent of devolved expenditure (Sandford 2015: 13). The budget of the Scottish Government would become increasingly determined by the changes in devolved taxation rather than being a consequence of the application of the Barnett formula, although replacing part of the block grant has been seen as meaning less predictable tax revenues, which may bring volatility to Scottish tax revenues.

Greater fiscal devolution for Wales

The legislation establishing devolution for Wales, unlike Scotland, did not give the Welsh Assembly tax-raising powers. A review of devolved powers in Wales five years later concluded that tax-varying powers, similar to those proposed for Scotland, were desirable but not essential (Richard Commission 2004). However, following the 2007 Welsh Assembly election, the new programme for government included a commitment to review Assembly funding through an independent commission. The Holtham Commission had two major terms of reference: one to look at the pros and cons of the present formula-based approach to the distribution of public expenditure resources through the Barnett formula; and the other to identify possible alternative funding mechanisms including the scope to have tax-varying powers (Independent Commission on Funding and Finance for Wales 2009). In practice, the work of the Holtham Commission focused on an analysis of the Barnett formula. The Commission found that the formula causes spending per head in Wales to converge over time on the average level of English spending per head, with a failure to take real account of need. It was recognized that the Barnett formula had benefits in avoiding political quarrels and making the annual distribution to the devolved administrations as low key and uncontroversial as possible. However, it found that Wales had relative needs 14–17 per cent higher than England. The main recommendation was that the funding formula should be changed to a needs basis. In the meantime, it was suggested that a floor should be placed under the Barnett formula. The final Holtham report discussed the details of a needs-based formula using demographic, deprivation and cost factors (Independent Commission on Funding and Finance in Wales 2010).

This report did consider which taxes collected across the UK were suitable for devolution. Income tax was considered as by far the strongest candidate to have an impact on the accountability of the Assembly. At the same time, the Calman proposal for Scotland was regarded as problematic for Wales. The Holtham Commission went on to suggest that other taxes be considered, including taxes on property and land, minor taxes of value as policy levers, such as aggregates levy and air passenger duty, and some new taxes on goods and activities. Corporation tax was considered as a feasible devolved tax, but a budgetary risk was identified as receipts would be deducted from the block grant. The Commission also noted the strictly limited borrowing powers of the Assembly and also made a recommendation that the UK government and the Welsh Government should jointly agree a new ministerial concordat on the funding arrangements for Wales.

Holtham's recommendations were greeted with caution but there was widespread acceptance of the finding that Wales received less than its fair share of funding through the block grant (Trench 2015). Welsh ministers did suggest that the fair funding issue had to be dealt with before going into tax-varying powers (Roy 2011). The Chief Secretary to the Treasury responded by saying that the wider reform of Barnett was not a priority, but also indicated that the proposal for a Barnett floor would be considered, and there was a commitment to explore tax devolution for Wales (Wyn Jones and Scully 2012). The new UK coalition government made a commitment to establish a process for the Welsh Assembly similar to that recommended by the Calman Commission. It appeared that the UK government placed more emphasis on the devolution of tax powers than on any reform of the Barnett formula and how the block grant was calculated (Roy 2011: 41). It also appeared the UK government would prefer similar elements of tax devolution along the lines of the proposals for Scotland. Following the action to increase legislative powers, an independent commission on devolution in Wales was established to examine financial and constitutional issues.

The Silk Commission was to issue its first report in 2012 on the question of devolving financial powers to Wales. The Commission's terms of reference were to review the case for the devolution of fiscal powers to the Assembly and to recommend a package of powers that would improve the financial accountability of the Assembly, and that were likely to have a wide degree of support. The main finding in the first report was that the current funding arrangements did not meet the requirements of a mature democracy and were anomalous in an international context (Commission on Devolution in Wales 2012). The Commission therefore recommended funding arrangements that brought more tax powers under the control of the Assembly and ministers, thereby increasing financial accountability. The main recommendation related to income tax, that the income tax basis should be shared between the UK and Welsh Governments. An initial 10 pence should be deducted from each of the main rates of income tax, with the Welsh Government able to set a Welsh rate for each band. The scheme differed from that contained in the Scotland Act 2012 in omitting the lockstep, which means that the Scottish Government cannot change the steps between the higher and lower bands. It was also recommended by the Silk Commission that the devolution of income tax should be subject to a referendum in Wales. It also proposed the devolution of four minor taxes, similar to what had been proposed for Scotland. These were: stamp duty land tax; landfill tax; air passenger duty; and aggregates levy. There would be an accompanying reduction to the block grant. As in Scotland, the Welsh Assembly would be given powers to legislate for the introduction of new taxes in Wales. In relation to borrowing, Welsh ministers should be able to borrow to increase capital investment within an overall limit.

Thirty-three recommendations were made by the Silk Commission, with the UK government fully agreeing with the key recommendations. The detailed response accepted that sharing income tax would contribute to enhancing the accountability of the Assembly. However, concern was expressed that the proposed ability of the Welsh Government to set unrestricted individual rates for each band could distort the redistributive structure of the income tax system (HM Treasury/Wales Office 2013). The UK government proposed to devolve equivalent powers to these legislated for in Scotland, but the Bill was amended to allow different rates to apply to different bands. It was agreed that the people of Wales should be able to decide in a referendum whether an element of income tax should be devolved. The UK government's command paper accepted the Silk Commission's recommendation that stamp duty tax and landfill tax be devolved, but it would keep under review the devolution of an aggregates levy. In relation to air passenger duty, the UK government stated that it was not convinced of the case for devolution (HM Treasury/Wales Office 2013: 6). The UK government announced its intention to publish a draft Wales Bill to include provisions to devolve tax and borrowing powers, and a consultation was carried out on the collection and management of devolved taxes, with a proposal for a Wales Revenue Authority. The passage of the Wales Act 2014 did not mark the completion of consideration of the Silk recommendations. The political parties were committed to further negotiations to advance financial reform (Armstrong 2015). The UK government's St David's Day Agreement included three further financial commitments: to further review the potential for devolving air passenger duty; to examine the assignment of a proportion of VAT revenues; and to introduce the funding floor, to be agreed in the next Spending Review. Stamp duty tax and landfill tax would be introduced in 2018. The Welsh Government still argued that until there was a fair funding settlement, it would not in the best interests of Wales to devolve any element of income tax, as the block grant would still account for 80 per cent of funding.

After a period of preparation and the creation of a Welsh Revenue Authority, it was possible to introduce the new taxes on land transactions and landfill disposal tax, to be collected from 2019. More progress was made with the introduction of the Welsh income tax when the UK government made the decision to remove the requirement for a referendum in advance of the devolution of a portion on income tax. This marked a savings in time and resources, but there was some critical response in Wales that the consent of the Welsh people was not to be sought. The need for a referendum was dropped in the Wales Act 2017. From April 2019, the Welsh Government has been able to vary the rates of income tax paid by Welsh taxpayers. The process means that the UK government will reduce the three rates of income tax: the basic rate from 20 to 10 per cent; the higher rate from 40 to 30 per cent and an additional rate from 45 to 35 per cent. The Welsh Government will then decide the Welsh rates of income tax that are added to the reduced UK rates.

An important feature of the financial arrangements following the relevant legislation was the agreement between the Welsh Government and the UK government on the Welsh Government's fiscal framework (HM Government/ Welsh Government 2016). The agreement covered the new block grant funding arrangement whereby a new needs-based factor would be included in the Barnett formula. The needs factor would be based at 115 per cent following the Holtham report's proposal to implement a new funding floor mechanism from 2018/19. This additional funding to the Barnett calculation was a recognition of the more dispersed population and greater prevalence of poverty. The formal agreement had agreed a methodology for assessing and updating funding and also set out the framework for additional capital borrowing, budget management tools, financial reporting arrangements, a new Welsh reserve to help manage its budget and a dispute resolution process (see Figure 4.1).

2004	Richard Commission
2010	Holtham Commission
2012	Silk Commission – devolving financial powers
2014	Wales Act
2016	Agreement on the Welsh Government's fiscal framework
2017	Wales Act
2019	Welsh Rate of Income Tax

FIGURE 4.1 *Timeline for change in devolved finances in Wales*

The Welsh funding system has evolved into two separate streams: one, the revenues from the Welsh rate of income tax, devolved taxes and business rates; and the other, the adjusted block grant. Developments towards greater fiscal devolution were marked by a difference in emphasis between the Welsh Government and the UK government. There was an emphasis in the Welsh approach on making the Barnett formula fairer while the UK government put an emphasis on the devolution of taxes. The final outcome was strongly determined by the work of two independent commissions, the Holtham and Silk Commissions. This gave authority and backing to recommendations for change in the fiscal arrangements and made it difficult for the UK government to reject the majority of recommendations. There was strong support for the case that Wales was underfunded by the Barnett formula as analysed by the Holtham Commission. Widespread agreement was expressed on the desirability of increasing the financial accountability of the Assembly and also on the need to devolve some minor taxes and borrowing powers, largely following the Scottish model. The UK government, in dealing with funding for Wales, appeared always anxious to make it clear that arrangements must operate within the framework of the UK fiscal system. Some degree of caution and concern over the introduction of a Welsh income tax was evident with divisions among the parties and among the business community. Income tax did introduce a particular Welsh factor, as different income tax rates from England could lead to behavioural responses, encouraging people to relocate across the Welsh border. The tax system was set for the 2019/20 tax year. HMRC administrates the Welsh rate of income tax as part of the UK system and the Welsh Government receives the revenues. To date, however, the Welsh Government has set the Welsh rate at 10 per cent, so the overall income tax rates are the same as those in England and Northern Ireland. It has not been policy to take more in the Welsh rate of income tax from Welsh families at least as long as an economic impact of COVID lasts (Welsh Government 2021c). There did appear to be continuing support for greater financial accountability and for effective policy levers to respond more effectively to problems (Cole and Stafford 2015: 69). The mixture of block grant, Welsh income tax and devolved taxes was projected as accounting for 20 per cent of Welsh revenue, with council taxes 30 per cent.

Finance in Northern Ireland

The Barnett formula has been used in Northern Ireland since 1979/80. Although after devolution in 1999 there was a view among the parties that Northern Ireland was being treated unfairly under Barnett, some contrary evidence did emerge. Midwinter (2006) found insufficient evidence to demonstrate that Northern Ireland had been disadvantaged by the application of the Barnett formula since devolution and that identifiable public expenditure had been growing. Statistical information does clearly show that the public expenditure per head in Northern Ireland has been consistently higher than in Scotland, Wales and England (Table 4.1). Subsequently, there was little interest expressed by the Northern Ireland Executive in pursuing amendments to the Barnett formula. Rather, the Executive maintained an emphasis on defending the size of the block grant (PricewaterhouseCoopers 2013). There was largely an absence of active discussion with the Treasury by civil servants on the operation of the formula (House of Lords 2009: 24). Similar problems to those identified in Scotland and Wales had been noted: the lack of control over the size of the budget; limited accountability for the relationship between taxation and spending; uncertainty over Treasury calculations; and disincentives to increase economic performance (Pidgeon 2010). If the Executive wished to increase spending different from the UK government, the only means to achieve additional revenue was through the regional rate. The Northern Ireland Assembly Committee for Finance and Personnel (2015) did eventually carry out a review of the operation of the Barnett formula. Assembly research service reports had identified key proposals for change from the Scottish and Welsh experience. One report highlighted the implications of developments relating to the Barnett formula in Scotland and Wales, the devolution of part of income tax and new taxes and the level of Treasury control (Northern Ireland Assembly 2014). There was concern about the sustainability of the Barnett formula in the context of potentially wide-ranging changes in devolved finance in Scotland. A review by an Assembly committee of the operation of the Barnett formula focused on identifying the key factors that could influence the ways in which the formula would change. The Committee's recommendations were limited to a proposal that the Department of Finance and Personnel and the Executive study how a new needs-based methodology could best be designed to take account of Northern Ireland circumstances, that the Executive minister was to act with Scottish and Welsh counterparts to make joint proposals to improve the operation of the formula, and that the Executive should be more proactive in developing longer-term funding arrangements (Northern Ireland Assembly Committee for Finance and Personnel 2015: 26).

The possible devolution of other taxes did not receive much attention in Northern Ireland, with the exception of two taxes. For several years, there was a view that the Republic of Ireland had benefited from a lower level of corporation tax than existed in Northern Ireland, when there was competition for investment. In 2011, the UK Chancellor announced a Treasury review of the case for a reduction in the rate of corporation tax in Northern Ireland to make it more competitive with the Republic of Ireland. The Varney Review concluded that, overall, considering both costs and benefits, a clear case could not be made for devolving corporation tax (HM Treasury 2007). Northern Ireland would have to bear the financial consequences of a reduction in the block grant possibly of up to £400 million per year. Reducing the block grant had to be balanced against the likely benefits of an increase in investment and employment, seen as a somewhat uncertain exercise (HM Treasury 2013 34). The loss of revenue posed risks for funding public services. A continuing debate indicated much support among businesses and among the main political parties for the proposal to devolve corporation tax rate-setting powers (Murphy 2010).

Eventually, in 2014, the Chancellor announced that the UK government was willing to take the matter forward and the final decision was made within the Stormont House Agreement, as part of a package of measures to increase financial sustainability. Theresa Villiers, the then Secretary of State, announced that legislation would be introduced as soon as possible in Parliament to enable the devolution of corporation tax. This led to the passage of the Corporation Tax (Northern Ireland) Act 2015, which devolved the power to set the main rate of corporation tax in respect of certain trading profits. This would apply to micro, small or medium-sized enterprises and also to large companies with a Northern Ireland trading presence (Seely 2018). Following the legislation, the Executive declared its intention to introduce a rate of tax set at 12.5 per cent, similar to the Republic of Ireland, beginning in 2018. The power was not devolved because of the collapse of the Executive. The UK government was committed to work with a restored Executive to consider a commencement date, adding a caveat that the Executive's finances should be in a sustainable position. The Act has not been implemented and Corporation Tax rates have been changed in the UK and the Republic of Ireland with the unionist parties in Northern Ireland not post-Brexit wishing to endorse economic differences with Great Britain.

One minor tax also drew the attention of the Northern Ireland Assembly supported by business interests, namely air passenger duty (APD). The issue of competition with the Republic of Ireland was again a factor. In 2011, the Executive gained an exemption from the higher APD tax rate that had applied to the long-haul, transatlantic route (PricewaterhouseCoopers 2013: 25). The Finance Act 2012 devolved the power to set the APD rate on direct long-haul flights from Northern Ireland with effect from January 2013. All the rates relating to short-haul and connected flights from Northern Ireland would continue as normal. HMRC would administer the system on behalf of the Northern Ireland Executive.

All the political parties in Northern Ireland have expressed little interest in pursuing an increase in fiscal powers or interest in the principle of fiscal accountability. No real debate occurred on devolving any aspect of income tax and discussion did not move beyond the case for corporation tax and some attention to APT for long-haul flights. The process of implementing the devolution of corporation tax has not taken place, while the one direct long-haul route has ceased operation. There also has been little interest in the argument for increasing democratic accountability through fiscal devolution. In terms of Northern Ireland politics, appeals based on fiscal accountability are not likely to count in influencing the electorate.

Northern Ireland, therefore, contrasts with Scotland and Wales in not considering the possible benefits of the devolution of any income taxes or other taxes. The main consequence is that Northern Ireland is dependent on the block grant, with very limited control over any tax resource other than local government rates. The financial package for the Stormont House Agreement (Northern Ireland Office 2014) had suggested a consideration of how devolution could bring about economic benefits, including devolution of aggregates levy, stamp duty land tax and landfill tax (see Table 4.5). The other possibility of raising revenue through major charges – for example, introducing water charges – is not popular with most political parties.

Other UK funding

The UK government provides certain funding separate from the Barnett formula and block grant, where appropriate. Reasons for funding outside spending reviews include: changes in financial arrangements; to deal with a national crisis; to deal with local crises; or negotiated for political reasons.

Since the spending review of 2020, with the exceptional circumstances related to Covid-19 and the end of the EU transition period, programme-level comparisons were applied to Covid-19-related funding and replacement EU funding to ensure that devolved administrations received comparable funding. Payments to procure Covid-19 testing and then vaccines were arranged on a UK direct-funding basis. The UK government allocated £16 billion for public administration as a consequence of all Covid-related expenditure for 2020/1. Additionally, £10 billion was added to the block grant spending on public services and business support. The United Kingdom Internal Market Act 2020 contained a general power that allowed UK ministers to provide financial assistance for a range of purposes including economic development, infrastructure and training.

City Region Deals are funding agreements between the UK government, the devolved administrations and local councils. City Region Deals and Growth Deals exist in all three devolved nations, with the UK Treasury contribution ring-fenced. In addition to this direct funding, the devolved administrations also receive Barnett consequentials because of funding allocated to the Department for Communities and Local Government to spend on City Deals in England (Ward 2020). Further support was given to Scotland, given the scale of Scotland's new tax and welfare powers. As part of the Fiscal Framework Agreement, the UK government contributed £200 million to the administrative costs. Extra funding was also given to Wales as part of the Fiscal Framework Agreement. Other more detailed funding has gone to single items. In 2017, rail funding was provided outside the Barnett formula for the period from 2019/20 to 2023/4. A new Victoria and Albert Museum in Dundee was allocated £5 million.

TABLE 4.5 *Other sources of funding*

Scotland
Devolved taxes – land and building transaction tax and Scottish landfill tax
Local taxation – council tax and non-domestic tax
Scottish income tax
Receipts and charges
Scotland reserve – to move funding from one year to another
Borrowing – capital and non-capital
VAT – first 10 per cent assigned to Scottish Government budget
Wales
Devolued taxes – land transaction tax and landfill disposals tax
Local taxation – council tax and non-domestic taxes
Welsh rate of income tax
Receipts and charges
Wales reserve – no limits on payments into
Borrowing – capital and non-capital
Northern Ireland
Devolved taxes – long-haul air passenger tax and corporation tax (not yet implemented)
Local taxation – domestic and non-domestic rates
Receipts and charges
Borrowing – for capital and non-capital purposes
Reserve – no reserve but budget exchange system, unallocated funds can be carried forward

Source: Based on HM Treasury (2020).

A major aspect of UK Treasury funding for Northern Ireland has been special additional funding to promote political and economic stability, usually at times of political breakdown with devolution. This may be construed as a process of Barnett bypass or Barnett-plus. Following the St Andrews Agreement in 2006, which restored devolution after a political breakdown, the UK government agreed a funding package over the next ten years. Over the next four years, the spending commitment totalled £35 million, which was equivalent to over £50,000 per household (HM Treasury 2006). The package included a capital investment plan totalling £18 million to underpin long-term economic growth, especially through research and development. There was further extra funding as part of the Hillsborough Castle Agreement in 2010, which completed the devolution of justice and police powers and brought about some political institutional developments.

This involved a funding settlement with the promise of a capital budget to maintain police operational capacity and training as well as access to the Treasury reserve to meet exceptional pressures related to policing and justice. There would also be a legal aid allocation from the Treasury, and the UK government gifted four former military bases for use by the Executive (Northern Ireland Office 2010).

The pattern of extra funding to sustain the devolution settlement was again demonstrated by the Stormont House Agreement in 2014. This Agreement was an attempt to resolve disputes in the Assembly over issues concerning dealing with the legacy of the past, and it also dealt with providing flexibility in welfare reform implementation and public sector reform in reducing the number of government departments. The Stormont House Agreement was accompanied by a package of almost £2 billion in financial support from the UK government (Northern Ireland Office 2014). A year later, it was clear that the implementation of the Stormont House Agreement had stalled, leading to a risk of the devolved institutions collapsing. Talks between the Northern Ireland parties, the UK government and the Irish government took place to deal with a number of challenges, particularly dealing with the past, but including Executive finance and problems around flags and parades. This led to a strategy called 'A Fresh Start: The Stormont House Agreement and Implementation Plan'. This plan had two main objectives: to secure the full implementation of the Stormont House Agreement and to deal with the impact of paramilitary organizations (Northern Ireland Office 2015). 'A Fresh Start' was underpinned by a financial package from the UK government that would give the Executive £2 billion in additional spending power. The UK government would provide direct additional support of £650 million. This included up to £150 million over five years to help fund the bodies to deal with the past and a contribution of up to £500 million of capital funding for shared education. Flexibility was also given to repay loans from the Treasury and support welfare mitigations, from asset sales and capital budgets. In giving this support, the UK government recognized the specific challenges facing Northern Ireland but stated that support must also reflect the continuing difficult fiscal environment and the need to be fair to all parts of the UK (Northern Ireland Office 2015).

These Barnett-plus payments had attracted relatively little comment from Scotland and Wales but this changed following the Conservative–DUP confidence-and-supply agreement in 2017 after the UK general election. The DUP promised voting support for the minority Conservative government in exchange for extra financial support of £1 billion to the Executive over two years for infrastructure development, health and education and broadband development, plus tackling pockets of deprivation. The Scottish and Welsh Governments expressed their profound disagreement with the additional funding. They argued that the matters receiving the funding were mainstream devolved services, which should give rise to Barnett consequentials, estimated as £2.9 million for Scotland and £1.7 million for Wales. The UK government held to the view that it had not broken rules in the Treasury Statement of Funding Policy and that the funding represented a targeted intervention to address a specific set of circumstances with exceptional funding outside Barnett (Birrell and Heenan 2020).

Devolution collapsed between 2017 and 2020 and the eventual agreement to restore it led to a new document, *New Decade, New Approach* (Northern Ireland Office 2020), which again provided additional support. This funding was focused on health and budget pressures, transforming public services, infrastructure delivery and Northern Ireland's unique circumstances, including legacy issues and paramilitarism. All this additional funding lay outside Barnett.

Fiscal subvention

A question had arisen concerning the extent to which the devolved nations rely on a fiscal transfer or subventions from the UK government. This analysis is based on a calculation of the differences in each administration between the received revenue from all sources and expenditure. The ONS produces data for eight regions of England as well as the devolved nations. The overall position has been seen as showing the nature of fiscal deficits and also, in practice, a transfer between regions. It is worth noting that the Independent Fiscal Commission NI found that only 45 per cent of this funding had been drawn down (see Table 4.6).

TABLE 4.6 *Fiscal balance by region 2019*

	Net fiscal balance £	Fiscal balance per head
Scotland	16,081	2,948
Wales	14,368	4,556
N. Ireland	10,283	5,430
North-West	22,745	3,086
North-East	11,007	4,121
West Midlands	17,318	2,915
East Midlands	7,004	1,1417
Yorkshire/Humber	12,231	2,220
South-West	612	1,088
East of England	−3,619	−580
South-East	−19,702	−2,146
London	−36,162	−4,035

Source: ONS (2019).

TABLE 4.7 *Revenue and expenditure by devolved nations 2019–20, per head £*

Region	Revenue	Expenditure
Scotland	12,269	14,417
Wales	9,848	13,698
Northern Ireland	10,465	14,821

Source: HM Treasury (2020).

Scotland, Wales and Northern Ireland all have a negative balance, but this is not dissimilar from most of the other regions of the UK, as Table 4.6 shows. The North-West has the largest net fiscal deficit. Only three regions – London, South-East and East of England – have a net fiscal surplus. A comparison based on population is clearly more meaningful, and Table 4.7 also examines the fiscal position per head (Keep 2020). Keep (2020) shows how revenues per person are highest in London, South-East and East of England, while spending per person is highest in Northern Ireland, Scotland and London.

Northern Ireland has the highest fiscal deficit per head and Wales the second highest; however, Scotland has a lower fiscal deficit than the North-West of England and is similar to several other regions. London, the South-East and the East of England all had negative surpluses per head, which protect spending in the rest of the UK. This variation reflected the dominant economic position London and adjoining areas. It has been suggested that the positive performance of the three regions in England tends to mask the poorer performance of the other English regions, and, on occasions, this can shed unduly negative light on the other three devolved nations (Scot Fact 2018). Although in nineteen of the past twenty years London and the South-East have been in surplus, other UK regions have experienced a deficit in all twenty years (Keep 2020). Nevertheless, between 2011 and 2019, all regions saw an improvement in net fiscal balances.

If a comparison is made between revenue and expenditure per head, revenue is similar between Wales and Northern Ireland while expenditure is similar between Scotland and Northern Ireland. In 2020, Northern Ireland had the highest expenditure per head at £15,910, while for Scotland the figure was £15,070. Revenue from sources other than taxation was highest in Northern Ireland at £2,191 compared to £1,791 for Scotland and £1,545 for Wales (Independent Fiscal Commission 2021: 62).

Borrowing powers

Scottish ministers can borrow to fund both capital expenditure and other purposes. The system was very similar for Scotland and Wales and not very different for Northern Ireland. The main legislation changing financial arrangements tended to increase borrowing powers. Provisions in the Scotland Acts 2012 and 2016 enabled borrowing to fund capital and other defined purposes, although a maximum and annual limit on borrowing was fixed. Scotland can borrow for capital purposes up to £3 billion, with an annual limit set, by the Treasury, at 15 per cent of the cap. The Scottish Government can borrow for purposes other than capital expenditure up to a set limit through the Secretary of State from the National Loans Fund or from commercial lenders or from bonds issued by the Scottish Government. Borrowing can be used in cash management because of fluctuations in receipts or forecasting errors. The Wales Act 2017 enabled the Welsh Government ministers to borrow for capital purposes up to £1 billion, with annual capital borrowing set at 15 per cent. As in Scotland, borrowing was through the Secretary of State from the National Loans Fund or commercial sources or bonds issued by the Welsh Government. Wales can borrow for purposes other than capital expenditure up to a maximum of £500 million, in order to meet fluctuations in tax receipts or in-year excess expenditure. The Northern Ireland Executive can borrow for capital purposes up to £3 billion, available from the Secretary of State through the National Loans Fund, with a limit set, by the Treasury, at £200 million for 2021/2. Northern Ireland can borrow over the short term for cash management, to provide a working balance or meet an in-year excess. UK governments have granted Northern Ireland increased capital borrowing powers to support economic regeneration, and such extensions have taken place as part of the financial incentive packages in the main agreements to promote political stability. The transfers have been facilitated in recent years by the UK government's ability to borrow at low interest rates as a percentage of GDP. Scotland had a deficit of 7.7 per cent, Wales 17.9 per cent and Northern Ireland 19 per cent (Tetlow and Cheung 2021). The Scottish Government also intends to push for greater fiscal flexibilities around borrowing. All four nations' fiscal positions have deteriorated because of Covid-19.

Private finance initiatives

Private finance initiatives (PFI) had been introduced in the UK just before devolution as a means of using the private sector to deliver projects in partnership with the public sector. In most such public–private partnerships, the private sector designed, financed, built and delivered a project in return for a revenue payment. These payments, sometimes known as a unitary charge, covered debt, interest and dividends as well as management and maintenance costs. PFI arrangements were popular in the early period of devolution in all three devolved nations. Public–private partnerships were established between the devolved administrations and private contractors mainly to support infrastructure projects relating to schools, hospitals and roads. PFIs had an appeal as often the only option, given capital constraints. Changes were made to the scheme in Scotland in 2008, with the adoption of a no-profit distribution (NPD) model and the establishment of a quango, the Scottish Futures Trust (SFT), to administer the process. This initiative was aimed at removing excess profits and costs, limiting the returns to the private sector and simplifying the contractual terms. The SFT was responsible for operating the new NPD system using five territorial hubs in Scotland, working with public sector bodies to identify buildings needed to support the delivery of community facilities. The SFT saw its task as working to attract additional funding to support the construction of public buildings and facilities immediately and deliver the best possible value. Additional funding for infrastructure investment was being provided at a time of a rapid decline in capital budgets.

The SFT is an independent company, set up to deliver value across infrastructure investment. It has developed programmes in the last ten years across the construction sector, delivering £22 billion in investment in 200 projects. This provides resources and knowledge to public sector organizations to support their plans and to fund and deliver construction projects. The SFT has an operational budget for 2020/1 of £10.7 million. The company uses public funding to work with public and private sector partners to achieve new infrastructure outcomes, including planning, investment, procurement, innovation, technology and use of public assets.

The Welsh Government had originally developed a private finance unit but there was a degree of political caution, and, in 2007, in the One Wales programme for government, the use of PFI was ruled out within the Welsh health service. The Welsh government's preference was that the private sector take a fixed rate of return with the public sector having greater control and with surplus profits returned to the public sector. After the economic crisis, the hostility in Wales towards bringing private sector finance to public infrastructure to mitigate capital budget cuts lessened, and some of the less attractive aspects of PFI were removed (Cole and Stafford 2015: 72). PFI were also used in Northern Ireland, with concern at calculations of the final cost to taxpayers. The use of PFI projects in both Wales and Northern Ireland was limited compared to Scotland. In 2017, Wales initiated a mutual investment model to lever in private capital to support public sector projects, with a minority share held by the state. The cost of thirty-three projects up to 2010 was calculated as costing the taxpayer £5 billion more than their value in 2043. Northern Ireland changed to an amended PFI model in 2012, copied from England, in which the government became a co-investor. There was clearer transparency and frontline services were removed. Trust in PFI was affected by strong criticism by the Northern Ireland Public Accounts Committee in 2014 over the arrangements for a new further education college building. The cost was £44 million, of which £20 million was supplied by the government department, but the private contractor was to be paid £200 million over 25 years. UK government scrutiny bodies, particularly the National Audit Office and Treasury Select Committee, had been very critical of the various forms of PFI, raising issues of inefficiency and value for money. In 2018, the Public Accounts Committee criticized PF1 and PF2 schemes in England for their inflexibility and as a fiscal risk to government (HM Treasury 2018). A decision was made by the UK government that it would no longer use PF2, the existing model of PFI. This announcement did not affect the devolved administrations but raised questions about its future use. Revised forms of PFI were developed, to avoid the negative aspects of the original PFI model, and these were intended mainly to offset cuts in the Treasury block grants, as capital budgets were under unprecedented pressures.

EU funding

Prior to Brexit, all three devolved governments were eligible for both pre-allocated and competitive EU funding. The two most significant pre-allocated funding channels were the European Structural and Investment (ESI) funds and the European Agricultural Guarantee Fund. For the funding period 2014 to 2020, the UK had been allocated €17 billion and €22.5 billion, respectively. In total, EU funding on the UK was €6.3 billion in 2017 and €7.1 billion in 2016 (Brien 2018). The ESI funds are intended to assist less well-developed regions. There were three main funds: the European Regional Development Fund, to promote the reduction of regional imbalances; the European Social Fund, to promote employment objectives; and the European Agricultural Fund for Rural Development. The three devolved administrations were responsible for the delivery of ESI funds in their own jurisdictions. ESI funding was not distributed evenly across the UK and it was Wales that received the most per person, through the weighting towards less-developed areas. For 2014 to 2020, Wales received £123 per person, Scotland £40 and Northern Ireland £50. Some 63 per cent of the population of Wales lived in the less-developed region of West Wales (House of Commons Library 2021). The breakdown for the European Agricultural Fund for Rural Development was more akin to population proportions. For the period 2014 to 2020, Scotland received 16 per cent, Wales 13 per cent and Northern Ireland 4 per cent, with 67 per cent for England. The European Agricultural Guarantee Fund was the primary financial mechanism for the implementation of the EU's Common Agricultural Policy, with direct payments to farmers to stabilize their revenues. For 2014 to 2020, of the UK total of €22.5 million, Scotland received €4.1 million, Wales €2.2 million and Northern Ireland €2 million. This funding did not require national co-funding. In the competitive EU funding stream, organizations could apply directly to the European Commission for support. Among the most important have been the Horizon 2020 project supporting research and innovation and Erasmus+ supporting education, training and youth. Questions have been asked as to whether the devolved nations received more from the EU than they contributed. As funding was often calculated on a

UK basis, it was difficult to quantify financial inputs and contributions. The Scottish Government produced data on Scotland's illustrative contribution to the EU budget and allocated EU receipts. For the period 2007 to 2013, the contribution was calculated as €7,787 million and allocated EU receipts as €6,007 million, showing Scotland was a net contributor to the EU (Scottish Parliament 2015: 10). While no official figure existed for Wales, one calculation made was an estimated annual investment of €653 to €747 million per year, compared to an estimated annual contribution of €630 per year (Full Fact 2014). Unlike Scotland, Wales seemed to receive more than it contributed. It appeared that Northern Ireland received more than a proportionate estimate of contributions.

Concerns were expressed in the devolved nations at the potential loss of funding with Brexit. An analysis by the Scottish Government suggested that under a hard Brexit, resources for public spending would be up to £3.7 billion lower and that the economic output would reduce by 8.5 per cent (Scottish Government 2016: 10).

Scotland, in particular, had been successful in securing Horizon 2020 funding, representing 11 per cent of UK funding awards. Outside the main funding streams, there was one unique fund for a devolved administration. The EU Programme for Peace and Reconciliation in Northern Ireland and the border region of the Republic of Ireland is a unique structural fund to promote a more peaceful and stable society. From its introduction in 1995 until 2020, tranches of the fund had delivered €2,265 billion. This funding is not available in any other part of the EU and was not dependent on matching support from the UK government. EU Peace funding will continue through Peace Plus funding combining Peace and INTERREG programmes along with UK funding. The European Investment Bank (EIB) is jointly owned by EU member states to develop jobs and growth and climate change. UK payments to it amounted to €3.5 billion in capital and loans received amount to €118 billion (Brien 2019). The main areas funded have included energy, transport and universities. Projects in the devolved administrations included financing of: energy efficient housing in Scotland; Cardiff energy from a waste plant; social housing in Northern Ireland; and the universities of Strathclyde, Bangor and Ulster. An offshoot of EIB was the European Investment Fund, which supports small and medium enterprises by providing risk finance.

After the European Union (Withdrawal) Act 2018, the UK government guaranteed to maintain all EU finding at EU levels until 2023, covering structural funding, payments to farmers and research funding. The UK intends to participate in some EU programmes in the period 2021–7, including Horizon Europe, Euratom nuclear fission and fusion research, training and Earth monitoring. Mainly, the UK government will provide domestic programmes to the EU funds. This includes funding for farmers and land management in Scotland, Wales and Northern Ireland for 2021/2 of £1.1 million; funding of £20 million to support fisheries in Scotland,

Wales and Northern Ireland in 2021/2; and training schemes as a domestic replacement for Eurostat backed by £100 million. Most significant is the UK Shared Prosperity Fund as the domestic successor to EU structural funds, operating UK-wide and using new assistance power from the United Kingdom Internal Market Act 2020. Some £1.5 billion was allocated to match lost EU funding, with £200 million to help prepare for its introduction. The fund covered investment in communities, local businesses, training and deprived areas. A pilot was set up as a community renewal fund for transport, town centre renewal, and arts and culture. There have been criticisms that gaps with replacement funds remain, such as EU rural development programmes. A major issue for the devolved governments is that the UK government would not devolve these funds but would control how EU replacement funds were allocated. There is concern on whether the devolved administrations will play any role in the funding's governance.

Direct UK financial intervention

The most recent period of devolution has seen the development of a set of strategies involving greater UK government direct expenditure in the devolved nations. The UK government has taken responsibility for replacement funding for the main EU structural funds through a Shared Prosperity Fund (UKSPF). The fund provided £2.6 billion over three years, giving priority to community and place, local business and people and place. Funding would be delivered by Westminster through local authorities in Scotland, Wales and England and working with the Scottish and Welsh governments. In Northern Ireland, the UK Government would have oversight of the scheme working with local partners (Department for Levelling up, Housing and Communities 2021). It was specified that projects in the devolved administrations should link with existing strategies. Each part of the UK received a centrally determined allocation for each of the three years for local authorities and regional economic partnerships in Scotland and Wales and a single allocation to Northern Ireland. To support preparation for the introduction of the UK Shared Prosperity Fund, a Community Renewal Fund was designed in 2021. An allocation of £220 million was made for bids from lead local authorities in Great Britain and one allocation to Northern Ireland. This fund was described as investing in people, places, business and communities. In practice, there was a focus on skills and training. In the 2020 Spending Review the UK Government announced a new levelling up strategy (HM Treasury 2021c) through a fund of £4 billion for England and £0.8 billion for infrastructure and economic development over three years. The aim was twofold, to assist neglected areas and to support recovery from Covid. In the first round, £1.7 million was allocated to Scotland, £120 million to Wales and £49 million to Northern Ireland. In 2021–2 the focus was on town centre regeneration, upgrading transport and cultural investment. Local authorities would take the lead in making bids, except in Northern Ireland where a range of bodies could be involved. The levelling up fund was a central part of a package of complementary UK-wide interventions directly determined from London. A further scheme was the Community Ownership Fund in 2021 to support local areas to protect community assets, again funding allocated centrally to the three devolved administrations. The package of funding interventions also included the Freeport Programme, and the UK Infrastructure Bank. Sitting alongside this funding were programme such as the Towns Fund which produced financial transfers through the Barnett formula. Although all these funds were treated as falling under the levelling up policy, the first such UK-wide funding policy took place earlier with the City deals or city devolution programmes, in 2012/3, eventually becoming the City and Growth Deals. These were a bespoke package of funding from the UK Treasury and other bodies. The initiative was to maximize economic growth, employment and infrastructure. From 2014, Glasgow became the first area outside England to negotiate a City Deal and the scheme was extended to other regions of Scotland, Wales and Northern Ireland supported by devolved government funding as well as private contributions (Ward 2020). City and Growth Deals were designed to promote more collaboration but could also be seen as more deeply involving the UK government in directing devolved government activity including local government which was a devolved matter. Scotland received some £1.5 billion, Wales some £790 million and Northern Ireland £617 million. While the devolved administrations largely cooperated with City and Growth Deals, the role exercised by the UK funding over the Shared Prosperity Fund and the levelling up funds were to lead to much criticism in Scotland and Wales. Two main criticisms were made that the EU replacement funding was much lower than the receipts that would have come from the EU. The estimated drop in Wales was from £1.4 billion to £632 million (Senedd 2021) and in Scotland a loss of £337 million over three years (Hudson 2022). The second criticism was more political and constitutional, namely, that these financial interventions were a threat to devolution and did not respect devolution, with key decisions made by the Secretary of State for Levelling Up, Housing and Communities. The UK government continued to take the view that it would invest directly across all parts of the country.

In March 2021, the three devolved finance ministers issued a joint statement to register their concern at the UK government decision to bypass devolved arrangements to deliver levelling up and community renewal funds (Welsh Government 2021d). They also expressed the view that money to replace EU funding should be allocated through devolved structures rather than through the separate layers of centralized UK bureaucracy. As the new arrangements would be based on bidding, to a degree this would bring more uncertainty. Funding allocations from the first round of Treasury levelling up funding were seen as poor for the devolved administrations. Further direct UK government intervention was signalled by the Internal Market Act 2020 which gave UK ministers broad powers to spend money directly in the devolved nations and on devolved competences. This was likely to be directed at economic development, infrastructure, education, training, and sport. There was no requirement to seek the consent of the devolved administrations. The power to provide funding to local areas across the UK was described as an assault on Welsh devolution and using a sledgehammer to crack a nut, creating new tensions (Drakeford 2021). The Act had the power to usurp devolved expenditure planning and even totally undermine devolution.

Concerns have been expressed at the potential loss of funding following Brexit. An analysis by the Scottish Government suggested that, under a hard Brexit, resources for public spending would be up to £3.7 billion lower annually by 2030 and that economic output would reduce by 8.5 per cent, with growing poor economic impacts (Scottish Government 2021d). Post-Brexit, arrangements may be made for the UK to continue to participate in programmes in science and education, with a fair and appropriate financial contribution from the UK as a third country (Brien 2018: 40). Much concern has also been expressed about the implications of the UK government taking responsibility for EU replacement funding and levelling-up funding. For the first time since devolution, the UK government has assumed wide powers in areas which are clearly devolved.

Conclusions

The original devolution settlement was based on principles that gave the three devolved administrations almost complete control over the allocation of funding for devolved matters but with very limited responsibility for raising revenue. All the administrations were predominantly dependent on the funding allocation from the Treasury through the Barnett formula. This operated to deliver a roughly similar level of funding and expenditure per head for Scotland, Wales and Northern Ireland, although Northern Ireland had a higher level of subvention per head. As devolution developed, concerns were expressed over the two issues for the fiscal future: the desirability of a needs basis for reforming the Barnett formula and options for increasing the financial responsibility and accountability of the devolved governments for revenue raising. In Scotland and Wales, a major role in promoting change was played by independent commissions and reports: Calman and Smith in Scotland and Holtham and Silk in Wales. The work of these commissions led to the eventual acceptance of many of the recommendations by the UK government. Increasing fiscal powers through the devolution of taxes was strongly supported by the UK government and Scotland moved ahead with the partial devolution of income tax and several minor taxes, followed by a similar pathway enacted for Wales. No commission was established in Northern Ireland until 2021 and, apart from decisions relating to two taxes, no other change occurred and much of the efforts of the main political parties was directed at obtaining special funding from the Treasury to resolve political logjams and disputes.

The devolution of financial powers, taking effect from 2018 onwards, gives the devolved administrations in Scotland and Wales more choice on tax-and-spend relationships and some levers to influence economic growth, social investment and income redistribution. The implementation of fiscal devolution has progressed slowly and with caution, exemplified by the adoption of the no-detriment provision relating to charges. Block grants are adjusted to reflect the devolution of new tax powers or welfare responsibilities (Keep 2020: 21). Discouraging the radical use of devolved taxes, including corporation tax, was the block grant adjustment from the UK to the devolved revenue. The position of the Treasury remains that it alone is responsible for UK fiscal policy and directly for public expenditure allocation. Budget control by the devolved administrations has to be exercised within the framework of public expenditure limits and controls. Further issues of territorial finance are likely to arise. While there is no consensus about what the appropriate share of total spending raised by local taxes should be, Scotland and Wales may move to a higher share. More fiscal devolution may impact upon the degree of Treasury control. Questions may also be asked on whether the Barnett formula is compatible with a semi-autonomous system of fiscal devolution. The Treasury Statement of Funding Policy has received criticism, and in Scotland and Wales there were negotiated agreements on producing a written fiscal framework. Further fiscal devolution should provide an increasing proportion of the financial resources available to the devolved administrations. The most likely scenario is continuing development towards a model of partial fiscal devolution covering part of income tax, and a range of other minor taxes in addition to local government taxes and business rates.

5

Political parties and systems

Introduction

In the last decade the electoral choices and systems used across the four nations of the UK have changed in a fundamental way. The choices across the state were once largely common, but increasingly voters are being presented with an array of different options. A wide range of voting systems are used to elect members of the devolved assemblies in England, Scotland, Wales and Northern Ireland. Electoral options are differentiated along national lines. All nations continue to elect to a single parliament in Westminster, but from distinct, separate electoral systems (Awan-Scully 2018). The devolved legislatures in Northern Ireland, Scotland and Wales are elected using different voting systems to that used in UK general elections (first-past-the-post (FPTP)) to elect MPs to Westminster. The systems used by the devolved legislatures were intended to challenge the dominance of single-party governments associated with Westminster elections and facilitate a wider range of views in the political process. This chapter deals with political parties and political systems in devolved countries, including party support, political representation, electoral systems and changing trends. The ideology of political parties and the salience of national identity are also discussed, alongside the formation of coalition, power-sharing, majority and minority governments.

The devolved electoral systems

The electoral systems in each of the three devolved nations deviate from the Westminster FPTP approach. Each uses a form of proportional representation. Elections to both the Scottish Parliament and the Senedd Cymru (Welsh Parliament) use a version of the additional member system (AMS). The single transferable vote (STV) system has been adopted by the Northern Ireland Assembly. The power to amend these systems was devolved to Scotland and Wales in 2016, and in both nations several reforms have been introduced (Institute for Government 2021).

Like much of the rest of the UK, the FPTP system dominated elections in Scotland for most of the twentieth century. This system meant that many MPs were elected to 'safe seats' and appeared remote and disconnected from their voters. The Scottish Constitutional Convention, created in 1989, paved the way for the establishment of the Scottish Parliament. The Convention called for a new electoral system that could challenge the outdated, stale two-party politics of Westminster (Sullivan 2019). The Scottish mixed-member proportional (MMP) system, also known in the UK as the additional member system (Lundberg 2007), is used to elect the 129 MSPs – seventy-three from the constituency vote, which uses FPTP, and fifty-six from regional lists. Divided into seventy-three constituencies and eight regions (each region having a total of seven MSPs elected from the lists), voters in Scotland have two ballots: the constituency vote, where they elect one MSP, and the regional vote, where they choose a party. The regional list element of the system, that is, the proportional component, is used to 'top up' the constituency results, thus offsetting the distorted results produced by FPTP. This is achieved using the D'Hondt formula, which divides the number of votes a party receives by the number of constituency seats won plus one (votes/seats + 1). As Mitchell and Henderson (2020) explain, a party that succeeds under the constituency vote is less likely to secure many seats on the regional list. Smaller parties, however, which are traditionally punished by the FPTP system, and which achieve around 5–6 per cent of the regional vote, have a chance of gaining seats. This proportional system was designed to ensure fairer representation of smaller parties such as the Greens, and also to prevent any single party from gaining a majority. Notwithstanding, in 2011, the Scottish National Party (SNP) won a majority of seats, proof, according to Mitchell (2014: 273), 'that while proportional systems tend to eschew majoritarian governments, they are not equipped to withstand a strongly expressed popular public opinion'.

The regional list element of the electoral system provides for a more proportional overall result. However, seats awarded at the regional level represent only 43 per cent of seats in Scotland and just 33 per cent in Wales, which is too few to fully compensate for the fact that large parties (the SNP and Welsh Labour, in recent elections) often win the lion's share of constituencies. The Senedd is made up of sixty Assembly members elected by the AMS, a form of proportional representation. Each voter has two votes: one for a constituency member and one for a member from a regional list. Wales has grown somewhat less proportional over time, as smaller parties such as UKIP, the Green Party and the Abolish the Assembly Party have won a greater share of the vote without (except for UKIP in 2017) winning any seats. The Northern Ireland Assembly was designed to 'ensure that all sections of the community can participate and work together successfully' (UK Government/Irish Government 1998) to facilitate power-sharing between unionists and nationalists. In order to facilitate fair representation of parties and communities within power-sharing arrangements, Northern Ireland uses an STV system, in which voters rank candidates in multi-seat constituencies. However, this power-sharing model has proved to be fragile and has collapsed on a number of occasions, including between 2002 and 2007 (Heenan and Birrell 2018) and, most notably, for a three-year period between January 2017 and January 2020. Indeed, even before the most recent collapse of power-sharing, there were signs of escalating tension between unionist and nationalist parties, with growing use of the 'petition of concern' process that enables either side to exercise a veto.

The Scottish political system

Politically, Scotland has long appeared a place apart from the rest of the UK. The crowded political landscape leaves parties struggling to establish their own identity, address often conflicting agendas and consolidate their membership in a fractious political scene (Frain 2019). The 2010s will be remembered as one of the most momentous decades in modern Scottish political history, largely because it delivered a referendum on independence from the UK. In the early years of devolution, the parties remained closely aligned to the period prior to the regional settlements. Politics was controlled by the Labour Party, which had been the dominant political force since the 1960s and held seats across Scotland. While the debate over independence defined this decade, it also ushered in significant changes to the Scottish Parliament. The nation's political landscape has shifted dramatically with the collapse of Labour and the phenomenal rise of the SNP.

The rise of the SNP

The SNP is a centre-left, civic nationalist, social democratic party that campaigns primarily for Scottish independence. Founded in 1934, it was at the margins of politics for decades before devolution threw 'an electoral lifeline' (Curtice 2009: 55) and enabled the party to become the dominant force in Scottish politics. Prior to devolution, the electoral system was heavily weighted against the SNP in elections to the House of Commons. Furthermore, Scottish politics were afforded little attention or priority in the Westminster system. The establishment of a Scottish parliamentary system introduced an electoral system more advantageous to the SNP, which has consequently created a context more conducive to winning support and translating this into seats. Rather than killing 'nationalism stone dead', as predicted by shadow Scottish Secretary George Robertson, devolution has provided a platform for a remarkable reversal of fortunes (Mackay 2009).

The leadership of the party has also had a significant impact on its transformation. The SNP was widely dismissed as a movement of oppositionists (Mitchell et al. 2009) marked by internal divisions and dissent. Under the leadership of Alex Salmond and Nicola Sturgeon, it has evolved into a professional political party of government. Given how divisive support for devolution had once been viewed, the unity behind core aims and objectives is remarkable. In the period between 1999 and 2000, there was turmoil within the party, with battles between the fundamentalist wing, which was unwilling to accept anything less than independence, and others who viewed devolution as a means of moving towards independence through a referendum. A new era began for the party in 2004 when Alex Salmond easily won the leadership contest and Nicola Sturgeon was elected as his deputy. The internal strife and factionalism were put aside in an attempt to present a more modern, dynamic political machine. The issue of independence, so long derided by unionist politicians as marginal, was propelled to the top of political agenda (McTavish 2016) and remains one of the main fault lines in Scottish politics (Hassan 2009).

The first eight years of the devolved parliament were governed by a Labour–Liberal Democrat coalition; however, in 2007, after narrowly defeating Labour, the SNP formed a minority government in the Scottish Parliament. Opinion polls following this success in the Holyrood election indicated that the SNP would replicate this success in the 2010 UK general election. However, as the election became imminent, voters turned back to Labour. It has been suggested that from the late 1980s, Labour supporters saw the SNP as their second choice, and vice versa, and this had become a fixed pattern (Mitchell 2015). In the Scottish elections, Labour and the SNP would compete to become the dominant party in Holyrood, but in elections to Westminster, Labour was in the ascendancy. Mitchell (2015) asserts that the explanation for this pattern was relatively straightforward. At the ballot box, voters focused on the party that could secure power and the potential to form a government. In the devolved parliament, the SNP represented a viable alternative to Labour; in contrast, the race for seats at Westminster was between Labour and the Conservatives, with the SNP largely inconsequential.

The 2010 general election witnessed a 5 per cent swing from Labour to Conservative; however, Scotland recorded a swing in the opposite direction. It has been suggested that this may be largely explained by Scottish support for the then Labour leader, Gordon Brown, and his party. Labour recorded another resounding win, securing forty-one seats in Scotland's fifty-nine Westminster constituencies. It seemed that the Labour Party had an iron grip on Scottish representation at Westminster.

Building on its momentum in 2011, the SNP secured what the *Guardian* described as 'the most stunning victory in recent Scottish political history' and one that had the potential to radically alter the constitutional fabric of the UK. In this thumping victory, Salmond had led the party to its first overall majority and won sixty-nine of the 129 seats. Significantly, the SNP quickly asserted that this result afforded it the moral authority to deliver on a key manifesto pledge: a referendum on Scottish independence. Such was the scale and significance of this victory that while constitutional matters are reserved for Westminster, the Conservative-led coalition government in London accepted the need to enter negotiations with the Scottish government on the issue. This completely changed the face of Scottish politics, culminating in a referendum on Scottish independence in September 2014. Following the referendum (discussed later) and in the run up to the 2015 general election, the SNP more than tripled its membership, becoming the third biggest political party in the UK, with more than 110,000 members (McHarg 2015).

The sea change in Scottish politics continued with the 2015 general election; in a historic victory, the SNP won all but three of Scotland's fifty-nine seats in the House of Commons. Curtice (2019) suggests that it was a result that appeared to make a mockery of any suggestion that Scotland continued to be an integral part of a common political battleground comprising Scotland, England and Wales. The phenomenal success of the SNP in the wake of the previous year's independence referendum was the headline story in what was an otherwise lacklustre general election. This landslide victory affirmed the seismic shift in the political landscape, consolidate the SNP's position as the new dominant force (McHarg 2015). While the 2019 general election saw Boris Johnson and the Conservative Party swept to power in London, it also confirmed that the quest for self-determination had not dissipated, as the SNP gained seats.

Scottish Labour

The last decade has witnessed a remarkable turnaround in the fortunes of the Labour Party in Scotland – moving from its position as Scotland's foremost political force to being relegated to the almost unthinkable status of fifth place and largely in the political wilderness. In the initial years of the Scottish Parliament, devolution entrenched Labour rule in Scotland. Scottish Labour defined Scotland: it was electorally dominant until 2010 and appeared to have an iron grip on power. 'Labour Scotland', as Hassan and Shaw (2012) refer to it, was a powerful political identity that represented Scotland's insurgent voice against Westminster. However, during the 2000s, instead of galvanizing this position, it allowed the SNP to move into this terrain. By 2014 and the fiercely contested independence referendum, Labour represented Westminster's voice in Scotland at a time when people in Scotland were increasingly dissatisfied with the London-centric nature of British politics. Fighting for the maintenance of the constitutional status quo cost Scottish Labour dearly. This stance meant that it relinquished its position of being the natural party to challenge the Westminster Conservative–Liberal Democrat coalition. The electoral impact was devastating. According to

Henderson and Mitchell (2018), 82 per cent of the Scottish people who voted Labour in 2010 and 'yes' in 2014 switched to the SNP in 2015. In Scotland during 1999–2007, Labour was in government with the Liberal Democrats. However, as Shaw (2019) has asserted, since then, it has been downhill all the way, with a succession of dismal election results.

In the 2016 elections to the Scottish Parliament, Labour secured just 22.6 per cent of the vote. This disastrous result was the worst for the party in Scotland since 1910 and relegated it into third place behind the Conservatives. The SNP made significant gains in totemic Labour heartlands such as Glasgow and Clydeside, securing eleven constituencies from Labour. Labour won twenty-four seats – less than half of those secured in 1999, and a significant decrease from the party's performances in 2007 and 2011. Ironically, Labour was initially sceptical about the use of regional lists, assuming that this proportional element benefited its political opponents. However, in 2016, these regional lists rescued Scottish Labour from electoral annihilation, as 88 per cent of the party's overall seats were gained via the D'Hondt method (Anderson 2016). Despite the extraordinary backdrop of Brexit, Scottish Labour only managed to win seven seats in the 2017 general election. The party's ambiguous position over Brexit, compounded by internal divisions over the issue and its hesitation to support a 'People's Vote', meant that it failed to capitalize on the opportunity provided to use the campaign as a pro-European platform in Scotland.

A huge swathe of its traditional working-class base has abandoned Scottish Labour to support the SNP, and the party's mixed messages around Brexit and independence have compounded internal strife and divisions. Charges of complacency and arrogance concerning the position of Labour in Scotland have long blighted the party (Hassan and Shaw 2012). Its lack of clarity and struggle for relevance have been compounded by numerous changes of leadership. Scottish Labour's attempts to appeal to both unionists and independence supporters have caused confusion and frustration amongst both its supporters and the public. The party's recent electoral performances have been dismal, attracting less than 10 per cent of the vote and currently it seems that it has neither the people nor the policies to have any realistic hope of returning to its glory days. Labour in Scotland had difficulty in producing areas of policy distinctiveness (McTavish 2016: 66). The election of Keir Starmer as Labour leader nationally may boost hopes of an electoral recovery as the Scottish question will have a profound impact on his hopes of becoming prime minister.

Scottish Conservatives

The decline of the Conservative Party in Scotland has been traced back to the 1960s when, it is argued, it failed to adapt to the changing social and economic conditions north of the border (Pearce 2011). The neo-liberal

Thatcherite policies of the 1980s attracted scant support in Scotland, further toxified the brand and hampered any hope of renewing its political fortunes. The legacy of Thatcher's premiership cast a long shadow and led to the Conservatives being widely characterized as anti-Scottish. For a considerable section of the Scottish electorate, the Conservatives are the 'other' (Mitchell 2015: 95), a label they have struggled to shake off. It has been asserted that the major problem with the Conservative Party in Scotland was its failure to engage in the national question (Finlay 2008). Unlike its Labour and Liberal Democrat peers, the Scottish Conservative Party refused to embrace devolution. After failing to secure a single seat in Scotland in its 1997 general election, the Scottish Conservative Party was compelled to undertake an internal review. This resulted in new organizational structures, which diluted the central powers in London and afforded more autonomy to the Scottish grouping.

Renewing unionism in Scotland has been challenging, as there was no clear path to power for the Scottish Conservatives. However, David Cameron's leadership of the Conservative Party marked a considerable change in attitude towards devolution. Convery (2016: 30) asserts that at the outset Cameron 'made clear that he was willing to go to extraordinary lengths to repair the damaged Conservative brand in Scotland'. He was much more supportive of devolution than previous Conservative leaders and adopted a pragmatic approach to territorial issues. As part of this accommodating style, Cameron made a number of highly significant interventions into Scottish politics. Under his leadership, the coalition government passed the Scotland Act 2012, which implemented the majority of the recommendations of the Calman Commission on devolution in Scotland. Through the Edinburgh Agreement (2012), Cameron granted the Scottish Government the power to hold a referendum on independence and agreed to abide by the outcome. Finally, on the morning after the referendum, he announced the Smith Commission to find a cross-party consensus for further devolution of powers to strengthen the Scottish Parliament within the UK (Convery 2016). The Commission reported in 2014 and set out the agreement reached by the main political parties on an extensive package of new fiscal powers for the Scottish Parliament. This 'extra devolution' was welcomed by David Cameron as a way of making the UK stronger.

The 2011 Scottish Conservative leadership election was significant as it was the first contested leadership election since the devolved settlement and as such provided a platform for a debate about the future of the party. During this campaign, two camps emerged: one contending that devolution should not be enhanced any further and that Scottish Conservatives should remain closely integrated to the UK Conservative Party; and another arguing that the Scottish Conservative Party had become more autonomous and should be shaping the debate on further powers to the Scottish Parliament (Simpkins 2018). Ruth Davidson, representing the former view, was narrowly elected as leader. It therefore appeared that change was unlikely, and that the Conservatives would remain opposed to any extension of the Scottish Parliament's powers. However, following a speech in February 2012 in which Prime Minister David Cameron acknowledged that the independence referendum did not have to be the end of the road, he asserted that following the vote he was 'open to looking at how the devolved settlement can be improved further'.

Ruth Davidson was forced to review her initial position and in response established a commission to ascertain how the powers of the devolved institutions could be strengthened to provide a clear alternative to independence. In May 2014, the Commission on the Future Governance of Scotland published its report and set out modest proposals for extending devolution to Scotland, including tax and welfare powers. Simpkins (2018) contends that, notwithstanding their lack of ambition, these proposals could be considered as a revolution for the Scottish Conservative Party, as they signalled that it was finally reconciled to devolution. As leader, Ruth Davidson presided over a coherent, conservative unionist agenda that incorporated increased Scottish autonomy. Her ebullient style and background represented a significant shift away from a 'traditional' conservative, and the media hailed her as an authentic, genuine leader. Her focus on the advantages of the Union rather than the downsides to independence appeared to strike a chord with a weary electorate with little appetite for a second referendum. Not long after the disaster of the Conservatives winning only one seat at the 2015 Westminster general election, Davidson led the party into the 2016 Scottish election, in which it doubled its number of Scottish Parliament seats to thirty-one and replaced Labour as the second largest party in Holyrood behind the SNP.

Against all predictions, the Scottish Conservatives made a shock electoral comeback in the 2017 snap general election, winning thirteen seats and saving Theresa May's Conservative government. It has been suggested that this reversal of fortunes was largely due to Davidson's integration of a distinct Scottish dimension into this previously centralist party.

Scottish Liberal Democrats

The Scottish Liberal Democrats are one of the three state parties within the federal Liberal Democrats, the others being the Welsh Liberal Democrats and the English Liberal Democrats. The Liberal Democrats do not contest elections in Northern Ireland.

Following the Liberal Democrats' decision in 2010 to go into coalition with the Conservatives in Westminster, their popularity and electoral support plummeted. The party's electoral malaise in Scotland and Wales appears to be inextricably linked to this coalition at Westminster. Polling data below reveals that the Scottish Liberal Democrats suffered a marked decline in support almost immediately after the coalition was formed (Evans 2015).

The party endured humiliation and defeat in both Holyrood and London, suffering huge defeats in constituencies that it had spent years cultivating (Denver 2011).

In the 2011 Scottish election, the party lost eleven seats and was reduced to just five, a tally that it managed to maintain in the subsequent 2016 election. This represented a devastating fall from grace for a party that had formed coalition governments with Scottish Labour from 1999–2007. In the wake of the coalition government in the UK, the party was reduced to just one MP in the 2015 general election, though by 2019 it had managed to increase this representation to four MPs.

In the political discourse there is widespread acceptance that the unpopularity of the UK coalition government meant both the Scottish and Welsh Liberal Democrats suffered at the ballot box (Bort 2012; Cutts and Russell 2015). This assertion is supported by evidence from 2011 electoral surveys that saw both the Scottish and Welsh Liberal Democrats record the biggest decline in support for any party in their respective nations (Evans 2015). For many voters, the Liberal Democrats had relinquished their status as the party of protest and were now the main focus of public disaffection and distrust. However, Evans (2015) argues that whilst it would be tempting to blame all their problems on the UK coalition government, Scottish Liberal Democrats must shoulder significant blame for this collapse and their continuing electoral woes. The calamitous coalition simply exposed many of the long-standing structural issues that have bedevilled the Liberal Democrats federally. The party has been organizationally weak, has attracted a small membership and, notwithstanding formal constitutional autonomy, has historically been highly dependent on the federal party (Bratberg 2009). This inherent weakness has led to the party occupying a precarious position in the Scottish political landscape, and it is precisely this historical frailty that made the coalition government's impact so damaging.

Additionally, the Scottish Liberal Democrats suffer from an identity crisis and have failed to carve out a unique, distinctive platform. Consequently, they become the squeezed middle. The party is broadly aligned to the social democratic, centre-left consensus that, as we shall see, dominates Scottish political life (McGarvey and Cairney 2008). A distinctive offering is simply crucial when contesting in this crowded and competitive electoral landscape that includes both the SNP and Labour. Indeed, it is exactly on this issue of being distinctive that the Scottish Liberal Democrats appear to have fallen short. As Lynch and McAngus (2012) note, many of the party's flagship policies are largely carbon copies of those of their opponents; for example, the SNP had similar policies on the Iraq War, Trident and the use of nuclear power. Furthermore, the Liberal Democrats' alignment with Labour and the Conservatives over the Calman Commission and the subsequent Scotland Act, coupled with a decision to govern with only Labour at Holyrood, has substantially restricted the party's ability to offer something different (Lynch and McAngus 2012). The party continues to be vulnerable and fragile as it has been unable to develop a defining vision (Evans 2015). In 2018, it won five seats and was replaced as the fourth Scottish party by the Green Party, with six seats.

The independence referendum

Divisive constitutional debates are a longstanding feature of Scottish politics, with the independence issue by far the most significant dividing line in recent times. The referendum of 2014 has cast a long shadow; indeed, it has been suggested that independence has permeated every aspect of Scottish policymaking and politics (Frain 2019). Following the securing of an overall majority in Holyrood in 2011, the SNP's manifesto commitment to an independence referendum became inescapable. The prevailing wisdom in Scotland was that securing support for constitutional change would be an enormous task. The polls suggested that only between a quarter and a third of Scots supported independence and that the contest would represent a straightforward win for the SNP's opponents. Furthermore, it was presumed that a significant defeat would inflict lasting damage on a fractured and demoralized SNP, facing obliteration and humiliation at the 2015 UK General Election and 2016 Scottish elections. Alex Salmond, the then SNP leader and Scottish first minister, had attempted to include a third option of enhanced powers on the ballot paper. The refusal by the prime minister to endorse a multi-option poll resulted in a more polarized debate. The stakes in this referendum were very high and it witnessed unprecedented levels of public engagement and debate. Mitchell (2015) contends that the 'Scottish question' is complex and not simply about national identity, nor constitutional status, but is also about the nature of society that people imagine for Scotland. *The Better Together* campaign, which was the main umbrella group of the Vote No camp, including the Labour, Conservative and Liberal Democrats, was an uneasy, unlikely alliance; it failed to catch the public imagination. Its promotion of the status quo was generally considered to be negative and uninspiring (Simpkins 2018 and this lack of ambition lingered long in the public consciousness. The victory for the Union was unambiguous – 55 per cent against 45 per cent – but post-referendum politics was not as expected, given the exceptional levels of public engagement and the defensive stance of the SNP's main political rivals. In the aftermath of the referendum, it was quickly apparent that the SNP was not a spent force. Rather than retreating wounded, following its defeat, the party was emboldened and determined to build on its momentum. As Mitchell (2015: 89) noted, 'instead of damaging introspection, supporters of independence celebrated progress in the belief that independence was within sight'.

Very shortly after the announcement of the result of the referendum, Alex Salmond announced his resignation as leader of the SNP and first minister of Scotland. He had spearheaded the campaign and he had been the focus of *Better Together* attacks. His immediate exit from the political stage allowed the focus to quickly shift away from the defeat to consolidating support and future campaigning. In his resignation speech, Salmond promised that 'the dream would never die'. The leadership was passed unchallenged to his deputy, Nicola Sturgeon, signalling the beginning of a new era and a smooth transition for the party from defeat in the referendum to energized campaigning for the 2015 election. The subsequent decision by the UK to leave the European Union (EU) has profoundly affected the context of independence debates and has provided a backdrop for growing demands for a second independence vote and support for the idea of the sovereignty of the Scottish people (Page 2016). In the 2016 Brexit referendum, 62 per cent of Scottish voters supported remaining in the EU while 38 per cent voted to leave. The result led Nicola Sturgeon to assert that Scotland was being taken out of the EU 'against our will', and this represented a significant and material change to the circumstances in which Scotland voted against independence in 2014 (Hepburn et al. 2021). The Scottish Parliament election of May 2021 was described by Johns (2021) as an 'as you were' election. Changes in vote shares were marginal and very few seats changed hands. He contends that this stasis can by largely explained by the fact that voting in Scottish elections remains largely a reflection of support or opposition to independence and that attitudes are deeply entrenched.

The Welsh political system

The main Welsh parties have all embraced devolution. Bradbury (2008) notes how the parties reorganized to fit with the requirements of this political system.

TABLE 5.1 *Welsh parliamentary election 2016*

	Constituency seats	Regional	Total
Labour	27	2	29
Plaid Cymru	6	6	12
Conservatives	6	6	12
Liberal Democrats	1	0	1
UKIP	0	0	0

Welsh Labour

Welsh Labour, a branch of the federal UK Labour Party, is the largest and most successful political party in modern Welsh politics. Labour has dominated Welsh politics for over a century. Even in the most difficult circumstances for the party, such as 1983, it has managed to hold on to a majority of Welsh parliamentary seats. Throughout the two decades of devolution, Labour has remained the largest party in the Welsh Assembly. It has won between twenty-six and thirty of the sixty Assembly seats at each of the five elections until 2016, with regional vote shares of between 30 and 37 per cent (Paun et al. 2019), see Table 5.1. The party has won the most seats in every Assembly election since its formation in 1999 and has been at the heart of every Welsh government during this period. An overview of its performance suggests that it has a stronghold on power in Wales; despite many setbacks, it has demonstrated remarkable political resilience. The preponderance of the Labour Party in Wales has extended to its representation in Westminster, where it has consistently held the majority of the forty seats. In recent years, its parliamentary strength has declined, with the number of seats held falling from twenty-eight in 2017 to twenty-two in the 2019 general election.

Since devolution there has been considerable internal wrangling about the structure of the party, accompanied by regular calls for an autonomous Welsh Labour Party. In 2002, Rhodri Morgan made his now famous 'clear red water' speech, in which he argued that there were nation-specific problems in Wales that required different solutions, advocating that the Welsh Labour movement was distinct and should be recognized as such within the broader Labour Party. The rhetoric of Morgan and his Welsh Labour ministers in his first two terms as first minister was underpinned by a twin-track argument: firstly, that the unique characteristics of Wales – particularity its smallness, culture and socio-economic legacy – required different policies from those in England; secondly, that these characteristics necessitated the rejection of neo-liberal politics favoured in England and the adoption of bespoke 'made in Wales' social democratic policies (Moon 2013).

Both Morgan and his successor, Carwyn Jones, were fluent Welsh speakers, which was viewed as symbolically important, as the language had been oppressed by the English for decades. Unlike its Scottish counterpart, Welsh Labour has successfully adapted to devolution and developed a distinctive brand. The appropriation of a different approach to the UK/ national Labour Party has allowed it to represent nation-specific values and appeal to a broad section of the electorate. The Welsh Labour Party maintains a distance between itself and the national Labour Party. However, the national Labour Party has demonstrated a strong preference for exercising single-party control, even when in minority government (Cole and Stafford 2015: 38).

In December 2018, Mark Drakeford replaced Carwyn Jones as first minister. A vocal supporter of Jeremy Corbyn, he promised radical socialist traditions in the style of Aneurin Bevan, Michael Foot and Rhodri Morgan. Yet, in the 2019 British general election, the Welsh Labour Party focused attention on Drakeford's leadership, with scant reference to the party's national leader, Jeremy Corbyn. During the Covid crisis, it was his assured, measured approach that won him support rather than his socialism or radicalism. Prior to the pandemic, there was some speculation that the political reign of Welsh Labour could come to an end in the 2021 Welsh Assembly election. Drakeford's leadership and enhanced visibility in response to the global emergency bolstered the party's electoral prospects (Elias 2021). In the 2021 Welsh Parliament election, Labour won thirty of the sixty seats, matching its best-ever Senedd election result, just one seat short of a majority.

Plaid Cymru

Independence in Wales has remained a largely dormant political issue, both within Wales and the wider UK context (Nyatanga 2020). It has been suggested that compared to the SNP, Welsh nationalism is the dragon that never roared (Lewis 2019). Nationalism in Wales has been largely focused on tradition and language rather than the creation of a separate state. The Welsh nationalist party Plaid Cymru (the Party of Wales) was formed in August 1925 by a diverse mix of individuals and organizations united around a shared objective of establishing a government in Wales (McAllister 2001). The party's initial focus was preserving and supporting indigenous culture and traditions. According to Davies (1994), describing Plaid Cymru as a political party before the end of the Second World War is a misnomer; during the 1920s and 1930s, it was no more than an educational and cultural movement. It was not until the 1970s that Plaid Cymru had developed into a mainstream political party in that it adopted an extensive range of policies and competed on existing lines of political division. A fundamental difficulty for Plaid Cymru has been developing a narrative that could attract support across the whole of Wales. Davies (1994) has highlighted the difficulties in articulating a common Welsh experience, due to the fragility of the Welsh identity.

Historically, Wales has not displayed the strong national confidence enjoyed by Scotland, and its people have often displayed ambivalence towards independence. Support for Welsh independence is increasing but remains a minority position. The party's electoral strength is concentrated in constituencies in north and west Wales, which have a relatively high proportion of Welsh speakers. Plaid Cymru is on the left of the political spectrum; Dafydd Elis-Thomas, party president from 1984 to 1990, aimed to develop it into a political force that would compete with the Labour Party. It has been contended that Plaid Cymru is more of a socialist party than a nationalist one, and consequently it cannot be described as a 'niche' political actor (Sandry 2011). In the 2007 Assembly elections, the party won fifteen seats and entered a formal coalition government with the Labour Party, which marked its first foray into government. Labour had already been sworn in as a single-party minority government, but its then leader, Rhodri Morgan, was keen to secure a majority through a coalition. In the 2011 elections, it lost four seats, dropping to a total of eleven, but in the 2016 and 2021 elections it arrested this decline, increasing to twelve and thirteen seats, respectively.

In the wake of Brexit and the global pandemic, there is a new political reality in Wales. There is a broad agreement that the Welsh government managed the coronavirus more effectively than the Westminster government. Additionally, the global emergency has tangibly demonstrated the importance of devolved competence over health. While support for independence in Wales has increased, regularly reaching between a quarter and a third of those sampled, this has not translated into increased support for Plaid Cymru (Basta and Henderson 2021). Despite renewed momentum in the independence campaign, Plaid Cymru has been unable to consolidate its position as the dominant political force in all but a few parts of north and west Wales.

Welsh Labour has emerged from the pandemic as the party best placed to advocate for Wales. The combination of pandemic and the implications of Brexit has strengthened support for devolution, invigorated calls for constitutional reform and witnessed the emergence of a non-party political campaign for Welsh independence. In January 2020, there were just 2,000 members of the pro-independence campaign group YesCymru, but by January 2021, membership of YesCymru had grown to 17,000. Constitutional instability in the UK has lifted the lid on the Pandora's box of Welsh independence with increasing support for the view that Wales could flourish as an independent nation.

The other smaller parties in Wales

The Welsh Conservative Party support for devolution has oscillated over the past two decades. It has shifted from a position of hostility to supporting devolution and has been viewed as more devolution-friendly than the Conservative Party in Westminster (Cole and Stafford 2015). The Liberal Democrat Party has declined dramatically in Wales and Scotland, losing over two-thirds of its seats between 2007 and 2016, after entering government at Westminster in coalition with the Conservatives. In Wales, the party won just one seat in 2016. But the proportional element of the electoral system has also enabled various smaller parties to secure representation at various points. The Scottish Greens have won seats at every election, without ever winning in any individual constituency, while in Wales, the UK Independence

Party (UKIP) won seven (12 per cent) of the sixty seats in 2016, although most of its elected representatives now sit as independents, after a series of splits and defections.

Northern Ireland's political system

Devolution in Northern Ireland has a long history, dating back to 1921. However, the unionist-dominated majoritarian system put in place by Westminster gave rise to discrimination against the Catholic minority, culminating in a sustained period of violence and civil unrest beginning in the 1960s which became known as 'the Troubles' (Paun et al. 2019). The parliament of Northern Ireland was prorogued between 1972 and 1999, with devolution suspended and replaced by direct rule from London. After almost three decades of conflict and prolonged negotiations, the Belfast/ Good Friday Agreement (GFA), signed in 1998, restored devolution. The GFA established new political institutions based on power-sharing. These unique arrangements were designed to ensure that both communities would be represented in government and to protect minority rights.

The Executive was appointed on the proportionate D'Hondt principle, with five parties holding ministerial posts. This created unique challenges: those who were once bitterly opposed were now required to co-govern, and deal with divisive issues relating to the legacy of a bitter conflict (Paun et al. 2019). Since the establishment of devolution in 1999, Northern Ireland's power-sharing governments have been fragile and prone to crisis. Following the prolonged negotiations leading to the GFA, the Northern Ireland Act and its implementation, there has been a series of breakdowns and suspensions of devolution, as well as times of severe threats to the continuation of the institutions. The most significant breakdown occurred in 2002 and it was not until 2007 that the St Andrews Agreement led to the restoration of devolution, underpinned in this case by the Northern Ireland (St Andrews Agreement) Act 2006 (Heenan and Birrell 2017). Following a decade of relative stability and cooperation between nationalists and unionists at Stormont, hopes were high that the devolved arrangements had finally become embedded and more resistant to collapse. This optimism was dashed when Sinn Féin brought down the devolved institutions in January 2017. Unlike previous occasions, this collapse did not signal the re-introduction of direct rule from London. In the absence of a power-sharing government, senior civil servants assumed responsibility for running Northern Ireland; however, their powers did not extend to making decisions normally made by ministers. Following a three-year impasse without devolution or direct rule, devolution was formally restored with the resumption of power-sharing at Stormont in January 2020. The power-sharing government that promised a new approach was led by the DUP and Sinn Féin.

TABLE 5.2 *Northern Ireland Assembly election results 2016*

DUP	28
Sinn Féin	27
SDLP	12
Ulster Unionists	10
Alliance	8
Other	5

In Northern Ireland, a key trend over the first two decades of devolution has been the increasing dominance of the more 'extreme' DUP and Sinn Féin (see Table 5.2). This was largely at the expense of the more moderate unionist and nationalist parties that were dominant in the first Northern Ireland Assembly elections, the Ulster Unionist Party (UUP) and the Social Democratic and Labour Party (SDLP). The UUP and SDLP have both lost more than 40 per cent of their voters over the first two decades of devolution. However, Northern Ireland also has the most balanced multi-party system of any of the four UK nations, with the two smaller parties (UUP and SDLP) securing around a quarter of the seats in the 2017 election (Institute for Government 2021).

The Northern Ireland Assembly election in May 2022 delivered seismic changes to the region's political landscape. For the first time, Sinn Féin won the largest number of seats in the Assembly. This historic win means a nationalist party is entitled to the First Minister post for the first time since the State was founded in 1921. The main unionist party, the Democratic Unionist Party (DUP), was pushed into second place, a position entitling the party to nominate a Deputy First Minister. However, the party has refused to join a new government without major changes to the post-Brexit trading arrangements known as the Northern Ireland Protocol (Tonge 2022). This Protocol agreed by the UK government and the EU in 2019 aligns Northern Ireland with EU rules and has imposed checks on some goods entering Northern Ireland from the rest of Great Britain. In a move designed to add pressure on the UK government to take action on the 'detested' protocol, in February 2022, the DUP withdrew its First Minister, Paul Givan, from the ruling Executive. Under the power-sharing system, Michelle O'Neill, as Sinn Féin Deputy First Minister, lost her position. Only a small number of caretaker ministers in the devolved government remained in place. Given that these ministers were unable take new or significant decisions, Stormont was effectively suspended. This 'zombie' government can continue for six months at most, when the Secretary of State will be compelled to call an election.

Whilst attention has focused on Sinn Féin becoming the largest party and deadlock over the Protocol, the 2022 Assembly election was also significant as it marked by the best-ever performance by the party of

TABLE 5.3 *Northern Ireland Assembly election results May 2022*

Sinn Féin	27
DUP	25
Alliance Party	17
Ulster Unionist Party	9
SDLP	8
Others	4

the centre ground, the Alliance (see Table 5.3). It more than doubled its previous Assembly seat tally and raised questions about the direction of travel in the North's political landscape. Rather than two political blocs, Northern Irish politics is now dominated by three minorities, unionist, nationalist and the non-aligned.

Democratic Unionist Party

Unionism in Northern Ireland is a broad church, complicated and multi-layered, incorporating a number of diverse groups and actors; it is a movement beset by political, class, cultural, geographical and religious tensions and conflicts. The DUP has replaced the UUP as the main unionist party. The Protestant/unionist/loyalist (PUL) community in Northern Ireland is defined by internal strife: the secular versus the religious; the rural versus the urban; the dogmatic versus the pragmatic; the elite versus the grassroots (Murphy and Evershed 2019). While Northern Ireland unionists may be divided along a number of significant fault lines, they share a fundamental political aspiration: defending the Union between Great Britain and Northern Ireland. Significantly, they see themselves as not only defending against an intractable threat posed by Irish nationalism, but also from the apathetic gaze of the London government. Farrington (2001: 69) refers to the unionist sense of 'siege and anxiety' over their political future in response to both Irish republican hostility and mainland British ambivalence.

The DUP was formed in 1971 by the firebrand Reverend Dr Ian Paisley, following his election to the Northern Ireland Parliament. The influence of the fundamentalist and evangelical Free Presbyterian Church, of which Paisley was the founder and long-serving moderator, on the party has been significant. In his implacable defence of Northern Ireland's position within the UK, he opposed all compromises with Irish Catholics, nationalists and republicans. Despite this stance, in 2006, astonishingly, he agreed to share power with Sinn Féin and lead the devolved government. In their definitive book, Tonge et al. (2014) trace the trajectory of the DUP from a religion-dominated protest party in the 1970s to a pragmatic party of government in the 2000s. They analyse the transformation of the party, outlining how it has embraced a more modern party structure and progressive ideals, detailing the tensions that this change has created both internally and externally. On a range of social and moral issues, such as abortion and same-sex marriage, the party was and remains deeply conservative. Post-Paisley, the dominance of the Free Presbyterian Church has diminished but religiosity remains a prominent aspect within the DUP and continues to be a hallmark of the party (Tonge et al. 2014).

As the electoral fortunes of the UUP declined, those losses largely translated into gains for the DUP. By 2003, the DUP's unrelenting denouncement of the GFA paid off, as it eclipsed the more moderate UUP to become the dominant unionist political party in Northern Ireland. As Murphy and Evershed (2019) noted, with ascendency came political responsibilities. If the DUP was to transform from a party of opposition to one of power, it would have to embark on a different route, involving compromise and pragmatism. The party claimed that revisions to the GFA contained in the St Andrews Agreement addressed fundamental flaws in the 1998 settlement. Importantly for its electoral base, the party claimed that concessions won had forced Sinn Féin to support policing and the courts. This provided a platform for what had previously been represented by the DUP as completely unthinkable and saw the party's leadership agree to share power with their sworn Irish republican adversaries. However, when Ian Paisley assumed the position of first minister in May 2007, it nonetheless marked a significant watershed in the DUP's move 'from hardline bystander to major governing force' (Tonge et al. 2014: 4). As power-sharing became embedded, the DUP's support stabilized. Since May 2007, the Northern Ireland Executive has been led by the two dominant parties: the DUP and Sinn Féin. In January 2016, Paisley's successor, Peter Robinson, stepped down and was replaced by Arlene Foster. In May 2016, she led the party to victory in Assembly elections, with the DUP retaining all of its thirty-eight seats. Foster remained first minister in a newly formed power-sharing government with Sinn Féin.

Following almost a decade of uninterrupted devolution and power-sharing, the Northern Ireland Executive and Assembly collapsed in January 2017. The devolved institutions imploded when the first minister was forced from office after the resignation of the then deputy first minister, the late Martin McGuinness. This move was in protest at the DUP's mishandling of a sustainable energy scheme, the Renewable Heat Incentive (RHI), coupled with a perceived lack of respect for Irish culture and identity. Divisions between the parties were also intensified by Brexit, which the DUP supported and the other parties did not. In response, the UK government called an Assembly election in March 2017. The result meant the DUP had just a one-seat majority over Sinn Féin, the narrowest ever margin between the two dominant parties. Intense talks failed to resolve the political stalemate; deadlines came and went, but despite calls from unionists, the UK government steadfastly refused to implement direct rule.

TABLE 5.4 *Westminster December 2019 election results*

DUP	8
Sinn Féin	7
SDLP	2
Alliance	1
UUP	0

Government in Northern Ireland went into abeyance for three years and civil servants were left to oversee the day-to-day management of the region. Research has highlighted the detrimental impact of this impasse on Northern Ireland's already grave economic and social problems.

The political dynamics of Northern Ireland took an unexpected turn in 2017 following the snap Westminster general election. Given her failure to secure a majority, the then prime minister Theresa May decided to enter into a confidence and supply agreement with the DUP's ten MPs to prop up her minority government. The DUP would support the Conservatives on major financial and Brexit votes in the House of Commons in return for additional funding for the Northern Ireland Executive (Tonge 2017). This highly controversial confidence and supply agreement not only ensured the survival of Theresa May's government but also become a central focus in the UK negotiations for exiting the EU (Birrell and Heenan 2020). The agreement ended badly when the DUP was cast aside by May's successor, Boris Johnson, who reached a Brexit deal that aligned Northern Ireland much more closely to the EU than the rest of the UK – the opposite of what Johnson had pledged to the DUP at its party conference the previous year.

In the December 2019 general election, both the DUP and Sinn Féin suffered losses (see Table 5.4). For the first time, unionism no longer held the majority of seats for Northern Ireland in Westminster. The DUP and Sinn Féin's inability to find compromise, which resulted in almost three years of political limbo, was punished by the voters (Hayward 2020). The DUP, having won a record ten seats in 2017, lost two of its three Belfast seats, including the North Belfast constituency of Westminster leader Nigel Dodds. Sinn Féin's winning of seven seats matched its 2017 result, but the party's vote share fell everywhere beyond North Belfast. Perhaps the most notable feature of the election was the swing from both sides towards middle-ground voting, which brought significant gains for the Alliance Party and the SDLP (Tonge and Evans 2020).

Sinn Féin

Sinn Féin is a left-wing Irish republican party active both in the Republic of Ireland and in Northern Ireland. Its name translates into English as 'we ourselves'. The party is currently the second largest in the Northern Ireland

Assembly, as well as the largest Irish nationalist party. It currently sits in government in Northern Ireland alongside the DUP. Michelle O'Neill is the party leader in the North of Ireland, and also Northern Ireland's deputy first minister.

By the early 1980s, Sinn Féin shifted from a military focus to becoming more politically active, winning over 100,000 votes in the 1983 general election, in which Gerry Adams – party president from 1983 to 2018 – was first elected as MP for West Belfast. The 1998 GFA provided the party with a guaranteed share of executive power based on the proportion of votes it secured, and that presented a potential route to a united Ireland. Significantly, the party viewed the Agreement not as a political settlement but rather as a basis to further advance its aims (Whiting 2018). The Northern Ireland peace process witnessed a remarkable change in Sinn Féin's political strategy. Despite having pledged to destroy Northern Ireland as a political entity, Sinn Féin accepted the GFA and has supported the political institutions created under that deal. Evans and Tonge (2012: 39) likened the party's backing for political institutions 'to the zeal of converts' with the once 'unequivocal support' for the IRA's 'armed struggle' replaced by participatory politics. Sinn Féin participates in Westminster elections, but its MPs do not take up their seats as they refuse to swear an oath of allegiance to the Monarch.

Social Democratic and Labour Party

The Social Democratic and Labour Party (SDLP) was formed in 1970 from an amalgamation of several smaller parties. Like Sinn Féin, this nationalist party is committed to a united Ireland; however, a significant difference between the two parties is the SDLP's rejection of the use of violence. The SDLP and the UUP were the main architects of the 1998 GFA, prioritizing the peace agreement before party fortunes. Its leader, John Hume, promoted a post-nationalist agenda: respect. This moderate party was adversely affected by a system that has favoured the extremes within each communal bloc. In the 1998 Assembly election, it attracted more votes than any other party in Northern Ireland, receiving a 22 per cent share. By 2003, the roles were reversed, and the SDLP was returned as the fourth largest party with 17 per cent, while Sinn Féin was the second largest with 23.5 per cent. In the post-GFA period, politics in the region have lurched to the extremes, with Sinn Féin successfully depicting itself as the stronger defender of nationalist interests (McGlinchey 2019). In the June 2017 general election, the Westminster representation the SDLP had enjoyed since its foundation was wiped out. All three of its MPs lost their seats and the party appeared to be in an intractable decline. However, in 2019, the party won back two Westminster seats, a result widely viewed as a revival of constitutional nationalism. Cognizant that Sinn Féin was the only all-island party with significant electoral presence in both jurisdictions, after much speculation, the SDLP decided to formally address this issue. In January 2019, the

SDLP and Fianna Fáil (a Republic of Ireland-only party) announced a new partnership, backed by almost 70 per cent of party members at a special party conference. While the party hailed the move as historic, it had little if any effect on policies and appears now to have been quietly dropped.

Ulster Unionist Party

The Ulster Unionist Party (UUP) is the oldest political party in Northern Ireland. Its electoral fortunes have recently shifted from a position of dominance, in the period 1921–2, to a position of increasing marginalization (Murphy 2009). Historically, the party had strong links with the Conservative Party but by the mid-1980s these had significantly declined. The period from the late 1960s onwards has seen the emergence of other unionist parties. Despite these challenges, the UUP remained the largest unionist party in Northern Ireland and was instrumental in drafting the 1998 GFA. The party leader from 1995 to 2005 was David Trimble; in 1998, he was a co-recipient of the Nobel Prize for Peace with the SDLP leader John Hume. The party participated in the newly created Northern Ireland Executive as the largest political party in Northern Ireland and David Trimble served as first minister. In the first elections to the new Northern Ireland Assembly in June 1998, the UUP emerged as the largest party, winning twenty-eight of the 108 seats. Thereafter, its electoral fortunes began to decline. Growing opposition to the Agreement from the Protestant community, coupled with a strong electoral challenge from the DUP, caused internal conflict and division, and the party struggled to maintain cohesion. By 2003, the DUP had replaced the UUP as the largest unionist party in the Assembly. The next Westminster general election, in 2005, produced the worst ever election result for the UUP; the party was reduced to a single MP to the DUP's nine. In May 2021, Doug Beattie was elected as the new leader of the party, its fifth in nine years, with no MPs at Westminster and just ten MLAs at Stormont. While the UUP is widely viewed as more moderate and liberal than its rival unionist parties, it has struggled to develop a compelling narrative to staunch the flow of support to the centrist Alliance Party. In their overview of the party, Hennessey et al. (2019) assert that, despite its hegemony, covering almost five decades, relatively little has been written about the party. They assert that despite being key architects of the GFA, the UUP has failed to become a significant custodian of this historic peace deal and is unlikely to regain its halcyon days of being the standard bearer for unionism.

Alliance Party

The Alliance Party was established in 1970 as a pro-union, but non-sectarian, cross-community party (Eggins 2015). It is liberal, progressive, pro-European and internationalist in its outlook. The party has links to the Alliance of Liberals and Democrats for Europe (ALDE) (previously the European Liberal Democrat and Reform Party) and a sister party to the Liberal Democrats. It rejects the traditional binary constitutional politics of support for Northern Ireland's place in the UK versus backing for a united Ireland and now claims neutrality on Northern Ireland's constitutional future (Tonge 2020). Uniquely in Northern Ireland, this political party aimed to attract electoral support from both the nationalist and unionist constituencies. Often depicted as the party of the 'neithers', it rejects this simplistic binary depiction and argues that there are far more identities than the traditional green or orange and that many people hold multiple identities (Farry 2019). In the 1980s and 1990s, it attracted approximately 10 per cent of the vote. It was a strong advocate for the GFA and won six seats in the first Northern Ireland Assembly election. Its leader, Lord John Alderdice, was Speaker of the Assembly from 1998 to 2004.

The Alliance Party has occupied the middle ground of politics in the region, but despite a number of earlier false dawns, it failed to make a significant impact at the polls. Its traditional support base has been in the Greater Belfast area, with little apparent interest in nor impact on constituencies outside this bailiwick. Power-sharing in Northern Ireland was designed to broaden the relatively small middle ground but instead has witnessed an increasing polarization of politics, with support for more moderate parties withering. However, the stand-off between Sinn Féin and the DUP that left the region without a government, the decision to leave the EU and tensions around the DUP/Conservative Party confidence and supply agreement have led to rising support for this centralist party. In an evolving political landscape, Alliance's recent electoral successes have pushed it into becoming the third largest party, ahead of two former political giants, the UUP and the SDLP. In 2016, Naomi Long, a former Belfast Lord Mayor, became leader of the party and she has presided over the most successful elections in Alliance's history. Having struggled for decades as a non-aligned party in a sharply divided political system, 2019 proved to be a momentous year. In May, it secured twenty-one extra seats in the local elections, representing a 65 per cent rise in councillors, and in the European elections Naomi Long won one of Northern Ireland's three seats in the European Parliament. This was a ground-breaking victory, as the region had returned two unionists and one nationalist to the European Parliament since 1979. Alliance has been outspoken in its opposition to Brexit and was particularly critical of the DUP's pro-Brexit stance. In this historic win, Long attracted support from both sides of Northern Ireland's constitutional divide, almost trebling the support for her party from the previous election, in 2014. Significantly, in the FPTP Westminster election in December, it was able to maintain this momentum and attracted just under 17 per cent of the vote share, making significant gains in many constituencies. According to Tonge (2020), there are two broad explanations for this electoral surge. The first is the range of contextual factors pertaining to the elections in 2019. The second is the broader political trend of ideological dealignment within Northern Ireland reflected in a number of social attitudes surveys. For the Alliance Party, this success has been a long time coming and, given its support in three elections, cannot be easily dismissed as a flash in the pan. The question is: what impact will Alliance moving into third place and increasing its influence have on the politics of Northern Ireland? Although the political discourse remains dominated by the constitutional question the rise of the Alliance party has challenged the tribal nature of politics. Their electoral gains raised serious questions about the consociational architecture of the devolved government and the cross-community voting formulas. The party contends that they are disadvantaged by a power-sharing system which rewards and perpetuates division.

The May 2022 Assembly election

In a move designed to add pressure on the UK government to take action on the 'detested' protocol, in February 2022 the DUP withdrew its First Minister, Paul Givan, from the ruling Executive. Under the power-sharing system, Michelle O'Neill, as Sinn Féin Deputy First Minister, lost her position. The Northern Ireland Assembly election which followed in May 2022 delivered seismic changes to the region's political landscape. For the first time Sinn Féin won the largest number of seats in the Assembly. This historic win meant that a nationalist party is entitled to the First Minister post, for the first time since the State was founded in 1921. The main unionist party, the Democratic Unionist Party (DUP) was pushed into second place. This position entitled the party to nominate a Deputy First Minister. However, the party has refused to join a new government without major changes to the post-Brexit trading arrangements known as the Northern Ireland Protocol (Tonge 2022). This Protocol, agreed by the UK government and the EU in 2019, aligns Northern Ireland with EU rules and has imposed checks on some goods entering Northern Ireland from the rest of Great Britain.

However, unlike previous periods of collapse, new legislation meant that Ministers could remain in post as 'caretakers' for a twenty-four-week period. During this period, government was significantly reduced. Without an Executive it was not possible to make new decisions that were significant, controversial or cross-cutting. Caretaker ministers could manage their departments and provide limited direction but were compelled to follow previous policies. Those twenty-four weeks began on 13 May and ended on 28 October. From then, the caretaker ministers were no longer in post, and it fell to unelected civil servants to make the decisions. When the twenty-four weeks elapsed, the Secretary of State was legally obliged to call an election within twelve weeks. Despite repeatedly insisting that he would call an election, the Secretary of State Chris Heaton-Harris announced that he would bring forward new legislation to allow him to delay taking this step.

Conclusions

All of the devolved regions operate multi-party systems. It can be argued that all have significant nationalist parties, as the UUP and the DUP can be classified as British nationalist parties. The partial proportional electoral systems in Scotland and Wales designed to produce more politically pluralistic legislatures have not achieved this aim. The SNP has dominated Scottish politics. In Wales, Labour has been the main party of government throughout the first two decades of devolution. Notwithstanding the DUP confidence and supply arrangement with Theresa May's Conservative government, regionally, there has been relatively limited government alignment with the Westminster government. In Scotland and Wales, both the Conservatives and Labour have sought to carve out identities distinct from their English counterparts. In Northern Ireland, the whole structure of a functioning government is underpinned by a legal requirement that the main unionist and nationalist parties form a power-sharing coalition.

6

Devolved political institutions

Introduction

The implementation of devolution in 1999 brought into existence forms of parliaments for Scotland, Northern Ireland and Wales. Legislation in 1998 established the Scottish Parliament, the Northern Ireland Assembly and the National Assembly for Wales. To a large degree the devolved elected bodies were based on a mini-Westminster model, or at least a unicameral mini-version with the absence of a second chamber. The major broad areas of work and procedures would reflect House of Commons practice, with the main functions covering legislation, scrutiny, financial approval, questions, debates and ministerial statements. The original model for Scotland was to prove the most sustainable over the twenty years of devolution. A major difference existed from 1999 in relation to Wales as the Assembly did not have responsibility for primary legislation, unlike the Scottish Parliament and the Northern Ireland Assembly. This was to change in 2011 when, following UK legislation and a referendum, the National Assembly for Wales became directly responsible for primary legislation, replacing a complex system involving Westminster approval for Welsh legislative measures. In 2020, legislation changed the name of the Assembly to Senedd Cymru or Welsh Parliament, to be commonly known as the Senedd. The Northern Ireland Assembly had the longstanding devolved model of parliamentary and legislative devolution of the Stormont system. An Assembly replaced the previous Stormont House of Commons and Senate, although this was to be subject to political breakdown for periods since 1999.

Procedures adopted in the devolved Parliament and Assemblies were closely aligned to Westminster practice, but some changes were introduced originally to reflect the requirements of the devolution settlement, differences in size and capacity, and the political environment. Various amendments to operating practices were introduced following reviews and inquiries into aspects of procedures, including relations with the public, the role of an opposition, media coverage and procedures for individual members' legislation. The continuing degree of similarity in operating procedures and issues encountered make it possible and useful to compare the work and performance of the devolved bodies in relation to their common main functions.

Types of legislation

The legislative function can be seen as the most significant delegation of power produced by devolution as control over primary legislation passed from Westminster to the legislatures for devolved matters. Some aspects of the devolved legislative function remained similar to Westminster practice, including the different types of legislation and the dominant position of government-sponsored legislation. The amount and focus of legislation reflected more strongly differences between the three nations in terms of the nature of the respective governments, ideological differences and the role of opposition parties. Devolution also brought some unique aspects, particularly through the provisions for legislative consent motions. The main types of legislation are similar in each of the three devolved jurisdictions. Government bills are the main category of legislation and are public bills introduced by the devolved governments to give effect to government policy. Members' bills are public bills introduced by an individual member and must follow certain procedures. Committee bills are public bills introduced to give effect to a proposal from a committee of the Scottish Parliament or of the Assemblies for Wales or Northern Ireland within the subject remit of the committees. Private bills are introduced for the purpose of obtaining powers for an individual, a body corporate or an association. Hybrid bills are public bills that may make provision about general law as well as affect particular bodies. Statutory instruments are delegated legislation conferring detailed measures under parent primary legislation.

The amount and nature of government-sponsored bills can vary, reflecting factors such as whether the government in power has an overall majority. When the SNP government was in a minority position it could not rely on legislation as its primary policy vehicle (Keating and Cairney 2010). Opposition party attempts to delay or amend bills may also affect the legislative output. The output in Northern Ireland was dismissed by the period of collapse and continuing difficulties in reaching consensus in the five-party Executive. Legislative output in Wales was limited by the history of so much UK legislation.

The legislative process

From the outset of devolution, Scotland and Northern Ireland had to establish a system for enacting primary legislation, later to be followed for Wales. Arrangements were made to largely follow the legislative stages set down for primary legislation at Westminster but recognized some different features, for example, the absence of second-chamber stages. In Scotland, a pre-legislative stage was built in to allow Parliament and interested groups to be consulted about proposed legislation before it becomes a bill. This was seen as implementing a commitment that there should be an open and participatory procedure, encouraging and allowing access to the decision-making process. It also provides an opportunity for evidence to be obtained and may involve round-table discussions and fact-finding exercises (Johnson 2009: 30). A report on the pre-consultation must be attached to draft bills as a memorandum, which means that views supporting or opposing the proposals are published. This has been seen as mainly a method of making comments available to the committee and not as a mechanism through which to seek changes in government legislation (ibid.: 31).

Although there are different types of bills and different ways in which they may originate, all Scottish legislation must pass through three basic stages. In stage one, the bill is sent to a parliamentary committee, which writes a report for Parliament. Parliament then considers the general principles of the bill and votes on whether it should proceed. If successful, the bill then moves to stage two, where it undergoes a more detailed line by line scrutiny either by the appropriate committee or the whole Parliament. The relevant committee can ask witnesses – whether experts, researchers or members of pressure groups – to give evidence on the bill or recommend changes. Amendments to the bill can be made at this stage. In stage three, the bill is considered by the whole Parliament and up to half the bill can be referred back for further consideration. Amendments can be made at this stage. Once a bill has been passed, it may be challenged by the Advocate General or by the Secretary of State on the grounds that it is outside the legislative competence of the Scottish Parliament or adversely affects reserved matters. Otherwise, the bill is submitted for Royal Assent.

Wales has officially a four-stage process for the consideration of bills. Stage one involves the consideration of the general principles of a bill by a committee that focuses on the main proposals of the bill rather than the fine detail. The committee may also invite representations from interested parties and may take written and oral evidence to inform its work. Once the committee has reported, the Welsh Senedd will be asked to debate and vote on the bill's general principles, the stage one debate. Stage two involves the detailed consideration of a bill by committee and any amendments that Assembly members have tabled. There is no limit to the number of amendments but only committee members may vote. Agreement on a financial resolution may also be necessary at stage two. Stage three involves the detailed consideration of the bill as a whole and any amendments proposed by Assembly members and approved by the presiding officer. If the Senedd chooses, it may consider a bill at a further stage three report stage. At the last stage of the process, there is a vote to pass the final text of the bill – by a simple majority, other than in the case of a protected subject matter, when a super majority of two thirds of Assembly members is needed. After stage four, the bill can move to receive the Royal Assent.

The process was largely similar for legislation in the Northern Ireland Assembly although officially broken up into six stages. In the first stage, the bill is formally tabled, with the speaker having confirmed that it is within the legislative competence of the Assembly. At the second stage, there is a general debate on the bill's principles followed by a vote. This is followed by the third stage of referral to an appropriate statutory committee for detailed investigation and a report to the Assembly. A fourth consideration stage provides an opportunity for members to vote on the details of the bill, including amendments to it, and there is provision for a separate further consideration stage. At the final stage, the bill is passed or failed (no amendments may be made at the final stage) and then passes for Royal Assent.

Legislative output in Scotland

The total number of acts passed in recent years has been similar in number, sitting at seventeen for 2019, eighteen for 2020 and twenty for 2021 (see Table 6.1). The overwhelming majority of these acts were government legislation, with the number of members' acts and private acts small in number each year. This is indicated by the bills under consideration by the Scottish Parliament in 2020. There were seventeen government bills, two members' bills and one private bill. The subject of the legislation passed shows three main areas. Social policy dominates, comprising 25 per cent of the total legislation, followed by law-and-order matters (18 per cent) and financial matters (17 per cent). Clearly in fourth position are, perhaps

TABLE 6.1 *Acts passed by year 2014–21*

Year	Scotland	N. Ireland	Wales
2021	20	8	4
2020	18	6	3
2019	17	–	4
2018	15	–	3
2017	7	–	4
2016	22	30	5
2015	13	10	6
2014	19	12	7

surprisingly, governance issues. The remaining categories, of more limited significance, are business/economy matters, agriculture and transport.

The Scottish Parliament adopted an innovative approach in making provision for bills to be introduced by individual members. The intention was to give members a more realistic chance than at Westminster to initiate and take legislation through to completion. Support to introduce a bill was required from only eleven members and a non-executive bills unit was established to provide support for members in drafting legislation and carrying out consultations (Johnston 2009: 34). An issue with the need to prioritize an initial surge in member proposals led to a more rigorous procedure, with support from eighteen members required, a consultation process of at least twelve weeks and the need to have the support of at least half of the political parties, to ensure broad support. The amount of members' legislation passed was not to grow substantially, with a total of only three in the period 2003–7 and seven in the period 2007–11. The process was difficult and lengthy for members and on occasions government took up the substantive issue. The majority of members' bills fell at some stage. In the period 2017–18, only one or two bills advanced by members became law. In 2017, a Seat Belts on School Transport (Scotland) Act required school transport vehicles to be fitted with seat belts. In 2018, one of the few controversial members' bills was eventually passed, the Offensive Behaviour at Football and Threatening Communications (Scotland) Act 2018, which repealed a previous Act of the Scottish Government. This was based on the argument that the existing legislation had failed to tackle sectarianism and unfairly targeted supporters. In 2019, a member's bill, the Children (Equal Protection from Assault) (Scotland) Act abolished the defence of reasonable chastisement.

Introduced in 2019 was a Period Products (Free Provision) (Scotland) Bill and a Protection of Workers (Retail and Age-restricted Goods and Services) (Scotland) Bill. During the fourth period of parliament until 2017 no fewer than twenty-eight members' bills were introduced, but most fell. Many proposals are a response by some members to current issues relating to matters of public concern. The mechanism provides an opportunity for issues to be formally raised and suggestions for government legislative action made. The amendment process in Parliament also gives formal opportunities for individual and opposition members to influence and change legislative proposals, but most amendments to bills are made by the government.

Private bills do not play a major role and only a few such pieces of legislation are passed each year. While usually largely technical and relating to minor private organizations, the category has included powers to authorize major infrastructure projects, such as the Edinburgh Tram Bill and the Glasgow Airport Rail Link Bill. Most examples largely represent technical requirements, for example, the Edinburgh Bakers' Widows' Fund Act 2018, allowing the transfer of funds, and the Solicitors in the Supreme

Courts of Scotland (Amendment) Bill 2019, to amend powers of the body. The latter was the only private bill under consideration in January 2020 (Scottish Parliament Information Centre 2021).

Legislative output in Wales

It was only in 2011 that the National Assembly for Wales assumed primary legislative powers, and adjusting to the enhanced legislative powers required time. The quantity of primary legislation was not to assume the same proportions as Scotland or Northern Ireland. Between 2011 and 2016, the total number of Acts passed was twenty-five and this rate of output was not to increase, with the figure for 2019 four Acts, for 2020 three Acts and for 2021 four Acts. A review of the legislative process in 2015 was to state the view that the volume of legislative product should not be regarded as the measure of success (National Assembly for Wales, Constitutional and Legislative Committee 2015: para. 32). The Assembly faced an added difficulty at times in decoupling new Welsh legislation from existing English and Welsh laws, with further issues over the boundaries of legislative competence. The majority of legislation enacted was overwhelmingly government legislation. Members' legislation existed but did so on the basis of a ballot usually held once a year, in which only one of the bills that members proposed was successful and the member then given twenty-five days to table a leave to progress to a bill and then thirteen months to introduce a bill. In 2018, the proposed member's Autism Bill was defeated and in 2017, two members' bills, on older people's rights and the protection of Welsh historical place names, were rejected. There have been examples in recent years of a bill proposed by an Assembly committee being passed into law, for example, the Public Services Ombudsman Act 2019; a bill proposed by the Assembly Commission was at its final stage at the end of 2019, the Senedd and Elections (Wales) Bill.

This Bill led to the renaming of the Welsh Assembly to Senedd, reducing the voting age to sixteen and reforming electoral arrangements. An examination of the content of legislation passed between 2011 and 2020 shows that social policy is the dominant subject, representing twenty-three out of forty-one Acts, mostly covering health and education. The majority of the remainder represent largely equality, the environment, governance, agriculture and finance. The strong focus on social policies reflects the priorities of the Welsh Labour Party.

In 2015, the Welsh Assembly's Constitutional and Legislative Affairs Committee carried out a review of the quality, preparation and scrutiny of legislation and made a series of recommendations (National Assembly for Wales, Constitutional and Legislative Affairs Committee 2015). The report drew attention to a tendency for legislation to focus on a framework within which more detail would be added through subordinate legislation.

This was explained as reflecting the experience of the Assembly under the previous system of executive devolution and use of measures (ibid.: para. 39). Recommendations were made that bills should be more fully thought through, pre-legislative scrutiny should be improved and a compulsory report stage of scrutiny added for each bill. The review also recommended that a financial memorandum is published alongside all draft bills and there should be a review of procedures for bypassing stage-one scrutiny. The majority of recommendations were accepted by the Welsh Government, agreed totally or in part, or subject to consideration and review (Jones et al. 2016). The Government proposed a more coordinated legislative programme with no more than five or six bills each year, a strengthening of the pre-introduction assessment of bills and accepting an earlier identification of financial implications and more efficient stakeholder engagement. In 2016, the Law Commission in Wales had made recommendations relating to the consolidating and codifying law in Wales and made further recommendations relating to the quality, publication and availability of legislation. Following these two reports, the Welsh Government published a consultation on interpreting Welsh legislation, which led to the Legislation (Wales) Act 2019. This Act made provision about the interpretation and operation of Welsh legislation, including placing duties on the Counsel General and Welsh ministers relating to the accessibility of Welsh law. This included making Welsh law available to the public, dealing with language issues, and the clear formulation of law and amending and re-enacting subordinate legislation.

Legislative output in Northern Ireland

With the gap in the passage of legislation in the period 2017–19, legislation enacted between 2011 and 2016 provides the data relating to the nature of law making by the Assembly. In the short period of the new Assembly ending in 2017 only one Act, on the budget, was passed. Only two bills, an Executive bill and a private member's bill, were in the system when the Assembly was dissolved. Between 2011 and 2016, sixty out of sixty-seven bills passed were Executive bills, showing, as in Scotland and Wales, the dominance of the legislative process by the government. The number of private members' bills that were successful averaged one half per year – not significantly different from Scotland and Wales. Of the four private members' bills passed, three were controversial: legislation on special advisers to ministers, an Assembly and Executive Reform Act to facilitate an official opposition, and a Human Trafficking and Exploitation (Criminal Justice and Support for Victims) Bill making the purchase of sex services illegal. Five private members' bills were unsuccessful, including a Speed Limits Bill and a Human Transportation Bill. Two bills sponsored by a statutory committee were passed in the 2011–16 period, both relating to the reform of ombudsman offices. Only one private member's bill was passed in 2020–1, relating to the regulation of ministers' special political advisors. While the amount of legislation passed may appear large, for example, compared to twenty-five Acts in Wales during this period, an important factor is the more extensive range of devolved powers; for example, Northern Ireland had often to enact its own legislation on social security changes even when maintaining parity with Great Britain on such matters as pensions.

The amount of legislation passed may also seem large, given the operation of petitions of concern. This was a mechanism introduced to protect minorities, which meant that if thirty MLAs signed a petition of concern, a legislative proposal or a motion had to have cross-community support in the Assembly, i.e. 60 per cent of members or 40 per cent in each community designation. A widespread use of petitions of concern developed, with the mechanism used 115 times in the period 2011–16 (Smyth 2016). It was used eighty-six times by the DUP, which was the only party with over thirty members. Petitions could be used against proposals for amendments to legislation, not just the whole bill. Some 84 per cent of petitions related to fourteen bills, and mostly to a Justice Bill 2015 and the Assembly and Executive Reform (Assembly Opposition) Bill. It was not common for whole bills to fall because of petitions but this did happen to veto proposed bills to allow same-sex marriage. The mechanism was being used in ways different from the usual intention. Part of the agreed changes for the return of the Assembly in 2020 in the *New Decade, New Approach* document were amendments to the petitions of concern. Requirements were a fourteen-day consideration period, support from at least two parties was necessary and that it could not be used at every stage of the legislative process. Anything relating to the conduct of an MLA was removed (Torrance and Johnson 2021).

The topics covered by the Acts passed in 2011–16 are dominated by two areas, social policy and finance, accounting for almost half the legislative output (see Table 6.2). One quarter of Acts relate to social policy, ranging over health, education, housing and social security. The next two categories, at 10 per cent each, are business and governance, followed by the environment and law and justice. The remaining topics mostly cover roads, transport, agriculture and regulatory measures.

The Assembly had an accelerated passage procedure, which allowed a bill to pass all stages quickly, omitting the committee stage. There has to be an Assembly vote on a cross-community basis to allow accelerated passage. Budget bills were passed this way, as a consultation takes place within the Assembly before the bill is introduced. Social security legislation, for example, on pensions, may be accelerated if in parity with legislation in Great Britain. Between 2011 and 2016, seventeen of the sixty-seven bills

TABLE 6.2 *Northern Ireland Acts by topic 2011–16*

Topic	Percentage
Social policy	25
Finance	23
Business	10
Governance	10
Environment/planning	8
Law and justice	6
Other	17

were fast-tracked, on occasions for reasons of urgency, for example, the Air Passenger Duty (Setting of Rate) Bill. However, at times there has been criticism of the use of this procedure.

Legislative consent motions

The Scottish Parliament and the Assemblies in Wales and Northern Ireland are responsible for another form of legislative activity arising from devolution. This was the requirement for a legislative consent motion to be approved by the devolved legislature to allow the Westminster legislation on devolved matters to apply to Scotland, Wales or Northern Ireland. This convention that the Westminster Parliament would not normally legislate with regard to devolved matters except with the agreement of the devolved legislature was adopted from the earlier arrangements for the Northern Ireland Parliament. This convention was written into the Memorandum of Understanding between the UK government and devolved administrations in slightly different versions. The convention for Scotland, known as the Sewel Convention, applied to provisions in a UK bill that legislated for a devolved purpose or that varied the powers of the Scottish Parliament. Following the recommendations of the Smith Commission, the UK government agreed to put the convention on a statutory basis in the Scotland Act 2016, which recognizes that the Westminster Parliament will not normally legislate with regard to devolved matters without the consent of the Scottish Parliament. With Wales acquiring primary legislative powers a similar convention applied – that the UK Parliament would not make laws for Wales on subjects where the National Assembly for Wales already had powers without obtaining the Assembly agreement.

A similar clause to the Scottish Act was included in the Wales Act 2017 – that the Westminster Parliament will not normally legislate with regard to devolved matters without the consent of the National Assembly of Wales.

A similar convention covers Northern Ireland when UK legislation made provision for a devolved purpose or altered the legislative competence of the Assembly or altered the executive functions of ministers or departments. Although the statutory and guidance wording refers to devolved matters, what is covered is both proposed Westminster legislation on matters that could be legislated on by the devolved legislatures as well as Westminster legislation, which amends the scope of devolved legislative or executive competence (Hunt and Phylip 2018). The devolved legislatures have moved to similar procedures for dealing with legislative consent. A legislative consent memorandum is laid in the legislature by the devolved government minister following the second reading of the bill in the House of Commons, with the Parliament or Assemblies subsequently giving their assent. The memorandum sets out the provisions that engage the convention, explains the reasons for choosing a legislative consent mechanism and recommends whether the legislature should give its consent. In some cases, a statutory committee can be tasked to report on a detailed study of the memorandum. In Wales, the Constitutional and Legislative Affairs Committee considered an Animal Welfare Bill in 2019 and a Healthcare International Arrangements Bill in 2018. For a period, the Northern Ireland Executive gave its approval to legislative consent motions, but this changed to the adoption of a similar procedure to the other legislatures. Thus, the Serious Crime Bill in 2014 and memorandum did go to the Northern Ireland Justice Committee for scrutiny. It is rare for legislative consent to be withheld. Over 320 legislative consent motions have been tabled across the three devolved jurisdictions and only nine have been rejected: seven in Wales and one each in Scotland and Northern Ireland (Cowie 2018).

The number of legislative consent motions passed is quite significant, with around eight per year, and is indicated in Table 6.3. The numbers have been skewed downwards between 2017 and 2019 as many legislative consent motions lodged fell due to the calling of UK or devolved elections. The figure for the previous session, at forty-six passed by the Scottish Parliament between 2011 and 2016, gives a truer indication of the normal use of legislative consent motions. During 2019, eight legislative consent motions were introduced in the National Assembly of Wales but only two were passed, with six falling due to electoral disruptions.

TABLE 6.3 *Legislative consent motions on bills*

	Periods	Number of motions
Scotland	2021–3	37
Wales	2020–3	36
Northern Ireland	2020–1	29

Note: With collapse of Northern Ireland Assembly in 2022/3 process could not be used.

The use of legislative consent motions (LCMs) has attractions and benefits for devolved administrations, with a number of major rationales. These may be categorized thus:

1 Support for copying a Westminster bill so it is uncontroversial and saves time and work.
2 It may be appropriate to put in place a single UK-wide system or provision.
3 It is convenient to adopt a small part of a Westminster bill.
4 Something would not be so well legislated for through a unilateral piece of legislation by the devolved body.
5 The complex relationship between non-devolved and devolved matters can be more effectively dealt with in a single Westminster bill.
6 It is the most efficient way to deal with a minor or technical matter.

Examples of specific matters taken out of larger Westminster bills were the provision to set up a statutory adoption register, from the Children and Families Bill 2014, and the establishment of a Health Research Authority, from the Westminster Care Bill 2014, and relating to the retail packaging of tobacco, all in Scotland. An LCM extended a few measures from the Higher Education and Research Bill 2016 to Northern Ireland, although they were devolved matters, relating to assessment of Northern Ireland institutions under the Teaching Excellence Framework, advisory services and the funding of research in the arts and humanities. LCMs in Wales in 2019 related to aspects of a Westminster Census Bill and an Animal Welfare Bill. LCMs were useful for legislation with cross-border dimensions, often relating to water, rivers and drainage in Great Britain. Overall, the use of LCMs does not technically affect the boundaries between devolved and non-devolved matters.

Some of the major constitutional legislation in the Scotland Act 2016 and Wales Acts passed at Westminster that generated LCMs also produced no political controversy, but this was not to be the case with Brexit legislation. While integrated matters are reserved to the UK, much of the legislation to implement Brexit relates to devolved matters or amendments to the powers of the devolved institutions. The European Union Withdrawal Bill 2018 had implications for areas of competence including the environment, fisheries, agriculture and public services and had powers to modify retained EU law returning from the EU. A post-Brexit Subsidy Control Bill was seen by the Welsh Government as undermining the established devolved powers over economic development, agriculture and fisheries. Thus, under the Sewel Convention, legislative consent to parts of the Bill had to have the consent of the Scottish and Welsh Governments (Institute for Government 2018). The Northern Ireland Assembly was suspended at the time.

A complication arose when the Supreme Court ruled that Sewel was a political convention and that policing its scope and the manner of its operation does not lie within the constitutional remit of the judiciary. The devolved governments still attempted to enforce the legislative consent convention (Institute for Government 2018: 15). The Scottish and Welsh Governments acted to pass continuity legislation to try to stop the UK government passing legislation without consent, but a key clause was rejected when the issue was referred to the Supreme Court. Following negotiations in 2018, the UK government made a number of amendments to the first Withdrawal Bill. The National Assembly for Wales voted to give consent in an inter-governmental agreement. The Scottish Government remained opposed to the Bill, especially section 12, which would constrain the powers of devolved ministers (Cowie 2018), and the law could also change through the use of delegated powers that did not require consent. When the UK government proceeded to pass the EU Withdrawal Bill, the Scottish Government announced it would not seek the approval of the Scottish Parliament for this Bill and other Brexit legislation, including a Trade Bill and an Immigration and Social Security Co-ordination (EU Withdrawal) Bill. A dispute occurred over whether an Agricultural Bill needed a legislative consent motion. One exception was the Healthcare (International Arrangements) Bill. The UK government conceded that having to seek consent from the devolved administrations before it can use certain powers posed difficulties. While the convention did not provide a veto power, it did cover significant political influence (Institute for Government 2018).

In 2019, the Scottish Government recommended that the Scottish Parliament should not give consent to the new EU Withdrawal Bill and voted to refuse consent by ninety-two votes to twenty-nine. The Welsh Government similarly laid a legislative consent motion, which recommended to the Assembly that it should not give consent to the Withdrawal Agreement Bill. Disputes arose over the Brexit-related legislation and the need for legislative consent mechanisms. Mullen and Hunt (2019: 10) describe the issue as appearing to show that the UK government treating the status of international relations as a reserved matter was being used to bypass the requirement for devolved consent that undermines a convention that is fundamental to devolved government. Concerns by the devolved jurisdictions at UK legislation by passing LCMs continued. A Health and Social Care Act and a Police, Crime, Sentencing and Courts Act would allow UK ministers to confer obligations on devolved authorities (Senedd Research 2021). The Professional Qualifications Bill was not agreed in the Senedd in October 2011. It appeared that the UK government was using the LCM process to roll back the devolution settlement. Some provisions of the UK Elections Bill 2021, presented as an LCM, were not agreed by the Scottish Parliament, while consent was also refused in 2021 to the Professional Qualifications Act as it threatened devolved competences.

Scrutiny by committees

An extensive committee system exists in all three legislative houses. The scrutiny system was set up largely to replicate the system at Westminster but with the devolved system of committees covering the two main tasks: scrutiny of the actions of the Executive, departments and other bodies and scrutiny of legislative proposals. This is different from Westminster where there are separate types of standing committees dealing with legislation. In each of the devolved systems there are a set of committees dealing with broader procedural issues and specific processes and also subject or departmental committees whose configuration may vary between sessions to reflect reorganization of central administration or changing priorities. Other committees may be established on an ad-hoc basis, for example, a Covid-19 Recovery Committee in Scotland and a Special Purpose Committee on Senedd Reform in Wales. In order to clarify roles and also to facilitate a comparison it is useful to identify three types of committee: subject committees, process committees and ad-hoc committees.

Subject committees in Scotland

Subject committees in Scotland are established at the start of each session. Scrutiny of the Executive and policy evaluation takes up the most time of subject committees. This task has evolved into something of a division between major full inquiries and reports and forms of short investigations. Major inquiries undertaken have included the Health and Sport Committee inquiring into primary care, social care capacity and medicines and also a report on technology and innovation in health and social care (Scottish Parliament Health and Sport Committee 2019); an inquiry into teaching and workforce planning and also inquiries into social security and in-work poverty and social security support for housing, the gender pay gap, economic performance and teacher workforce planning. One annual topic for each committee is scrutiny of the budget for the subject area. Committees take a wide range of evidence, often undertake online surveys, hold an open consultation process and appoint expert witnesses. Among new initiatives on engagement has been the use of public panels reflecting populations across Scotland and holding inquiry sittings across Scotland. The number of full reports is in the region of four to seven per year. The reports may be debated in Parliament and the relevant minister will publish a government response, indicating which of a report's recommendations may be accepted. A major recommendation by the Equality and Human Rights Committee in 2018 that all prisoners should be allowed to vote was not accepted by the Scottish Government. A further recommendation by this committee on a human rights framework for Scotland did lead to a working taskforce (Scottish Parliament, Equality and Human Rights Committee 2018), see Table 6.4.

TABLE 6.4 *Subject committees in devolved legislatures*

Scotland
Health, social care and sport
Education, children and young people
Criminal justice
Local government, housing and planning
Justice and social security
Rural affairs, islands and natural environment
Equality, human rights and civil justice
Finance and public administration
Constitution, Europe, external affairs and culture
Economy and fair work
Net zero, energy and transport

Wales
Health and social care
Children, young people and education
Climate change, environment and rural affairs
Scrutiny of first minister
Culture, communications, Welsh language, sport and international relations
Economy, trade and rural affairs
Equality and social justice
Legislation, justice and the constitution
Finance
Local government and housing

Northern Ireland
Agriculture, environment and rural affairs
Communities
Economy
Education
Executive office
Finance
Health
Infrastructure
Justice

Committees can also carry out shorter forms of inquiry. A short inquiry was held into health hazards with Queen Elizabeth University Hospital in 2019. Other examples were a short inquiry in 2017 into reforms brought about by the Children's Hearing (Scotland) Act, and a short inquiry to consider options for criminal persecution of elder abuse. One-off evidence sessions are also used, for example, in 2019 on suicide prevention and the Scottish Government's action plan and also on a code of conduct for councillors. What is described as one-off round tables have been held on 'young people's views on health and sport', on personal and social education, on the young carer grant, and on alcohol licensing. One-off evidence sessions may be appropriate for the Parliament in reacting to recent events. In May 2019, there was a one-off evidence session on new devolved powers arising from the UK's withdrawal from the EU. A quick focus inquiry was held on the Scottish Welfare Fund while a mini-inquiry was set up into empty homes in Scotland. Some committees, including the Committee on Local Government and Communities, have committed to maintain a watching brief on issues, for example, on City Region Deals, on building regulations and fire safety and also on digital connectivity. Reports and recommendations from short inquiries often are sent directly to a government minister.

Committees also regularly hold one-off evidence sessions with public bodies or quangos to scrutinize their performance, outcomes and strategic direction. The Education and Skills Committee has examined bodies such as Education Scotland, Skills Development Scotland and the Scottish Qualifications Authority. The Local Government and Communities Committee annually holds a scrutiny session with the Scottish Public Services Ombudsman and the Scottish Housing Regulator. Scrutiny of a number of the NHS boards takes place each year and several scrutiny sessions have been held with the Scottish Ambulance Service on such issues as classification of 999 calls, response times and inappropriate calls. In practice, a number of committees now publish letters to ministers and others as the agreed output of inquiry work rather than formal lengthy reports. Some committees have also used a main findings approach in addition to recommendations.

The other main task for committees has been scrutiny of legislative bills. This role meant two to four bills had to go through a committee stage each year, although some committees could have more legislative work. In 2016/17 the Justice Committee considered seven bills, raising the risk that the legislative task dominated the committee's agenda (Scottish Parliament 2017). Legislative scrutiny at stage one can also involve a call for evidence to be submitted and can carry out online surveys, for example, with the Health and Care (Staffing) Bill 2019. As part of the scrutiny process for the Human Tissue (Authorisation) (Scotland) Bill, oral evidence was taken from patient and public groups. When a bill was considered on a restricted speed limit of twenty miles per hour, an online survey drew 6,585 responses. In a Finance Committee scrutiny of the Private Housing (Tenancies) Bill, a smart survey allowed respondents to provide submissions using social media. Extensive social media campaigns have been used on some matters such as by the Rural Affairs, Climate Change and Environment Committee in considering the Land Reform Bill (Scottish Parliament 2017).

Committees also have responsibility for considering the detail of legislative consent memorandums (discussed above). Some of this work may not be controversial or may be very specific, for example, on higher education research or the UK Ivory Bill. Others have attracted more detailed attention, for example, the Social Security Coordination (EU Withdrawal) Bill. Committees can hold evidence sessions, for example, on the Health Service (International Arrangements) Bill. A further legislative task for committees has been the consideration of statutory instruments made under parent legislation, under both negative and positive procedures. Usually, each committee considers twenty to thirty statutory instruments per year, but the number increased in 2018/19 because of notifications relating to the UK withdrawal from the EU. The Scottish Parliament has put much effort into promoting a high level of public engagement. There has been a marked increase in this activity, particularly through external meetings and fact-finding visits and in the use of social media (Scottish Parliament 2017). A recent development has been the use of citizens' juries, with a sample of people from wide-ranging backgrounds, including one to discuss land management to improve Scotland's natural environment.

Welsh Senedd subject committees

Since 2006's provision for a form of greater legislative powers for Wales, the National Assembly has had the discretion to determine its own committee structures. The initial response was a decision to set up permanent legislation committees, to an extent copying the Westminster model. The legislation committees had an element of subject specialization (Thomas and Roberts 2013). At the start of the fourth assembly in 2011 it was decided to establish committees that would have a dual legislative and policy role. By 2016, subject committees were to examine legislation and hold the Welsh Government to account by scrutinizing its expenditure, administration and policies. The role of committees grew in importance, despite the relatively small number of members. Nine subject committees operate, with each completing some four or five inquiries each year. In 2018, there were reports on human rights in Wales, poverty in Wales, rough sleepers and public service boards. In 2019, there were inquiries on diversity in local government, voting rights for prisoners, elective home education and perinatal mental health. Committees often respond to current events with inquiries: recent examples include an inquiry into fire safety in buildings, refugees and asylum seekers in Wales, electric vehicle charging infrastructure, the pandemic, hospital Wales, net zero Wales, hospital discharge, HGV driver shortage and the common framework. Composed of usually only five members, given the scale of work, one-day inquiries are popular. Aside from major scrutiny by the Finance Committee, other subject committees scrutinize the government's draft budget proposals. Joint inquiries can be carried out by two committees, for example, in 2019 between the Economy, Infrastructure and Skills Committee and the Finance Committee on retention payments in the construction sector.

The amount of primary legislation scrutinized by committees has to date been rather limited in number; since 2016, each committee has dealt with only a few bills. The Equality, Local Government and Communities Committee dealt with two bills in 2017, an abolition of the Right to Buy Bill and a trade union bill, and also two bills in 2018, a trade union bill and public service ombudsman bill. There was also consideration by the Children, Young People and Education Committee of the Children (Abolition of the Defence of Reasonable Punishment) (Wales) Bill. There have also been some examples of post-legislative scrutiny, for example, of the Higher Education (Wales) Act 2015 and the Active Travel (Wales) Act 2013. Legislative consent motions, requiring scrutiny, are also fairly limited in Wales, with some examples covering the digital economy, the UK Health and Social Care Bill and the Armed Forces Bill. Committees of the National Assembly can also scrutinize public boards. This area of scrutiny has included an annual scrutiny of the Future Generations Commissioner and the Public Services Ombudsman for Wales.

Northern Ireland committees

The structure of Committees in the Northern Ireland Assembly has remained very similar since 1999, with a system of statutory subject committees and standing committees representing process and procedural issues. The nine subject committees mirror government departments exactly on the Whitehall model and any changes in the configuration of subject committees has reflected changes in the structure of departments. A review of the committee system in 2013 noted satisfaction with the structure and recommended that the link between each executive department and a single statutory committee should be retained as a key strength of the system (Northern Ireland Assembly 2013). Committees ceased to operate between 2017 and 2019, but the experience prior to this can be quoted as well as the restoration of committee work. The official stated role of subject committees is to advise and assist ministers on the formulation of policy with respect to their responsibilities. A pattern developed of conducting a relatively small number of full inquiries, only one or two per year. In the period 2011–16, the Department of Finance conducted four inquiries, the Department of Justice four inquiries and the Department of Education three inquiries. In the period 2020–1, the Communities Committee, which covers social security, carried out no major inquiries. All seven published reports related to legislation or legislative consent memorandum. All ten published reports by the Justice Committee also related to legislative proposals. The Economy Committee had published three full reports including one on energy. Only one major report was carried out by the Health Committee, on Covid-19 in care homes. Committees resumed in January 2020 and the Education Committee launched a major inquiry into educational underachievement. Some of the relatively small number of full inquiries have been significant, for example, on historical sexual abuse in Northern Ireland, on the Barnett formula, on corporation tax, on judicial appointments and on shared and integrated education. Regular reviews took place on departmental annual reports, budgets and the programme for government. There was no separate Brexit committee but there was monitoring of developments and EU matters such as the Common Agricultural Policy and the Social Fund. Shorter reports have been published on policy areas such as education reports on school funding, area planning and STEM subjects. Some of the funding recommendations were accepted by the Department and included in the revised planning process. The review of the committee system had identified a need to enhance the capacity and effectiveness of committees and link inquiries more to strategic planning. In 2018, there was evidence that the relevant Stormont committee did not have the capacity to deal with the crisis over irregularities with a renewable energy heating scheme, a crisis that led to the downfall of the Executive.

There was provision for ad-hoc committees to be established, for example, on equality requirements and welfare reforms, as well as concurrent inquiries by one or more committees. In the period 2011–16, committees did deal with a substantial number of bills, usually between four and seven bills per committee. Frequently, the committees would report that the minister had accepted changes made by committees, for example, on the Tobacco Retailers Bill and the Human Transplantation Bill, road traffic speed limits and carrier bags. The number of legislative-consent scrutinies per committee had originally involved more technical matters, for example, the Health Services Medical Supplies (Costs) Bill 2016. By 2020–1, LCMs accounted for nearly 50 per cent of committee reports.

Public accounts/audit committees

The devolved Parliament/Assemblies have a number of other procedural and specialist committees but the most important is the committee in each legislature dealing with public accounts (see Table 6.5). This committee is modelled on the House of Commons Public Accounts Committee, which has a high status and reputation. The devolved committees have the power to consider and report on accounts laid before the Parliament/Assembly.

TABLE 6.5 *Procedural committees*

Scotland
Standards, procedures, and public appointments
Citizen participation and public petitions
Public audit
Delegated powers and law reform

Wales
Standards of conduct
Petitions
Public accounts and public administration
Llywydd's

Northern Ireland
Audit
Public accounts
Standards and privileges
Procedures
Business committee
Chairperson liaison review
Assembly and Executive review

In practice, the committees operate on the basis of reports prepared by the Auditor General and the respective Audit Office in each jurisdiction. In 2016, the Scottish Parliament's Public Audit Committee carried out four audit tasks. The four audit tasks of the committee are: to audit the accounts of Scottish Government and public bodies' accounts; to scrutinize the financial performance of the Scottish Government and public bodies; to examine the economy, efficiency and effectiveness of the public sector; to look at other government and financial issues raised by the Attorney General. Two main types of report by Audit Scotland are important: those examining the economy, efficiency and effectiveness of the public sector delivering specific services and those examining public sector bodies including NHS bodies, further education colleges, police and fire services. The Attorney General gives evidence to the committee on each report and the Public Audit Committee decides whether to have a full inquiry. Recommendations in a report from the committee have to be responded to by the Civil Service Directorate. The Public Audit Committee has examined some wider public policy areas, for example, accident and emergency services, reshaping care for older people and the mental health of children and young people. One of the most difficult issues the committee has dealt with is a high-profile inquiry followed a very critical report by the Attorney General on Coatbridge College. There was praise for the work of the committee as a strong example of efficient non-partisan working and meaningful scrutiny. Another body critically examined was the Crofting Commission. The committee also produced a very critical report on failures with an ICT project, NHS 24. In 2020–1, the committee has been investigating responses to Covid-19, including the vaccination programmes.

The National Assembly for Wales established the Public Accounts Committee in 2016 mainly to carry out functions related to the economy, efficiency and effectiveness of the resources employed in discharging public functions. The committee must report on the use of resources in excess of what has been authorized by the Assembly. The inquiries held by the Public Accounts Committee are usually based on value for money reports from the Attorney General and the Welsh Audit Office. However, the committee can initiate its own inquiries and inquiries of a more general nature rather than on individual institutions. These dominate the roughly ten inquiries and reports made each year. Inquiries in 2018/19 ranged from the specific, such as housing adaptations, to the whole of public procurement. Health-related inquiries have been prominent – on the informatics system in the NHS, on medicines management, on a health board's performance, and primary care out of hours. For 2020, the committee selected a major focus on the effectiveness of local planning authorities. Recommendations made in the committee reports are discussed in the published response and normally there has been a government response to largely accept the recommendations, which are based on a detailed and considered analysis. Thus, in 2018, recommendations on the Supporting People Programme led to revised guidance on engagement and evaluation. Also accepted were most recommendations relating to improved services for care-experienced children and young people, including drawing up specific outcome indicators. The main recommendations on the regulatory oversight of housing associations in Wales were accepted except for one relating to the external recruitment of the regulatory team. Outside the policy areas, the committee scrutinizes the accounts of public bodies including the National Museum Wales, Sport Wales and the Public Service Ombudsman. In 2021, this committee was renamed the Public Accounts and Public Administration Committee, extending the work to the quality and standards of the delivery of public services in Wales. A new committee, the Llywydd's Committee, was established in 2021 to scrutinize the financial estimates and plans of the Electoral Commission.

The Public Accounts Committee of the Northern Ireland Assembly has the main function of examining public spending with the benefit of hindsight, to highlight good practice and poor value for money, and to recommend improvements to the stewardship of taxpayers' money. The work of the committee has been to focus primarily on the consideration of Northern Ireland Audit Office reports, which can be annual financial reports of public bodies or reports on the economy, efficiency and effectiveness of public spending.

The bulk of inquiries are case studies into value for money, practices in management, use of external consultants, capital projects, whistleblowing and fraud. It is the practice to work closely with the Audit Office using its investigatory material. The committee takes evidence from ministers, civil servants and officials and issues a report with recommendations, which produces a formal response from the relevant department. In the period 2011–16, thirty-four inquiries were conducted. With the return of the Assembly the output increased to 12 per year by 2022. The Public Accounts Committee has achieved a reputation for objective and non-partisan inquiries and dealing with sensitive issues, such as the police use of agency staff. A critical inquiry into Northern Ireland Water resulted in the demotion of a senior civil servant. An inquiry cleared a whistleblower in the Fire and Rescue Service who had been suspended after publishing claims of financial irregularities. In 2016, the Public Accounts Committee reported on what it described as the biggest scandal in the history of the committee and was appalled at the level of mismanagement and impropriety associated with the Northern Ireland Events Company, which funded special events. The department involved was found to have failed in sponsoring the public body and the body itself found to be responsible for mismanagement of public funds. The collapse of the Assembly in 2017 meant that a very major inquiry into the Renewable Heat Incentive scheme, which had led to the Assembly collapsing, had to be suspended. A significant inquiry into reducing the cost of legal aid had also just taken place. During the period 2017–19, the Audit Office had continued to publish reports and government departments had to respond. The Public Accounts Committee resumed in 2020 with the first inquiry looking at an Audit Office report on major capital projects. Reports had been carried out by 2022 on the Driver and Vehicle Agency, on special educational needs and, perhaps most significantly, on capacity and capability in the Northern Ireland Civil Service. An evaluation of the work of the committee published in 2015 acknowledged that the committee had adopted an independent and non-partisan approach but identified weaknesses, including a tendency to focus on detail and an over-reliance on Audit Office reports.

Petitions committees

One of the most innovative features of the Scottish Parliament and National Assembly for Wales has been a petitions process largely organized through petitions committees. Individual citizens or groups can raise an issue with the Parliament or Assembly and request action. In Scotland, the petitions system was seen as part of the commitment to the principles of openness, accessibility and power-sharing and in Wales to increasing accessibility. Petitions submitted to the Scottish Parliament must refer to devolved matters and be relevant as a national issue, not just a personal or local matter. From 1999 to 2016, 1,607 petitions were lodged. From 2017, the number of petitions increased from 20 to 164 in 2019. In the shortened parliamentary year 2020/1, forty-two new petitions were published out of a total of 119 petitions and considered by the Committee (Scottish Parliament Public Petitions Committee 2021b); the demand for petitioning has continued to grow each year. A key role in the process is played by the Parliament's Petitions Committee, which examines all the petitions that are admissible, writes to relevant bodies with questions and takes further evidence from those submitting petitions. Open petitions can seek signatures of support. Petitions tend to call for changes in the law or executive action to make changes. If the matter is being considered by another subject committee it may be passed on or subsumed within an ongoing legislative process. Petitions have brought about changes in the law, including: mandatory custodial sentences for knife carrying; access to cancer treatment drugs; school bus safety; and increasing sepsis awareness (Scottish Parliament Public Petitions Committee 2021). The main areas for petitions have been business, health, communities, justice and the environment. In 2017, a petition to save Scotland's school libraries led to a national commitment to deliver a national school library strategy. The school bus safety petition led to compulsory seat belts on school transportation. A petition on tackling child sexual exploitation led to the Scottish Government introducing a national action plan. The petition process has been speeded up through a decision in 2020 to seek the views of the Scottish Government on new petitions. In 2020, petitions were successful on funding for increased security around places of worship, first aid training for primary school children, and mental health support for young people. There were frequent referrals of petitions to relevant subject committees to keep the petitions open. Changes were introduced in 2021 to improve accessibility and efficiency in the petitions process through the website.

In Wales, the petition process is similar, but 250 people must sign a petition for it to be discussed by the Petitions Committee. Again, it must be about something the Welsh Government or Senedd is able to change. The Petitions Committee can select a range of options similar to their Scottish counterparts. It can: seek further information from relevant bodies; ask another Senedd committee to look at the matter; invite petitioners and others to attend meetings of the Petitions Committee; conduct a short inquiry; set time for a debate (automatic if there are 10,000 signatures). In 2021, debates were held, following petitions, on protecting red squirrels, on sudden unexpected deaths in children, and on controls on the housing market in tourist and rural areas. Visits can be made and a site visit was made to investigate noise nuisance from wind carbines. The result of the process, and of pressing the government, can be a change in policy or influence on legislation, or it could lead to a debate or prompt a Senedd member to ask and pursue questions. Successful petitions have included a ban on goods packaged with single-use plastic, and a campaign to increase public awareness of sepsis. An unsuccessful example was a petition for more third-party rights in planning applications. At a minimum, the petition process in both Scotland and Wales facilitates the raising of issues, and an opportunity to present information, but the outcomes can be more significant. The actions that the Petitions Committees can take enable a range of outcomes and demonstrate individual citizen influence. Bochel (2012) sees this petition process as a significant input to the representative system of democracy, underpinning the legitimacy and functioning of democratic institutions in Scotland and Wales. Northern Ireland has had a different and more limited petitions procedure through which signatures to a petition could be collected and presented through an MLA, but no action was required. In 2016, just before the Assembly suspension, a proposal was agreed by the Procedure Committee to move to a new petition process based on 100 signatures but with referral to a relevant committee rather than a special petitions committee.

Cross-party groups

Cross-party groups bring together elected members from all parties around a subject of common interest. The groups function to promote issues, policies and changes relating to the subject matter. They represent a forum for the group to gain publicity for causes and they can engage with external representatives and bodies. The formation of a group has to be approved by a parliamentary committee. Groups in each jurisdiction are not formal committees, have no statutory role and are not allowed to make use of official secretarial services. Scotland has no fewer than 109 all-party groups covering a wide range of interests; major areas represented are health matters, with external organizations often providing secretarial support, for example, cancer, disability, dyslexia and palliative care. Some groups represent promoting relations with other countries, such as China, Japan, Germany and Poland. Others promote commercial activities, such as oil and gas, renewable energy and Scotch whisky. Others are of particular Scottish interest, for example, tackling sectarianism. The all-party groups do make a major impact into policy awareness, but they are not allowed to raise issues in Parliament or with the government. Wales has seventy-three cross-party groups. There are rules in Wales about a membership of ten and at least three parties have to be represented. Groups must also complete an annual report, with a record of meetings and a financial statement. Again, health groups lead the Welsh list of cross-party groups, including groups on strokes, cancer, diabetes, autism, long Covid, sepsis and mental health. Other groups in Wales deal with looked-after children, fuel poverty, policing, transport, small shops, the Welsh language, and Wales international. The Northern Ireland Assembly has forty-seven cross-party groups providing a forum for members from all parties to discuss and promote shared interests. A group must have at least ten members and represent the three designated categories of MLAs. Health groups dominate, with groups on cancer, autism, diabetes,

MS, and with other groups on renewable energy, industrial development, fair trade, animal welfare and motor insurance. During the period 2017–19, while the Assembly was suspended, the cross-party groups continued to meet and function, launch inquiries, take evidence and submit reports to government departments.

Use of parliamentary questions

Question time procedures are used in a mainly similar fashion in the Parliament, the Senedd and Assembly and are based on Westminster practice. Both oral and written questions can be put to ministers by members with the intention of holding government to account under slightly different rules. In Scotland and Wales, particularly, the first minister's question time is important politically and attracts public and media attention with live broadcasting of the questions and answers. In Wales, the first minister answers questions each week and Welsh ministers answer questions in a four-week rotation. A ballot is conducted to determine who can table questions. Each week, forty-five minutes are devoted in Scotland to First Minister's Questions. Written questions must be answered within ten working days. The practice of using scripted diary questions by party leaders to open First Minister's Questions was recommended for abolition by a parliamentary commission on reform. This was accepted to increase the spontaneity and attractiveness of parliamentary proceedings (Commission on Parliamentary Reform 2017). In all three systems there are provisions for urgent questions. In Wales, a topical or emergency question can be tabled with the approval of the presiding officer. In Northern Ireland, urgent questions can be put with the approval of the speaker and, since 2013, fifteen minutes are allocated to topical questions by ten MLAs successful in a ballot. In Scotland, the Commission on Parliamentary Reform recommendation that there should be a shift in focus from emergency questions to urgent questions to emphasize the significance of the timing of the question was implemented.

Conclusions

The Scottish Parliament and the Assemblies in Wales and Northern Ireland are at the core of a system of legislative devolution. They consider and approve proposals for legislation, scrutinize the details of legislation, pass legislation, approve expenditure, scrutinize the delivery of legislation, services, Executive action and the administrative actions of public bodies. Committees in the Scottish Parliament have been described as the engine room of the devolved Parliament (Commission on Parliamentary Reform 2017: 7), at the heart of legislative scrutiny and of holding government to account. At the same time, some weaknesses in the role of committees can be identified. An issue in Scotland and Northern Ireland, in particular, has been the use of party discipline to manage votes in committee and thus hinder the development of a consensus or on partisan agreement rather than replicating party dynamics. There is also agreement on the view that committees have to deal with too much legislation rather than develop their own agendas, with fewer opportunities to hold their own inquiries. In all three legislative bodies, it has been difficult for committees to undertake much pre- or post-legislative scrutiny. In Scotland, an initiative was made to give the post-legislative role to the Public Audit Committee. With the relatively small size of committees, especially in Wales, and change-over in members it has been difficult to build up expertise in some areas. In all three jurisdictions there have been initiatives to reach out to communities and hard-to-reach groups and areas. In Scotland and Wales, of particular importance has been the major innovation of public petitions to enhance public participation. Methods other than committee meetings have been introduced to promote further public engagement, such as through social media and online activities. Outreach activities relating to Parliament and the Assemblies and the availability of facilities to the public have also developed strongly to help promote their status and the value of the parliamentary buildings, outside the role of the working institutions.

7

Policy outcomes: Divergence and convergence

Introduction

Devolution has had a significant impact on public policy. A number of previous comparative studies analysed policies using a divergence and convergence distinction (Greer 2004; Jeffery 2007; Birrell 2009; Keating 2005). In principle, devolution affords the devolved governments the ability to develop policies that are tailored to the specific economic and social characteristics of their regions. As Jeffery (2006) noted, devolution presented the opportunity to create bespoke policy solutions to designed to address local problems. The new local assemblies provided the opportunity to reflect the unique identities and characteristics of the devolved regions. Importantly, however, capacity for policy innovation and transfer is also restricted by pressures to ensure that measures adopted by devolved administrations do not contradict those of the central state, encouraging policy convergence (MacKinnon 2015). The UK model of devolution is based upon a separation of powers between the UK parliament and the devolved parliaments (Keating 2002). This grants considerable latitude to the devolved governments to develop distinctive policies (Greer 2016) in devolved spheres of policy, while the central UK state retains the power to maintain common state-wide policies in reserved areas. The scope for divergence in policymaking varies in terms of the balance between reserved and devolved matters, which in turn varies between the three devolved nations. For example, Wales has no powers over justice and home affairs (such as policing, crime and fire services), while Northern Ireland has powers over transport and energy that are not devolved elsewhere (Paun et al. 2019).

Devolution presented the devolved governments with a tremendous opportunity to develop and share innovative and creative approaches to social policy. Key areas of social policy such as health, social security, education and housing were fully devolved. Devolved functions are so dominated by social policy competences that the legislatures had been characterized as 'social policy parliaments' (Birrell 2009: 13; 2010). Devolution has impacted upon a range of services the social rights of citizenship. However, it has been argued that devolved governments have largely failed to capitalize on the chance to create a 'living laboratory' for policy transfer and exchange. Rather, learning across the governments of the UK is limited and uneven. There is also a notable absence of mechanisms and formal structures to facilitate evidence exchange amongst civil servants across the jurisdictions (Paun et al. 2016). Assessing cross-national performance is often problematic as statistics and data are often not directly comparable. Additionally, as Paun et al. (2016) note, cultural differences in political control and policy style between the four governments may also curtail the desire for learning and sharing.

It has been argued by MacKinnon (2015) that since 2007 the UK has entered into a new phase of devolution and constitutional politics that has three distinctive features. First, nationalist centre-left parties entered into government in Edinburgh, Cardiff and Belfast in 2007 as either minority governments or coalition partners. Following this, the SNP's momentous victory in the Scottish election of 2011 enabled it to form a majority government for the first time and secure agreement from Westminster for a referendum on independence in 2014. In contrast, Labour was able to govern on its own in Wales after winning thirty of the sixty seats. Second, the politics of the UK had changed dramatically since the defeat of Labour in 2010 and the formation of a coalition government between the Conservatives and Liberal Democrats, followed by a Conservative government thereafter. This period has witnessed marked political divergence between the devolved territories and England, with Conservatives not in power in the devolved nations. Third, in response to the financial crisis of 2007 and 2008 and the subsequent deep economic recession, the coalition government adopted a programme of fiscal authority designed to drastically reduce public expenditure (Lowndes and Pratchett 2012). This reduction in public expenditure has been passed on to the devolved governments, which have experienced substantial cuts to their block grants since 2011. The devolved parliaments in the UK have relatively limited revenue-raising powers; consequently, the decade of austerity that has characterized the UK's public policy agenda has had profound implications for the devolved governments, including substantially reducing their budgets and requiring them to administer cuts locally. This has resulted in devolved governments having a reduced capacity to respond to local needs. It has been argued that devolution and re-balancing the regional economies were incompatible with an austerity agenda (Ethrington and Jones 2016). This chapter aims to identify and assess significant areas of policy divergence and convergence in the period from 2010 to 2020. It outlines convergence and divergence in key policy areas such as health and social policy and social security and gives a brief assessment of mechanisms to support collaboration and policy transfer.

Approaches to policymaking

The process of devolution to Scotland, Wales and Northern Ireland has now been in place for over two decades and continues to evolve, with further powers devolved. In the ten years since 2010, the devolved legislatures have taken the opportunity to adopt a different approach from Westminster, resulting in considerable legislative divergence across the UK. For instance, the UK government continued to focus on competition, markets and performance management, while policies in Scotland and Wales have emphasized social justice, reducing social inequalities and collaboration across sectors, e.g. through the single-outcome agreements between the Scottish government and local authorities. The Scottish and Welsh governments have also tended to favour universal free provision of public services such as NHS prescriptions, social care, hospital car parking and university tuition, while in England the UK government has emphasized means-testing and the targeting of resources. In Northern Ireland, there has been a focus on mitigating the effects of austerity and cuts to budgets with significant policy divergence in the area of welfare reform. The Welsh Government operated with a declared commitment to progressive universalism (Drakeford 2021). Overall, the devolved governments in the first decade of devolution operated in a more universalist and consensual fashion in social policy compared with the approach of the UK government in England (Welsh Assembly Government 2007; Scottish Government 2008; Birrell 2010; Lodge and Schmuecker 2010). This emphasis on social justice had been particularly strong in Scotland and Wales (Scott and Mooney 2009) but had been less of a feature in Northern Ireland (Birrell 2010).

The categories of divergence and convergence in policy are broad in meaning. Originally, the terms were mainly used to compare devolved policies with policies applied to England. Later, it became significant to make comparisons between the devolved administrations. The meaning of devolution can also move along a spectrum of degree, and an understanding of the context is also required to understand both divergence and convergence (see Table 7.1). Thus, divergence and convergence in policy can be considered under the following headings:

TABLE 7.1 *Divergence and convergence*

Divergence	Convergence
Innovations and initiatives	Policy copying
Continuing historical differences	Similar responses to needs
Major policy differences	Legislative consent motions
Detailed differences within policy areas	UK government/parliament action
Administrative differences	

Divergence–convergence analysis also requires a benchmark and this has usually been with England. However, it has to be noted that there can be a significant divergence between two, three or four of the component jurisdictions of the UK.

Continuing historical differences

Prior to devolution in 1999, all three nations had developed elements of policy divergence arising from the operation of a degree of territorial delegation through the Scottish Office, the Welsh Office and the previous devolved arrangements for Northern Ireland and, from 1972 to 1989, through the Northern Ireland Office. This historical divergence had covered not only administrative differences but also policy differences. Divergence in Scotland in this period had focused on education through the school system and examination system and on aspects of health care and social care, children and young people's services and justice services. In Wales, despite the original lack of primary legislative powers, divergence was also found in the organization of health and education. Action was taken in this period to promote the needs and values of Welsh communities (Zolle 2016), including a change in focus from acute health care to primary care and prevention and also ending school league tables. Northern Ireland had produced administrative differences in health, social care, education, housing and planning, as well as significant policy differences in education, housing and employment. In Scotland and Northern Ireland, divergence was facilitated by the existence of a separate legal system, whereas the legal system in Wales was integrated with the English system. Devolution brought opportunities for the new governments to demonstrate the value of devolution in introducing new distinctive policies, with a strong interest in formulating Scottish answers to Scottish problems. The coming to power of the SNP increased the enthusiasm for building on the historical foundations to create new, distinctive policymaking. Initially, the National Assembly for Wales was restricted by the lack of primary legislative powers, but the introduction of the reserved powers model led to a major increase in the Welsh legislative and policy capacity to develop more divergent policies. The restoration of devolution to Northern Ireland also opened the way for progressing from a strong historical basis, although issues related to establishing inter-party power-sharing and peacebuilding post-conflict played a more prominent role than implementing a wider range of new policies.

Elements of educational policy have historically differed between Scotland, Northern Ireland and England and these differences continued after devolution. Scotland has its own system of secondary school examinations and a comprehensive system of secondary education under local authority control alongside a small number of private schools. Northern Ireland has been characterized by the continuation of academic selection at age ten and a grammar school/secondary school division. All schools are either state schools, in practice, Protestant schools or Catholic schools funded by the state. Wales has, again, a largely comprehensive system of secondary education with very few private schools. England had mainly a comprehensive system, but with a significant number of private independent schools and a small number of grammar schools. The strategies adopted in England in promoting free schools and academies to reduce local authority control and introduce more entrepreneurialism were not copied in Scotland or Wales. Localism and democratic control continued to outweigh potential gains from managerialism approaches. In Northern Ireland, control of schools remained with a single education authority. Wales also introduced some distinctive education policies, including its own national qualification, the Welsh Baccalaureate, less rigorous school inspections and the development of nurseries in schools. The Scottish government has acted to increase spending on early years provision and increase free nursing provision for the under-fives, with differences of eligibility and scope of provision across the four nations. Much attention has been drawn to the differences in higher education fees between the four nations, with Scotland having no fee charges for Scottish students attending Scottish universities. England had the highest fees for all students attending universities in England. Wales and Northern Ireland have set fees at a much lower rate for students attending university locally.

Scotland's preference for policies reflecting equality and social justice was further demonstrated in several other policies. The Child Poverty (Scotland) Bill 2018 sought to repeal sections of the UK Child Poverty Act 2010, to set income-based targets to measure child poverty and to set reporting mechanisms for ministers' actions. Other measures tackled included aspects of homelessness and rough sleeping, support for carers and providing their restricted role. Wales has followed Scotland in a commitment to social justice and what was described as progressive universalism, but faced more difficulties constitutionally. Much emphasis was placed on increasing the supply of social housing. A law on tenancy reform was also passed and the right-to-buy provision ended. The Northern Ireland Executive has had a focus on setting more general aims or outcomes in its programme for government, usually without specific policies or principles, as made clear in Scotland and Wales.

Innovations and initiatives

The devolved governments have used their autonomy to introduce innovative reforms that have offered evidence for the other countries (Paun et al. 2016). A ban on smoking in enclosed public spaces was first introduced in Scotland in 2006 (following the Republic of Ireland) and the plastic bag charge in Wales in 2011 (again, following the Republic of Ireland). Despite initial scepticism about the enforceability and desirability of both of these innovations, they were later adopted in other regions in the UK, including England. In December 2015, Wales became the first part of the UK to institute an 'opt-out' or 'deemed-consent' organ donation system. Here, adults are assumed to have consented to organ donation unless they have opted out. Since 2011, the UK government has required people in England, Scotland and Wales to either opt in or out on the donation register when they apply for a driver's licence. The debate about minimum prices for alcohol was prompted by increasing concerns about high levels of drinking. At an early stage, both the Scottish and Welsh governments stated an intention to introduce minimum pricing for alcohol. The Alcohol (Minimum Pricing) (Scotland) Act 2012 led the way for the introduction of minimum unit pricing. This legislation was unsuccessfully challenged by the Scotch Whisky Association in the European and Scottish courts. A minimum price of 50p per unit has been in place since 1 May 2018. In Wales, the Public Health (Minimum Price for Alcohol) (Wales) Act 2018 enabled the introduction of minimum unit pricing on the grounds of public health. In March 2020, the UK government announced that there were no plans for the introduction of minimum unit pricing in England, but it would continue to monitor its impact in Scotland (Woodhouse 2020). In July 2020, the Minister of Health in Northern Ireland announced his commitment to a full consultation on minimum unit pricing within a year. Improving public health outcomes is the overarching policy objective underpinning all of these policies and, therefore, there is clear potential to learn about the efficiency of different approaches. As Paun et al. (2016) point out, this willingness to learn is more problematic in contested policy spheres such as welfare reform, where governments are often divided about ends as well as means. Devolution has thus increased the potential for divergence in social policy approaches between the different parts of the country, turning the UK into a 'policy laboratory', in which different solutions to common problems can be put into practice. This offers the opportunity for evidence exchange and policy learning across the UK.

Scotland had taken measures early in devolution that were distinctive from prevailing policies for England imposed by the UK government. In particular, the Scottish government introduced free personal and nursing care for older people, which was seen as a major achievement and a flagship devolved policy. Other significant innovations followed, with perhaps the most significant being the creation of a Scottish Income Tax. Certain tax powers were devolved under the Scotland Act 2016. Designed as part of a package for enhancing devolution after the referendum on independence, the Scottish parliament has the power to set all income tax rates and bands to apply to Scottish taxpayers' income. Excluded were savings income, and setting personal allowances remained a reserved matter. The UK body, HM

Revenue and Customs (HMRC), continued to be responsible for its collection and management and pays the money through the Treasury to the Scottish government. Under these arrangements, income tax is not fully devolved. The Scottish government can set five bands and rates from 19 per cent to 46 per cent. Four key tests were set for implementation: to raise additional revenue; to protect lower-earning taxpayers; to improve progressivity; and to support the Scottish economy. For 2020/1, the Scottish government increased the basic and intermediate rate thresholds by inflation, to protect the lowest- and middle-earning taxpayers. The additional £51 million for the Scottish government would help the economy and public services and the targets for reducing child poverty. These changes still meant that 56 per cent of Scottish income taxpayers will pay less than if they lived in other parts of the UK (Scottish Government 2018). A Welsh income tax was introduced in 2019 but has yet to have a significant impact. The rationale was similar to that relating to the Scottish scheme, to increase the financial accountability of the devolved government. In Wales, the income tax rate for each tax band remains unchanged while the UK government reduced the tax rate by 10p. For 2020/1, the National Assembly for Wales decided to keep the same rates as the UK, which meant no change to the basic, higher and additional tax rates, and the tax bands remained the same.

Another recent innovation by the Scottish government is the introduction of the Scottish Child Payment. This was available from 2021 for children under six, with a payment of £10 per week. It was designed as family support in the context of austerity cuts and was available to all families on qualifying benefits. Claiming the benefit had no effect on other entitlements. This payment was doubled to £10 per week. Another innovative measure relating to child poverty was Child Winter Health Assistance. Also introduced together were Covid hardship payments, made four times a year to families eligible for free school meals. A ban on smoking in enclosed public spaces was agreed at the end of 2004 in Scotland. Cairney (2007) notes that this legislation marked one of the most significant policy divergences between Scotland and England since the introduction of devolution. More recently, the Scottish government has introduced two further pioneering initiatives. First, in 2017, every baby born in Scotland received a box of gifts (known as a baby box) to help families and give babies an equal start in life. Second, in response to 'period poverty' legislation was introduced in 2021 to make sanitary products free to all, to be distributed by local authorities and education providers.

Wales was the first UK nation to introduce a plastic bag charge in 2011, to reduce consumption and the associated environmental impacts. Despite initial scepticism about the desirability and enforceability of both these innovations, they were later adopted by other administrations. In December 2015, Wales became the first country in the UK to depart from an opt-in system in organ procurement. New legislation introduced the concept of 'deemed consent' whereby a person who neither opt in nor opt out is deemed to have consented to donation. England and Scotland have also adopted this opt-out system and from spring 2023 Northern Ireland will also move to this system.

Policy differences in major services

Health policy was an area almost totally devolved (Smith and Hellowell 2012) and the largest service for which the devolved administrations have direct responsibility. However, all four administrations in the UK are committed to operating within the principles of the NHS as established throughout the UK. The principle of a service free at the point of delivery was maintained, and a similar range of core services was maintained to meet largely similar needs covering primary care, acute care, community health, mental health and public health. With the embedding of devolution, divergence began in aspects of policy areas, which opened up some differences, especially with England (Timmons 2013). Greer (2016) identified differences in underlying influences: an emphasis on markets in England; the influence of the medical professions in Scotland; and localism in Wales and Northern Ireland, which was marked by permissive managerialism. This appeared to suggest the possibility of four divergence systems and cultures. In revisiting the impact of devolution on health policy, Greer (2016) asserts that the three devolved systems differ from the system in England in a number of ways. However, NHS policies were strongly influenced by the dominant position of England and the UK government and, in the second period of devolution, by the Conservative Party's policies on a purchaser–provider distinction, use of the private sector, commissioning more competition, efficiency savings and consumer satisfaction. Over the past two decades, the NHS in England has been subject to almost constant review and reform. In practice, Greer (2016) notes that different governments for England – Conservative, Labour and coalition – had endorsed health policy reforms including private sector involvement, internal public sector competition, performance management and outcome indicators.

There are a number of other clear examples of policy differences within the NHS. All three devolved administrations have a policy of free prescriptions, leaving England as the only nation to retain charges, albeit with exclusions. Scotland and Wales have moved to free car parking at hospitals for patients and visitors, but Northern Ireland has retained charges at most hospitals, with only a few exclusions for certain categories of patients. England presents a mixed picture of charges and free car parking. Much attention has been drawn to Scotland's action in making a range of cancer drugs available to patients while they remain unavailable in Wales, England and Northern Ireland. Scotland has its own Scottish Medicines Consortium, which appraises drugs for use, distinct from the National Institute for Clinical Excellence, which covers England but also advises Wales and Northern Ireland. In 2020, in Scotland, four more cancer drugs were approved to lengthen life expectancy, displaying a difference in interpretation of what value for money indicates. All four administrations have developed commitments to user participation and involvement and in devising projects (Fleming and Osborne 2019). Again, Scotland has taken a lead in making user co-production a key element in the principles for planning and delivering health care.

The devolution of health, including public health, meant that responsibility for dealing with Covid-19 fell to the devolved administrations. This included the guidelines and regulations on protecting communities from the pandemic. The significance of devolution became more visible as the scope for divergence in approach between the four countries came into operation in 2019 and 2020. Information on the spread of the disease was shared across the four jurisdictions with, at times, attendance at COBRA meetings and joint announcements by devolved ministers or chief medical officers. In practice, rules and guidelines across health and education and governing lockdowns were not dissimilar. Some degree of divergence did occur with social distancing, school closures and restrictions on the opening of shops, restaurants and pubs, but these differences tended to be short-lived or minimal. Some differences remained for longer periods. While England had three phases or degrees of lockdown, Scotland had four phases and Northern Ireland five, while Wales had a traffic light system.

During the second wave of Covid-19, more differences appeared in attempts to suppress the virus (Sargeant et al. 2020). The devolved administrations introduced schemes of financial support, for example, there was a financial support scheme for families in Scotland and Northern Ireland gave a lump sum award to all health staff and gave £100 to each adult to spend locally to boost the economy. Schemes to give financial support for self-isolation had minor differences. England had experimented with local and city region lockdowns, to be followed in Scotland and Wales. Public libraries were opened early in Wales. While the Scottish and Welsh governments set up their own expert groups to give scientific and technical advice, Northern Ireland did not. In general, there was little sign of UK decisions to produce strategies to overrule the independent decisions and actions of the devolved administrations. The test and trace initiative was organized on a UK-wide basis.

Although in 2020 the vaccines were distributed nationally, with guidelines set by the Joint Committee on Vaccination and Immunisation, some differences arose in the implementation.

When the devolved administrations assumed powers in Scotland and Wales, they were excluded from policy discretion on social security matters. Social security was devolved to Northern Ireland as it had been before direct rule in 1972. The benefits system was administered by a Northern Ireland devolved department, not the UK Department of Work and Pensions. There was a policy of maintaining parity with UK government legislation, but separate legislation was enacted. The Northern Ireland Act 1998 did specify that the relevant Whitehall and Northern Ireland department consult to secure a single system of social security, care support and pensions for the UK. Unlike 2016, social security was at least organized on a GB-wide basis. This has been described as an expression of the UK's social union (Mackley and McInnes 2020). Disquiet and unease in the devolved nations over the welfare agenda perused by the Conservative–Liberal coalition was a driver of support for the emergence of divergence in areas of social security. With major welfare reform proposed by the next Conservative government, this was met with demands for additional powers in welfare to facilitate the development of more bespoke approaches to social security reform. The Scottish government stated its intention to radically review the existing system, removing what it saw as the adversarial nature of that system. The aim was to develop a more supportive ethos that was more closely aligned to the principles of the Scottish administration, which stressed that social security was a human right and respect for the dignity and fairness of individuals was at the heart of this vision. The Scotland Act 2016 and the subsequent Social Security (Scotland) Act 2018 devolved further powers to the Scottish government. Northern Ireland's Executive was able to act to mitigate some aspects of welfare reform, including the 'bedroom tax'.

In education policy, Wales shared the similar principle of Scotland and England, of largely a non-selective comprehensive system of secondary schools. Wales did not copy the initiative in England of free schools and academies, and nearly all schools are funded by the twenty-two local authorities. Wales continued with a major focus on a curriculum for Wales to raise the standards of literacy and numeracy. Linked to this were: improving the attainment gap; reforming teacher training; extending bilingual provision; and a whole-Wales approach to mental health in schools. There was a focus on all-round child development as opposed to a focus on academic status. Action taken earlier had phased out league tables and the use of SATS, still in place in England. However, an OECD study found that Welsh schools were not delivering the desired outcomes and were underperforming. Following this, a new national categorization of school performance was devised and a new plan added digital competence to literacy and numeracy. Also designed was a Welsh Baccalaureate. A pioneer initiative to forward this was led by teachers, resulting in an improved performance at A levels.

Scotland has a long tradition of a separate education system, with its own examinations and structures, but faces some similar problems. Scotland has a commitment to comprehensive secondary schools, which are the responsibility of local councils. There are around 100 independent/ private schools at primary, secondary and all through the levels – more than in Wales but proportionately less than in England. Two main principles dominate practice: a curriculum for excellence and delivering a young workforce strategy. A blueprint was developed from 2020 for an expansion of early learning and childcare. Education Scotland is a distinctive executive agency responsible for supporting quality and improvement. However, in 2021 the OECD proposed an overhaul of the Scottish system to keep pace with best practice, especially the reform of the exams and school inspection system and leadership on curriculum development. Northern Ireland has an education system that differs in four main respects from Great Britain: the almost total absence of private schools, the continuation of academic selection at the age of ten, the division into grammar schools and non-selective secondary schools, and the division into Protestant and Catholic schools, with only seven per cent of children attending integrated schools.

A major focus throughout the UK in the last decade has been the provision of affordable housing. A difference in the devolved administrations relates to increasing social housing rather than regarding low-cost private housing as the main aspect of affordable housing. Scotland has the highest proportion of social housing at 22 per cent, with 17 per cent in Wales and England and 15 per cent in Northern Ireland. The Scottish Government is committed to a high level of support for social housing and abolished the right to buy for social housing in order to preserve the housing stock. A new housing strategy for 2021–40 sets a target of 100,000 affordable houses, to include 70,000 units of social housing. In Northern Ireland, the centralized public housing authority stopped building new houses in 2020 but this will now change. Northern Ireland differed from Great Britain in not having any large-scale voluntary transfer of social housing and also in not having developer contributions of social housing in major new building schemes. All three devolved administrations have produced policies to tackle homelessness, often with a focus on preventative action, with some difference in emphasis. Scotland had initiated a rapid rehousing strategy along with close monitoring of homelessness. Homelessness in Wales is a high action level plan, which aims to utilize both the social sector and private rented sector. A homelessness strategy for 2017–27 is operating in Northern Ireland. A new tenant saver loan scheme aims to help private tenants in financial difficulty. Wales has also committed to a right to adequate housing. Northern Ireland has introduced a 'decent' standard of housing fitness. Shared and co-ownership schemes have been popular in the devolved administrations, to promote owner occupation. Scotland has pushed ahead with targets to reduce carbon emissions to zero for new housing.

There are many devolved policy areas in which there may be limited divergence in overall policy and objectives, but policy differences can be identified in activities to achieve the objectives. Thus, while there was a largely similar planning system in operation in each nation, some differences operated in the procedures for individual applications, consultation process, defining the impact of development, definition of use and enforcement of breaches of planning consent, for example, in the Planning (Wales) Act 2015. Public procurement policy for public service contracts differed somewhat in each of the UK nations. Early learning and childcare provision in each nation differed in scope of free provision and terms of eligibility. Scotland and Wales devoted more detailed study to tackling child poverty strategies and Scotland created a Poverty and Inequalities Commission to advise ministers. Scotland also produced opposition to the UK government proposal to replace the Human Rights Act. While there was acceptance of the guidelines of the UK Committee for Vaccination and Immunisation for priority groups for the Covid-19 vaccination, the Northern Ireland Department of Health decided to break the guidelines by moving to a lower age group before completing the first four groups.

Prior to devolution, the organization of the NHS had displayed a number of differences. With devolution, the systems in all three devolved administrations had to create a level of central administration that was aligned to a political tier of ministers. Below this central level, the devolved administrations produced a structure of health bodies and boards to deliver acute and community services and form partnerships with local government. Scotland had moved to a system of central administration based on directorates rather than large departments. Nine of the forty-three directorates relate to health. Wales and Northern Ireland have a more traditional single civil service department. The structure of administrative boards to deliver the NHS relies mainly on the model of quangos or non-departmental public bodies and also on a distinction between acute care, community health care, GP services and social care. The division between commissioning and providing was also built into the structures. In 2006, Scotland moved to a simplified system of fourteen territorial health boards, dismantling the purchaser–provider split and responsibility for the planning, funding and delivery of all frontline health services. Wales had a similar structure of seven local health boards for planning, securing and delivering acute and community health services. Northern Ireland has five integrated health and social service trusts, including social care, delivering health services but retaining a separate single commissioning board for Northern Ireland. England has evolved with a more significant delivery–commissioning system involving 211 clinical commissioning groups (CCGs), and with 244 delivery trusts, including hospital trusts, foundation hospital trusts and mental health trusts.

There are some devolved areas in which policy objectives are similar between the devolved administrations and England but the administrative structure to implement and deliver the policy differs. The integration of health and social care has been an important policy for all four administrations, with integration increasingly placed on a statutory basis. Such developments were a reaction to similar influences, demographic change, a move to community care from acute care and joined-up approaches to problems. Responsibility for integration and related legislation, organization, implementation and financing fell to devolved institutions in Scotland, Wales and Northern Ireland. Bringing together health services with social care and personal social services has resulted in different organizational formats. England has concentrated on collaboration between health bodies and local government social services through flexible arrangements, pooled budgets and joint management. There has been a continuous process of initiatives and experimentation, for example, with Vanguard and Pioneer schemes aimed at improved cooperation. In Scotland, there has been a more dedicated approach based on partnership working, originally setting up community health and social care partnerships. The Public Bodies (Joint Working) (Scotland) Act 2014 came into effect in 2016 and amended these to integrated authorities with a joint partnership board between health boards and local councils. Scotland's approach can be thought of as a model of formalized and uniform partnership underpinned by legislation. In Wales, the Social Care and Well-being (Wales) Act 2014 required that local councils must exercise their social services functions with a view to ensure the integration of care with health provision and implementing cooperation. There is some difficulty in that the seven health boards are not coterminous with the twenty-two local authorities. The Welsh approach has been dependent on local initiatives (Ham et al. 2013). The approach in Northern Ireland has been different, with a long-established system of comprehensive structural integration as a health and social care system. There is no entity called NHS Northern Ireland. A Health and Social Care Board acts as a commissioning and regulatory board delivered through integrated health and social care trusts. This includes acute care, community health care, adult social care and childcare. There is a single employer and a single funding body. The system has operated through shared management and IT systems and extensive colocation and benefits identified in hospital discharge (Heenan and Birrell 2018). In 2016, an element of further delegation was introduced through the establishment of seventeen integrated care partnerships to focus on four areas, including older people and stroke patients.

The devolved administrations are similar to England in having a number of centralized quangos, some to provide services and some to provide advice or run a specialist service. All have a quango to operate an ambulance service or regulation and inspection and public health. However, Public Health Scotland, Public Health Wales and the Public Health Agency in Northern Ireland differ in their configuration. Public Health Scotland operates as a central body but also with public health directors in each health board. The public health bodies in Wales and Northern Ireland have only one level of organization. In England, there is a central public health agency, but public health is also a local government function. Each jurisdiction has more unique bodies: NHS National Services Scotland supplies essential services including blood transfusion while the Golden Justice Foundation provides access to first-class treatment in carrying out planned procedures to reduce waiting lists. A unique structure in Wales is the Velindre University NHS Trust, which provides specialist cancer centres for the whole of Wales. Northern Ireland has a Patient and Client Council to provide a voice on behalf of users and carers.

Convergence

Convergence in policy can readily be identified, referring to a similarity in policy between two or three of the devolved nations and/or to similarities with England. This would reflect policies passed by the UK government for England. There is a strong basis of convergence throughout the UK, which reflects the historical basis laid down before devolution. A clear example is the uniform undermining principles of the NHS or the functions of the local government system. Substantial convergence in policy remained after the introduction of devolution simply through a lack of interest in making changes. A major determinant of convergence lies in the prescription of reserved and non-devolved services, which are the responsibility of the UK government and parliament. This includes such matters as immigration policy, Brexit policy, macro-economic policy and human rights policy. More attention has been paid to policy convergence as a product of a process of policy copying and policy transfer. This could include transfer between the three devolved administrations but also from or to England. There was an early expectation that this could be a common occurrence once devolution was established. Significant examples included the introduction of a children's commissioner, initiated by Wales, followed by Scotland and then Northern Ireland and eventually by the UK government (Birrell 2009: 111).

Although there may be time differences in the order in which new policies have been adopted, it may be difficult to identify policy copying as such, as the matter may be under discussion in two or more devolved jurisdictions; for example, with smoking bans, the ban was raised first in Wales but introduced first in Scotland. The plastic bag charge was more clearly introduced first in Wales. An opt-out mechanism or deemed consent for organ donation was also first introduced in Wales. Certain procedures have encouraged a degree of policy copying. Legislative consent motions are a mechanism to allow the devolved governments to give their consent to let Westminster legislation cover devolved matters. This may be acceptable for a number of reasons, where it is effective to have a single Act (e.g. a UK Child Poverty Act), or where it is convenient and saves time and resources, or where there is an overlap between devolved and non-devolved powers. International agreements may also require devolved governments to adopt similar provisions. This applies if the UK government signs UN conventions, for example, on the rights of a child, on the elimination of all forms of discrimination against women or the rights of people with disabilities. Until 2021, EU regulations had an impact on producing similar legislation, for example, the Working Time

Directive. The British–Irish Council (BIC), set up as part of the Good Friday Agreement, established a forum for all the devolved governments, the UK and Irish governments and also the governments of the Isle of Man and the Channel Islands to exchange information, share policy ideas and innovations and engage in collaborative projects. Paun et al. (2016) identify the policy copy contribution of the BIC but doubt its major influence. The Joint Ministerial Committee originally had potential in promoting policy copying, mainly through subcommittees such as a poverty committee, but this role did not develop. Brexit also led to greater application of UK government measures in relation to the repatriation of UK powers. This applies to the replacement of EU funding such as the Social Funds, Agricultural and Rural Development Funds and Structural Funds. The present Conservative UK government has also brought in the City Deals Initiative across the UK and other Levelling Up Funding has brought further convergence.

The Covid-19 pandemic capitulated devolution into the public consciousness and highlighted the differing responses from each nation. It was the most visible way of understanding the extent to which each territorial government could shape their own strategies and regulations. It offered a tangible opportunity to do things differently, to flex constitutional muscles and push back against Westminster's pandemic response. It also afforded the public to witness devolution in action.

Covid-19

Health is a devolved issue and, in the face of a global emergency, at the outset all four countries worked together to manage the pandemic (Sargeant et al. 2020). This initial period of cooperation was quickly followed by the decision to adopt different approaches as they grappled with the challenges of moving out of lockdown. It has been suggested that this decision was in part related to the British government's move to exclude the devolved leaders from COBRA meetings and consultations prior to key announcements. It was also deemed politically expedient to create distance from Johnson's dubious decisions and methods (Kenny 2022). Both the Welsh and Scottish leaders bemoaned the Prime Minister's disrespectful, dismissive approach to devolution. The idea that Whitehall knew best also drove divergent approaches. While these differences were confined to relatively minor differences in rules or guidance rather than substantive policy differences, the distinctive approaches helped to increase trust in the devolved leaders (Curtice 2020). Dealing with the pandemic has had significant repercussions on the inter-governmental relationships and solidarity within the UK. The global emergency raised the question of how, in the face of a national crisis, central government should interact with the devolved administrations given that key health powers and decisions are devolved. It also brought into sharp relief the lack of formal mechanisms for inter-governmental coordination and liaison with the UK.

Devolved governments repeatedly expressed their irritation at Westminster government's habit of conflating England's public health role with a UK-wide remit. The pandemic exposed the confusion around the dual role of Whitehall ministers, in making decisions for England in areas that are devolved, but simultaneously performing the role of central government for whole of UK (Kenny and Sheldon 2020).

Conclusions

The divergence–convergence spectrum remains useful for analysing policy differences and policy copying. There are processes, such as the BIC, and a range of pressures encouraging policy copying, for example, public opinion, lobby campaigns and the media, plus research evidence and parliamentary inquiries. Notwithstanding these influences, divergence has not developed as a major objective of the devolved governments. A problem-solving approach is more likely to dominate than the pursuit of policy learning and innovation. Overall, policy agendas reflect priorities based on strategic policies as set out in programmes for government plus special issues, for example, austerity, Brexit, Covid-19 expenditure crises and Scottish independence. Also influential in some areas of policymaking is the degree of autonomy exercised by local government and by non-departmental public bodies. Mechanisms for inter-governmental cooperation are not well developed except in a few critical areas, relating, for example, to financial discussions or COBRA meetings on emergency matters. The extent to which the devolved governments have functioned as policy laboratories has been worthy of analysis but is more a by-product of devolution than a clear commitment by governments.

8

Devolution and new models of public administration

Introduction

Just over twenty years ago, there was one government for the entire UK, usually led by a single political party. Today, with its asymmetrical model of devolution, the UK possesses four governments of varying powers and responsibilities, each led by different political parties possessing widely differing political ambitions. For the civil service, such differentiation has posed a deep leadership challenge. The UK ('Home') Civil Service provides the staffing both for the UK central government and the Scottish and Welsh governments; for Northern Ireland, since its very establishment as a distinct political entity, the Northern Ireland Civil Service (NICS), formed at the inception of the state, provides a parallel system of administrative support. Thus, 'the civil service' (encompassing the Home and NI components) forms an inseparable part of both the UK government and the governments of the three devolved nations. Executive decisions of government ministers are implemented by the civil service. The civil servants themselves are employees of the Crown and not of the UK Parliament or the devolved institutions. Civil servants also have some traditional and statutory responsibilities that to some extent protect them from being used for the political advantage of the party in power. Senior civil servants may be called to account to Parliament and, since devolution, to the respective devolved assembles and legislatures.

By convention, in UK parlance, the term *civil servant* does not include all public sector employees. Thus, while no fixed legal definition exists, the term is usually defined as a 'servant of the Crown working in a civil capacity who is not the holder of a political (or judicial) office; the holder of certain other offices in respect of whose tenure of office special provision has been made; [or] a servant of the Crown in a personal capacity paid from the Civil List' (Bradley and Ewing 2007: 272). As at the end of March 2018, there were 430,075 civil servants in the Home Civil Service. Of these, 83,500 are based in London – an increase of more than 5,000 since 2017. By far, the London region retains the most civil servants, now by a margin of over 30,000 (ONS 2017a, 2018).

Devolution has given rise to significant developments in respect of the systems of public administration within each devolved entity. Many of the key features of public administration remain like elsewhere in the UK, reflecting a perhaps inevitable early inertia and reluctance to depart too radically too soon from established practices and procedures. Moreover, for the first decade of devolution, with the Labour Party in office nationally and in both Scotland and Wales, it afforded a greater measure of consistency. However, as devolution was a process and not an event, the passage of time and changed contexts and circumstances have meant, inevitably, that administrative structures, patterns and processes have evolved. Therefore, there has been a steady deviation from the UK 'norm' and the Whitehall model. In part, these changes reflect the fact that, from 2010, Labour was out of office nationally, to be replaced first by the Conservative and Liberal Democrat coalition and, since 2015, a succession of Conservative administrations. Concurrently, while Labour remained dominant in Wales (albeit weakened over time), its hegemony in Scotland was shattered; a minority SNP administration came into office in 2007, becoming a majority government in 2011 and continuing, with the support of Greens and independents, to govern Scotland since 2015. Also, the period since the 2010 general election coincided with the commencement in earnest of a period of fiscal austerity, which, while its severity and impact has been disputed, has resulted in growing dissatisfaction with the political status quo as represented by the traditional 'two-party' domination of Conservative and Labour, particularly in Scotland but also in Wales. The convulsions of Brexit have merely compounded these tensions and trends. For Northern Ireland, already unique in its political dispensation and culture, after a fitful start (suspended four times before a four-year hiatus from 2003 to 2007), a somewhat more stable and sustained period of devolved government emerged. However, here, too, fundamental disagreements between the two major parties in government over how to respond to the implications of austerity together with rising tensions over an array of other social and cultural issues, culminating with Brexit, eventually resulted in a further three-year suspension of the devolved institutions in 2017, prompting many to question whether meaningful devolution, even if nominally restored in 2020, could function properly. It was later suspended again over the issue of the Protocol on Ireland/Northern Ireland following the UK's secession from the EU.

Building on existing arrangements

As Rhodes et al. (2003) observed, regionalization and differentiation are not new features of the British 'unitary' state. Since its creation, Northern Ireland has always been governed as 'a place apart' (to quote Rose 1971), first through devolution (1921 to 1972), direct rule via the Northern Ireland Office (NIO) (a UK government department) (1972 to 1999) and what has been styled 'devolution plus' (1999 to the present, with periodic interruptions), all supported throughout by the NICS. Scotland has the longest established territorial ministry (the Scottish Office, created in 1886); the Welsh Office was created in 1964.

The devolution settlement in the UK post-1999 is asymmetrical, with fundamental differences between each territory. The arrangements for all three resemble each other, albeit only partially. All three now possess a devolved legislature and an executive, enjoying primary legislative powers, on all matters not reserved to the UK Parliament. For the civil service, the devolution legislation passed in 1998 adopted a different concept for Scotland and Wales to that of Northern Ireland. There was no requirement to legislate for a specific Scottish civil service. Until 2010, the UK civil service remained constituted by means of an Order in Council.

Following devolution, only certain Scottish civil servants working in devolved subject areas would report directly to the new Scottish executive, whereas UK-wide departments, such as the Department for Work and Pensions, would continue to report to the UK government. In effect, two systems would operate in parallel in each jurisdiction – that of the national UK government alongside that of the newly devolved government. The systems were cemented through means of the three territorial offices: the Office of the Secretary of State for Scotland (formerly the Scottish Office, now the Scotland Office), the Office of the Secretary of State for Wales (formerly the Welsh Office, now the Wales Office) and the NIO. All three are UK government departments. They represent the UK government's interests in Scotland, Wales and Northern Ireland, and, theoretically, provide a voice for the interests of Scotland, Wales and Northern Ireland in the UK government. However, officials working for the governments of the UK, Scotland and Wales remain part of the same civil service organization and share the same culture and values as set out in the Civil Service Code for England & Wales, and for Scotland. Although a separate organization, the NICS shares the same culture and values as those set out in the Civil Service Code.

To varying degrees, in all three territories, the devolved arrangements built on pre-existing arrangements in each. Hence, to begin with, the process involved creating a framework of political accountability about existing structures, policies and processes. As the political institutions became embedded, so ministers in the devolved territories could move in earnest to put their own stamp on how government and public policy would function. As Parry (2012a) observed, after a decade or so of devolution, the devolved administrations have asserted their distinctiveness and identity while remaining within UK norms and traditions of public administration. That said, in clear contrast with the singular Northern Ireland model, he questioned whether the balance between institutional continuity and adaptive local practices amounted to Scottish and Welsh models of public administration. A further decade on, it is clear that key to the process of transitioning from different forms of administrative devolution in place prior to the newly established arrangements was the civil service. We consider each territory in turn.

Scotland

Prior to devolution, there had been a separate Scottish Office since 1885, which already operated an extensive form of administrative devolution, having responsibility for the various government departments in Scotland. With the 1997 referendum approving political devolution, the Scotland Act 1998 established the Scottish executive in 1999. Quickly increasing use of the name 'government' in place of 'executive' was made in common parlance, but UK politicians, in particular, remained hostile to a change in nomenclature. After 2007, however, although the Scotland Office continued to use the existing logo and terminology, the new SNP administration in Holyrood switched, adopting the term 'Scottish Government' and the flag of Scotland in place of the royal coat of arms. The switch carried no legal force (the issue being a reserved matter) although the name was formally changed in UK law by the Scotland Act 2012. In 2016, a refreshed version of the Scottish Government logo was launched and used on all government websites and letters of correspondence as part of the national Gaelic language plan.

Scotland's devolved government is formed by the first minister, cabinet secretaries (who attend cabinet) and ministers. All government ministers sit in, and are accountable to, the Scottish Parliament through which all devolved primary legislation must pass. The Scottish Government was granted power over all so-called devolved matters, namely, those not reserved to the UK Parliament by Schedule 5 to the Scotland Act 1998, as amended by subsequent revisions to the devolution settlement in the Scotland Act 2012 and Scotland Act 2016. Originally, the range of matters devolved included, inter alia, health care, education, policing and justice, most aspects of transport, environment, rural affairs and housing. Later legislation, namely the Scotland Acts of 2012 and 2016, transferred additional responsibilities including some taxation powers, notably full control of income tax on income earned through employment, land and buildings transaction tax, landfill tax, drink driving limits, Scottish parliamentary and local authority elections, some social security powers and the Crown Estate Scotland.

Each cabinet secretary has an individual portfolio, assisted in their work by junior ministers. The Scottish law officers, the Lord Advocate and Solicitor General, can be appointed without being a Member of the Scottish Parliament (MSP); however, they are subject to parliament's approval and scrutiny, being appointed by the head of state on the recommendation of the first minister. Collectively, the first minister, cabinet secretaries, junior ministers and the law officers are known as the 'Scottish ministers'. The Scottish Government has adopted a dual executive structure of a cabinet that invokes collective decision-making, as well as non-cabinet members as junior ministers. The title *cabinet secretary* means a member of the government who partakes in cabinet, whereas junior ministers assist cabinet secretaries but are not part of the Scottish cabinet.

As with national UK arrangements, Scotland's government takes collective responsibility for all aspects of Scottish government policy. The Scottish cabinet meets weekly. Normally, meetings are held on Tuesday afternoons in the first minister's official residence, Bute House. The cabinet consists of the cabinet secretaries, excluding the Scottish law officers (the Lord Advocate and the Solicitor General). Although not formally a member, the Lord Advocate attends meetings of the cabinet when requested by the first minister. The cabinet is supported by the cabinet secretariat. Like in Whitehall, the Scottish cabinet has subcommittees – at present there are two: one on legislation and the Scottish Government Resilience Room. A time-limited third one existed prior to the Commonwealth Games 2014 in Glasgow.

The Scottish Government is supported by the civil service. The civil service helps the government of the day develop and implement its policies as well as deliver public services. Civil servants are accountable to ministers, who in turn are accountable to parliament. Across the core Scottish Government directorates and agencies, there are some 16,000 civil servants. As responsibility for the civil service continues to be a reserved matter, Scottish Government civil servants work within the rules and customs of the Home Civil Service while they serve the devolved administration. Notwithstanding this fact, the Scottish Government has proceeded to develop revised arrangements to better suit its own perceived needs. The most senior civil servant in Scotland is the permanent secretary, who serves both the first minister and cabinet. S/he is part of the permanent secretaries management group of the Home Civil Service, being answerable to the most senior civil servant in Britain, the UK cabinet secretary (not to be confused with Scottish Government cabinet secretaries), for his or her professional conduct. S/he remains, however, at the direction of Scottish ministers. The Scottish model departs from its Whitehall counterpart insofar as it is divided into directorates rather than ministries. The thirty directorates execute government policy. Unlike in Whitehall, Scottish cabinet secretaries (as politicians, being equivalent to secretaries of state in the UK government) do not lead the directorates, nor do they have any direct role in their operation. Rather, the directorates are grouped together into 'directorates general' (DGs), each run by a senior civil servant who is titled a 'director-general'. Like its Whitehall, the structure is not immutable, changing in response to shifting priorities, preferences and events. Hence, the number of DGs can vary, having been six and currently eight (see Box 8.1).

BOX 8.1 DIRECTORATES GENERAL OF THE SCOTTISH GOVERNMENT IN OCTOBER 2022

- Communities
- Constitution and External Affairs
- Corporate
- Economy
- Education and Justice
- Health and Social Care
- Net Zero
- Scottish Exchequer

Directors general and their constituent directorates are responsible for progressing the Scottish Government's strategic objectives, as set out in the Programme for Government. Each directorate is supported by a variety of other corporate service teams and professional groups. As an independent prosecution service, the Crown Office and Procurator Fiscal Service is a ministerial department of the Scottish Government headed by the Lord Advocate. It is responsible for prosecution, along with the procurators fiscal, under Scottish law.

The Scottish Government possesses a strategic board, which is composed of the permanent secretary, the directors general, two chief advisers (scientific and economic) and several non-executive directors. The board is responsible for providing support to the government through the permanent secretary, forming the executive of the Scottish civil service. To deliver its work, executive agencies – either as part of government departments, or as departments in their own right – each conduct a discrete area of work. These include, for example, the Scottish Prison Service and Transport Scotland. Executive agencies are staffed by civil servants. There are also non-ministerial offices and departments that form part of the Scottish administration, and therefore the wider devolved arrangement, but answer directly to the Scottish Parliament rather than to ministers. These include the National Records of Scotland (formerly, the General Register Office for Scotland and National Archives of Scotland) and the Office of the Scottish Charity Regulator.

Additionally, the Scottish Government is also responsible for a large number of non-departmental public bodies including executive non-departmental public bodies (NDPBs), such as Scottish Enterprise; advisory NDPBs, such as the Scottish Law Commission; tribunals, such as the Children's Panel, and, until 2018, the Additional Support Needs Tribunals for Scotland; and nationalized industries operating as a statutory corporation, such as Scottish Water. These are staffed by public servants rather than civil servants. The Scottish Government is also responsible for some other public bodies that are not classed as non-departmental public bodies, such as NHS Boards, Visiting Committees for Scottish Penal Establishments or HM Chief Inspector of Constabulary for Scotland. Moreover, the policy focus of the Scottish Government has changed to one very much focused on an outcomes-based approach, diverging from Whitehall practice.

Wales

Prior to devolution, the Welsh Office had responsibility for the various government departments in Wales. Albeit by a far narrower margin than occurred one month earlier in Scotland, the 1997 Welsh referendum produced a 'Yes' vote leading to the Government of Wales Act 1998. The Act established a new National Assembly for Wales (NAW) in 1999. Initially, devolution in Wales differed crucially from that in Scotland and Northern Ireland inasmuch as the Welsh Government had no independent executive powers in law. That is, the NAW was established as a *body corporate* – the executive, as such, was simply a committee of the Assembly. The 'executive' or cabinet only had those powers delegated to ministers by the assembly as a whole. Any primary legislation that the NAW sought to introduce had to be channelled via Westminster.

Pressure quickly built for correction of what was widely viewed as both an anomalous and even demeaning treatment of Wales vis-à-vis its devolved counterparts. Consequently, in its third term, Tony Blair's Labour government enacted the Government of Wales Act 2006, formally separating the NAW and the Welsh Government. The move gave Welsh ministers independent executive authority, effective following 2007 Assembly elections. In a further development serving to underscore its status, the Welsh Assembly Government was formally renamed the 'Welsh Government' following the Wales Act 2014. The Senedd and Elections (Wales) Act, 2020, changed the name of the NAW to *Senedd Cymru*, or the Welsh Parliament.

Since separation, Welsh ministers have exercised functions in their own right. Further transfers of executive functions from the UK government can be made directly to the Welsh ministers (with their consent) by an Order in Council approved by the UK Parliament. The separation was designed to clarify the respective roles of the legislature and the executive. The Government of Wales Act 2006 provided for Welsh ministers to take decisions, develop and implement policy, exercise executive functions and make statutory instruments. The sixty legislative members scrutinize the government's decisions and policies, hold ministers to account, approve budgets for the Welsh Government's programmes and enact Acts on matters devolved to the Welsh administration. Thus, the position in Wales more closely paralleled the relationship between the UK Government and Westminster Parliament and that between the Scottish Government and the Scottish Parliament. Thus, all members of the Welsh cabinet are accountable to the Parliament as a whole, an arrangement better in keeping with a conventional legislature–executive relationship. Nonetheless, despite its initially minimalist provisions, the locus of administrative accountability has shifted from the Office of the Secretary of State for Wales to the Cabinet of the Assembly.

As the devolved government of Wales, the Welsh Government is led by the first minister, the leader of the largest party in the Welsh Parliament. To date, Labour has held this position uninterrupted. The first minister is joined by ministers, who attend cabinet meetings, and deputy ministers, who do not; there is also a counsel general. The Parliament's functions, including that of making subordinate legislation, in the main, transferred to the Welsh ministers upon separation. A third body, the National Assembly for Wales Commission, was also established under the 2006 Act. Since 2020, it has been restyled as the *Senedd* Commission. It employs the staff supporting the Welsh Parliament.

The Government of Wales Act 2006 provided for the appointment of Welsh ministers. The first minister is nominated by the Welsh Parliament and then appointed by the head of state. Then, the first minister appoints ministers and deputy ministers. The Act created a new post of Counsel General for Wales, to serve as the principal source of legal advice to the Welsh Government. Ministers and the counsel general are appointed by the head of state on the nomination of the first minister, whose recommendation must be agreed by the Parliament. The counsel general may be, but does not have to be, a Senedd member. The Act permits a maximum of twelve Welsh ministers, including deputy ministers, but excludes the first minister and the counsel general. Thus, the Welsh Government has a maximum of fourteen members.

With only secondary legislative capacity, aside from the problem of clogging up the busy Westminster legislative timetable, dissatisfaction prompted the outgoing UK Labour government to contemplate extending full law-making powers to Wales, following the recommendations of the Report of Lord Richard's Commission. Subsequently, the Conservative and Liberal Democrat coalition honoured that commitment, authorizing a referendum on approving the change. By a large majority, the referendum result in March 2011 approved the proposal to endow the NAW with primary legislative capacity. Thus, the Welsh Government became entitled to propose bills to the Welsh Parliament on subjects spanning some twenty fields of policy. Acts of the Welsh Parliament may make any provision that could be made by Act of Parliament at Westminster. The twenty areas of responsibility devolved to the Welsh Parliament are listed in Box 8.2.

BOX 8.2 AREAS OF RESPONSIBILITY DEVOLVED TO THE WELSH PARLIAMENT IN OCTOBER 2022

- Agriculture, fisheries, forestry and rural development
- Ancient monuments and historical buildings
- Culture
- Economic development
- Education and training
- Environment
- Fire and rescue services and promotion of fire safety
- Food
- Health and health services
- Highways and transport
- Housing
- Local government
- The Welsh Parliament
- Public administration
- Social welfare
- Sport and recreation
- Tourism
- Town and country planning
- Water and flood defences
- Welsh language

The Welsh Government is supported by the UK civil service. Even in the early period of devolution, such was the degree of idiosyncrasy combined with local custom and practice that Rhodes et al. (2003: 114) remarked: 'Wales has acquired its own civil service in de facto, if not yet, de jure, form'. Developments since this assessment have only served to reinforce this impression and nourished calls for a formally distinct Welsh civil service. There are approximately 5,000 full-time-equivalent civil servants working across Wales for the Welsh Government. Like Scotland, the civil service in Wales is a matter reserved to the UK Parliament at Westminster: Welsh Government civil servants work within the rules and customs of the Home Civil Service but serve the devolved administration rather than the UK government. The Welsh Government is divided into a series of directorates, being grouped into departments (previously five, currently eight), see Box 8.3.

BOX 8.3 DEPARTMENTS OF THE WELSH GOVERNMENT IN OCTOBER 2022

- Office of the First Minister
- Permanent Secretary's Office
- Chief Operating Officer's Group
- Covid Recovery and Local Government Group
- Climate Change and Rural Affairs Group
- Economy, Treasury and Constitution Group
- Education, Social Justice and Welsh Language Group
- Health & Social Services Group

Most senior leadership for the civil service in the Welsh Government is provided by the permanent secretary. Like their Scottish counterpart, s/he is also a member of the Home Civil Service and so part of its permanent secretaries management group, answerable to the most senior civil servant in the UK, the UK cabinet secretary, for their professional conduct. S/he remains, however, at the direction of the Welsh ministers. The permanent secretary also chairs the Welsh Government Board, which translates the strategic direction set by the Welsh cabinet and its committees into work that is joined up across Welsh Government departments. Rather than reflecting strictly functional responsibilities, board members constitute a collective leadership in support of the permanent secretary. Ordinarily, the board comprises the directors general (currently, six), directors (six) and non-executive directors (four); an additional director general was appointed in response to the Covid-19 pandemic crisis. Board members are appointed at the discretion of, and by, the permanent secretary.

Additionally, the Welsh Government is responsible for Welsh Government Sponsored Bodies (WGSBs). Like Scotland, given that a key argument for devolution in Wales was to increase democratic oversight of the various NDPBS that operated in the country, the Welsh Government moved swiftly to bring many such bodies back within its direct remit. Today, the remaining bodies are, respectively: executive WGSBs, which are non-departmental public bodies such as the Arts Council of Wales; advisory WGSBs, which are non-departmental public bodies; and tribunals such as the Mental Health Review Tribunal for Wales. The WGSBs are staffed by public servants rather than civil servants. The Welsh Government is also responsible for some public bodies that are not classed as WGSBs, such as NHS Wales, and the Welsh bureaux of the England and Wales legal offices. Historically, most Welsh Office staff were based in Cardiff. However, in 2002, the Fullerton Report had concluded that 'the assembly could no longer sustain having the majority of its operational functions located in and around Cardiff'. Therefore, since 2004, Welsh Government civil servants have been relocated across Wales, which involved the creation of new offices across the country. In 2006, the mergers of Education and Learning Wales (ELWa), the Wales Tourist Board and the Welsh Development Agency into the Welsh Government brought these agencies' offices into the Welsh Government estate. In April 2013, the first minister for Wales established the Commission on Public Service Governance and Delivery. It was tasked with examining all aspects of governance and delivery in the devolved public sector in Wales. A draft bill was introduced in the Fourth Assembly that would pave the way for local authority mergers, provide local authorities with the general power of competence and change the functions of councils and their members. However, following the 2016 assembly election, the proposals were abandoned.

Northern Ireland

Since the Good Friday (Belfast) Agreement in 1998, and the Northern Ireland Act 1998, the governmental structure of Northern Ireland became devolved, with an Assembly and executive, under the leadership of the first minister and deputy first minister. These arrangements were revised but otherwise reaffirmed by the Northern Ireland (St Andrews Agreement) Act 2006. They have endured intermittently, with several periods in which the devolved arrangements were suspended. During these occasions, Northern Ireland has also been governed by ministers under the Secretary of State for Northern Ireland, an arrangement known as 'direct rule', or a form of governmental limbo leaving civil servants in charge though shorn of power to make key decisions.

The Northern Ireland executive is referred to in the relevant legislation as the 'Executive Committee of the Assembly', exemplifying a form of consociational ('power-sharing') government. Uniquely, it has a dyarchy consisting of the first minister and deputy first minister (one from each of the two main communities, co-equal in status and powers), plus various ministers with individual portfolios and remits. The main Assembly parties appoint most ministers in the executive, except for the Minister of Justice who is elected by a cross-community vote.

Initially, as well as the Office of the First Minister and Deputy First Minister (OFMDFM), devolution provided for ten departments, later rising to eleven (with Justice being devolved). In 2016, the twelve departments were reduced to nine, following the dissolution of the Department of Culture, Arts and Leisure, Department of the Environment and Department for Employment and Learning (see Box 8.4).

BOX 8.4 DEPARTMENTS OF THE NORTHERN IRELAND GOVERNMENT IN OCTOBER 2022

- The Executive Office
- Department of Agriculture, Environment and Rural Affairs
- Department for Communities
- Department of Education
- Department for the Economy
- Department of Finance
- Department of Health
- Department for Infrastructure
- Department of Justice

Northern Ireland's executive is composed and functions on a different basis to those elsewhere. While it is normal for governments to carry on based on the continued confidence of legislators, in Northern Ireland's case, ministerial positions in the executive are allocated to parties with significant representation in the Assembly. With the exception of Justice, the number of ministries to which each party is entitled is determined by the D'Hondt system. Rather than a voluntary arrangement emerging, a 'compulsory' or mandatory (non-exclusionary) multi-party coalition is required. In effect, major parties cannot be excluded from participation in government and power-sharing is enforced by the system. While four of the five main political parties (the DUP, the UUP, the Alliance Party and some SDLP members) favour a move towards a voluntary coalition in the longer term, Sinn Féin remains opposed. Additionally, the executive cannot function if either of the two largest parties refuse to take part, as these parties are allocated the first minister and deputy first minister positions. However, other parties are not required to enter the executive even if they are entitled to do so; instead, they can choose to go into opposition if they wish. In 2015, the UUP announced that it would withdraw from the executive and form an opposition after all. In 2016, a new executive was announced (three weeks after Assembly election). For the first time in the Assembly's history, parties that were entitled to ministries (i.e. UUP, SDLP and Alliance) chose instead to go into opposition, following legislation providing parties with this choice. This meant that the executive was formed only by the two major parties, the DUP and Sinn Féin, thus giving them more seats in the executive (with the exception of the Department of Justice, which was given to an Independent Unionist MLA, Claire Sugden, due to this appointment needing cross-community support). In 2022, reflecting the continuing impasse at

Stormont and their disappointing election performance, the SDLP once again formed an opposition, nominating the first Leader of the Opposition.

The executive is co-chaired by the first minister and deputy first minister. Its official functions are to serve as a forum for the discussion of, and agreement on, issues that cut across the responsibilities of two or more ministers; prioritizing executive and legislative proposals; discussing and agreeing upon significant or controversial matters; and recommending a common position where necessary (e.g. in dealing with external relationships). Executive meetings are normally held fortnightly, compared to weekly meetings of the UK cabinet and Irish government. Under the executive's Ministerial Code, ministers are obliged to operate within the framework of the programme for government; support all decisions of the executive and Northern Ireland Assembly; and participate fully in the executive, the North/South Ministerial Council and the British–Irish Council. The Ministerial Code allows any three ministers to request a cross-community vote. The quorum for voting is seven ministers.

The current system of devolution succeeded long periods of direct rule (1974 to 1999 and 2002 to 2007), when NICS had a considerable influence on government policy. The legislation that established new departments in 1999 affirmed that 'the functions of a department shall at all times be exercised subject to the direction and control of the Minister'. Ministers are also subject to several limitations, including the European Convention on Human Rights (previously) EU law, other international obligations of the UK, and a requirement not to discriminate on religious or political grounds. Uniquely, ministerial decisions can be challenged by a petition of thirty Northern Ireland Assembly members, an action permitted for alleged breaches of the Ministerial Code and on 'matters of public importance'. The speaker of the Assembly must consult political party leaders in the Assembly (who are often also ministers) before deciding whether the subject is a matter of public importance. Successful petitions will then be considered by the executive.

With each new mandate, the executive develops a programme for government, incorporating an agreed budget. Additionally, under the St Andrews Agreement, the executive is obliged to adopt strategies on the following policy matters: enhancing and protecting the development of the Irish language; enhancing and developing Ulster Scots language, heritage and culture; and tackling poverty, social exclusion and patterns of deprivation based on objective need. However, to date, although the OFMDFM published a child poverty strategy in 2011, neither an Irish language strategy nor an Ulster Scots strategy had been adopted until recently. Subsequently, relations within the executive deteriorated – arguments over the extent to which Northern Ireland would implement austerity measures, a free-standing Irish language act, abortion reform, gay marriage, the Renewable Heat Incentive (RHI) scandal and Brexit all served to foster distrust. Eventually, the government collapsed in early 2017, after the deputy first minister resigned. For three years, Northern Ireland experienced a lacuna in its governance, with neither the local parties nor London taking direct responsibility. Complicating the situation was the 'confidence and supply' arrangement at Westminster between the Conservative Party, operating as a minority administration, and the DUP, on whose votes the UK government relied in order to remain in office. The arrangement broke down towards the end of that parliament and with the Conservative Party's emphatic victory in December 2019. In the meantime, the Northern Ireland (Executive Formation and Exercise of Functions) Act 2019 prevented another Assembly election, being designed to keep services running in Northern Ireland in the absence of a functional devolved government. Although the measures were intended to enable senior officials to make key decisions (a power neither sought nor desired by the civil service), legal action in the courts determined that those matters still required decisions by political leaders. In January 2020, following intense political activity in the aftermath of the UK general election, Northern Ireland's executive was re-formed, only to be suspended again in early 2022, this time over the issue of the Protocol on Ireland/Northern Ireland. A subsequent election saw Sinn Féin emerge as the largest single party, entitling the party to nominate the First Minister position. Devolution, however, remained deadlocked.

The changing civil service across the devolved nations

Across the devolved countries, there are civil servants working both for the UK government and the respective devolved administrations. Indeed, there are more civil servants in Scotland and Wales working for Whitehall departments than for the Scottish and Welsh governments, although the percentage of all civil servants in each country working for the devolved administration has increased (see Figure 8.1). Consequently, a higher percentage of civil servants working in each of the three devolved nations worked for the devolved administration by 2015 compared to 2010, a trend that has been maintained (see Figure 8.2). Even so, five UK secretaries of state have more civil servants at their disposal than any of the first ministers of the devolved nations (see Figure 8.3).

Concerning the period since 2010, the UK civil service was around 18 per cent smaller at the end of 2015, compared to the Spending Review in 2010. None of the devolved administrations have experienced staff reductions as deep as the UK civil service as a whole. The reduction is significantly deeper than in the Scottish Government and its related organizations (which stand 5 per cent smaller) and the Welsh Government and its organizations (6 per cent smaller). Both devolved governments reduced staff in early 2011 before small increases in 2015 and then another reduction. By contrast,

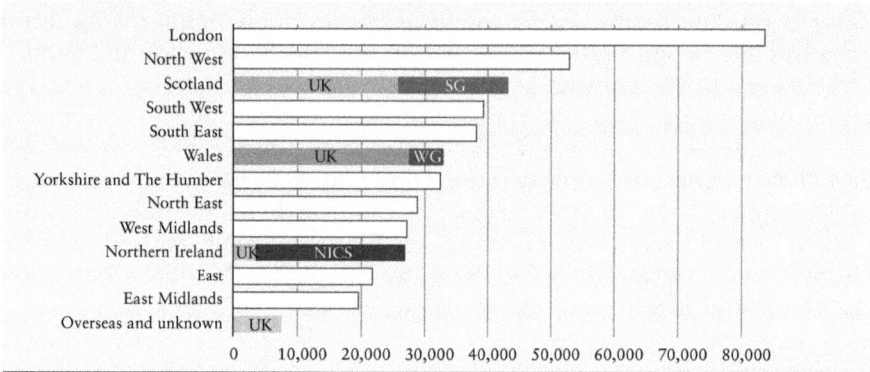

FIGURE 8.1 *The location of civil servants across the UK in 2018*
Source: Institute for Government (2020a).

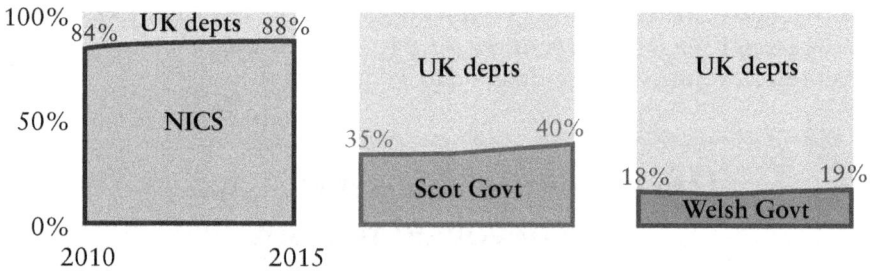

FIGURE 8.2 *Proportion of civil servants working for devolved administration in each nation, 2010–15*
Source: Ilott (2016).

the NICS is slightly larger (+1.4 per cent) now than at the start of 2010 (see Figure 8.4). This is largely due to the devolution of police and justice powers and resulting transfers of staff (1,000 staff in the NI Court Service and Youth Justice Agency in 2010, and the inclusion of 1,700 prison grade staff in 2012). A voluntary severance scheme, funded by the UK Treasury, was enacted during 2015, which saw the NICS cut from just over 26,000 at the start of 2015 to just under 23,500 at the end of it (as part of a commitment to slim down the public sector in Northern Ireland). Reflecting the longstanding differences there, the separate NICS employs 23,486 civil servants compared with 15,960 in the Scottish Government and 5,290 in the Welsh Government. Additionally, in Wales, after returning several large agencies back to government control, the Welsh Government has only one arm's-length body employing civil servants – Estyn, which inspects education and training. By contrast, most Scottish Government civil servants

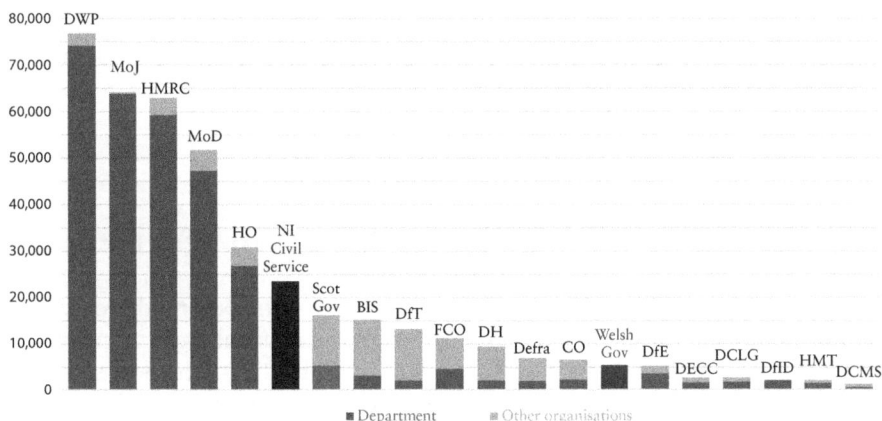

FIGURE 8.3 *The civil service in the devolved nations*
Source: Ilott (2016).

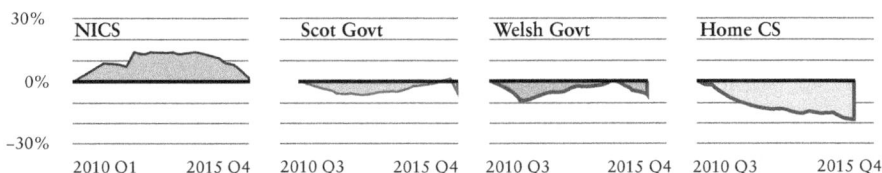

FIGURE 8.4 *Change in civil service staff numbers, 2010–15*
Source: Ilott (2016).

are employed in various arm's-length bodies, the largest being the Scottish Prison Service. Interestingly, the Welsh Government has a greater percentage of staff at higher grades than either of the other devolved administrations or the Home Civil Service, while having a higher percentage of women at every grade of the civil service than in Scotland or the UK civil service as a whole. Female representation has increased in both of the most senior grade bands between 2010 and 2015: from 44 per cent to 47 per cent at Grades 6 and 7, and from 38 per cent to 47 per cent in the Senior Civil Service. Additionally, just over 21 per cent of civil servants working for the Welsh Government (and Estyn) work in the two most senior bands of the civil service (the Senior Civil Service and Grades 6 and 7). This compares with 11.6 per cent in the Scottish Government and its agencies, 8 per cent across the UK civil service as a whole, and 6.9 per cent in the Northern Ireland Civil Service. This reflects the fact that significant aspects of delivering public services through front-line staff (more junior grades) have been devolved to both the Scottish Government (for example, prisons and justice) and Northern Ireland (welfare and other areas). While the civil service remains a UK matter in law, in practice, the Scottish Government and Welsh Government have autonomy over staffing, promotions and grading, and pay settlements. The single UK framework tends only to apply to the highest reaches of the Home Civil Service – the Senior Civil Service.

Implications – still a unified civil service?

Before devolution, 'there were Scottish departments before there was a Scottish minister, and a minister before there was a coherent ministry to serve him' (Parry 1982, cited in Rhodes et al. 2003: 71). The Scottish civil service had a degree of autonomy not enjoyed by other regional civil services, having always been distinctive within the wider UK firmament. Devolution did not bring any significant additional powers to Scotland (still less, Wales) in the organization and management of the civil service. Powers dealing with terms and conditions, for example, were already delegated. Scottish Office civil servants transferred to the new parliamentary structure, yet they remained part of a unified UK civil service, combining practical loyalty to the minister they serve and ultimate loyalty to the Crown. A similar pattern was evident in Wales. Reflecting on the first decade of devolution, therefore, Parry (2012b) contended that the unified civil service seems well entrenched.

In the early days of devolution, several commentators cast doubt on the continuity of the unified civil service. Hazell and Morris (1999, cited in Rhodes et al. 2003) predicted that a break up of the unified civil service was likely, with a separate civil service emerging in Scotland and Wales, like the NICS. Others even saw it as potentially desirable, with calls for a unified public service (Cole et al. 2003; Prosser 2003). Inevitably, the continuity of unified civil service arrangements in Great Britain has been questioned. As the pressures for bespoke solutions and responsiveness to specific Scottish and Welsh political imperatives have grown, the debate has steadily simmered concerning the case for forming separate civil service organizations for Edinburgh and Cardiff, paralleling that based in Belfast. Similarly, with their overlapping political cultures, built on a continuing major role for the public sector in Scotland, Wales and Northern Ireland, and limited privatization of provision, there has been a relatively heavier focus on the merits of joined-up governance and small-country government, which in turn has prompted discussion over the concept of a devolved civil service or unified public service. To varying degrees, too, devolution sparked fresh debate on the role of delegated governance through quangos and public bodies, the process of appointments and public accountability more generally in each jurisdiction, with various attempts designed to reduce quangos through mergers, simplification and abolition, internal reforms, more public participation and co-production through improved relations with the voluntary sector, in response to reports and inquiries into public service delivery.

The unified civil service serves as one of the binding agents that gives the UK continued coherence and form. It has facilitated inter-institutional relations post-devolution, promoting knowledge exchange and enabling interchange between the devolved administrations and Whitehall. That said, while formally remaining part of a unified civil service, it is clear that 'officials serve exclusively the ministers of the duly-elected administration that they serve. This has been supplemented by a shared understanding that any managerial arrangements consequential on the unified service do not compromise this exclusive loyalty' (Parry, oral evidence cited in Parliament 2016). Although it has its own arrangements, the NICS closely resembles the Home Civil Service in its underlying principles and modus operandi. Not only have these arrangements worked satisfactorily throughout the period since devolution, they are 'widely held to assist inter-institutional relations' (Parliament 2016). In his Commission on Devolution in Wales, having initially been disposed to a separate Welsh civil service, Sir Paul Silk eventually concluded that the advantages of retaining a shared civil service outweighed any disadvantages, a change of heart in part based on the opportunities the Home Civil Service can provide for career development and 'cross-fertilization' between the devolved administrations and Whitehall.

Indeed, Sir Derek Jones (as former permanent secretary to the Welsh Government) and Leslie Evans (his counterpart in the Scottish Government) have indicated that not only were they both well integrated at the heart of the Home Civil Service, but that there was frequent contact between the devolved governments and other UK government departments (Parliament 2016). Suggestions that there is a potential conflict of loyalty have been dismissed. While the UK cabinet secretary is the line manager to his Welsh and Scottish permanent secretary colleagues, both individuals serve their respective governments and view their duty as being to support their respective first ministers, as their chief policy advisers.

Political pressures for separate arrangements notwithstanding (predictably emanating most forcefully from separatist political parties), the public pronouncements of senior officialdom indicate that a broad consensus remains strongly convinced that the advantages of a unified civil service continue to outweigh the case for separation. Philip Rycroft, former Head of the UK Governance Group in the Cabinet Office, described the advantages as 'relatively straightforward', adding:

> We share the same set of values; we share the same senior leadership structure; we share the same training and leadership development opportunities. Colleagues from Scotland and Wales will join the High Potential Development Scheme for potential Director Generals and the equivalent scheme for potential Permanent Secretaries. That gives us

a context in which we are working together in a number of different contexts, which helps us to build the relationships that are so important to manage the good relationships between the various Governments.

(cited in Parliament 2016)

Even though the particular constitutional history of Northern Ireland accounts for the existence of a separate NICS, and there was little appetite to change matters, a former permanent secretary of the NIO, Sir Jonathan Stephens, emphasized that the NIO and the NICS manage to make their relationship work, aided by the fact that 'in many ways it [the NICS] is, although separate, identical to the UK Civil Service' (cited in Parliament 2016). He did not believe that the model was a suitable candidate for transfer to Scotland and Wales. While separate civil services were possible, the potential gains were outweighed by the drawbacks.

Despite two decades of devolution, there remains a tendency for the changed reality not to be fully appreciated in Whitehall. As identified by the UCL's Constitution Unit's report *Devolution and the Future of the Union*, 'too many officials and departments tend to treat the devolved governments as an afterthought, or like any other Whitehall department' (Hazell 2015). Arguably, the practice has become more evident as the policy stances within the different governments have diverged. In response, while not seeking to enforce or even engineer congruence, the UK Cabinet Office has responded with steps to raise devolution awareness and capacity in Whitehall. In 2015, the UK Governance Group was established to lead the UK Government's work on constitutional and devolution issues. It brings together under one command the Cabinet Office Constitution Group, the Scotland Office, the Office of the Advocate General for Scotland and the Wales Office. The group is tasked with improving civil service capability to support ministers in sustaining the United Kingdom and its constitutional settlement. In turn, the civil service unveiled a devolution toolkit to give advice to civil servants in UK government departments aimed at helping them to 'take devolution issues into consideration in your work' and providing advice on how 'you may best work with colleagues in the devolved administrations of Scotland, Wales and Northern Ireland' (HM Government 2019).

While the continuity or otherwise of a unified civil service has been debated, other commentators speculated whether the civil service in Scotland would be neither unified nor separate but become part of a more unified public service in Scotland (Ryan 1999). Commentators also wondered whether, in creating a more joined-up territorial polity, it might fuel fears of separation. With ministers being 'on the doorstep', scrutiny would rise but, with it, creeping politicization is a risk too. The traditionally strong role of civil servants in the Scottish polity has inevitably been pushed back as politicians have asserted themselves. Differentiation has remained a key feature of the public administrative landscape.

Conclusions

As Madgwick and Rose (1982: 1) observed, 'Territory is important politically'. Whitehall's writ no longer runs automatically beyond Offa's Dyke and Hadrian's Wall, not to mention the North Channel. The dynamic has shifted from one of proconsuls to that of emissaries. Progressively, Scotland and Wales have witnessed an 'indigenization' of the civil service in both territories, serving to build 'Team Wales' and 'Team Scotland' in governmental and administrative terms. Inevitably, it has become increasingly difficult to reconcile the familiar refrain in Westminster of 'joined-up government' and maintenance of a unified UK civil service with the reality of three devolved polities, each intent on following a separate path from the 'London' line. The recent variegated responses to Brexit and also, perhaps more tellingly, to Covid-19 have illustrated this fact starkly.

Inevitably, with new structures come new systems, processes and networks, with a corresponding transformation of intergovernmental relations (IGR). Hence, at the outset of the UK's devolution process – a unique experiment with no immediate comparator – Rhodes et al. (2003) remarked that the pattern of British IGR may resemble those of other states (such as Canada) with the Westminster system. 'Even in devolved systems, the pull of the centre remains strong' (Rhodes 2001: 31). Oscillating tension in and on the unified civil service is a central characteristic of how devolution occurs and has evolved. From 'matching' and aiding adjustment in the territories, we now have a conscious policy of de-alignment away from homogeneity. Pressures to politicize will intensify and with it a demand for formally separate and distinct civil services. To begin with, however, devolution reinforced existing patterns of functional differentiation with decentralized political authority.

Over time, however, the powers and responsibilities of the Scottish Parliament, Welsh Parliament and Northern Ireland Assembly have grown with the potential to go further over the next few years. As a response to the threat of Scottish independence, significant further tax powers to the Scottish Parliament, including most income tax, as well as (for the first time) aspects of the welfare system have been transferred to Edinburgh. A new fiscal framework governing the level of spending available to the Scottish Parliament has been established. While not as advanced, the direction of travel of – and, taking their cue from the Scottish experience, the aspiration for – the Welsh Parliament and Northern Ireland Assembly has been similar, seeing new powers and responsibilities devolved to Cardiff and Belfast.

Ironically, the different governments (national and devolved) are moving to apply different policy solutions to populations that share many of the same socio-economic characteristics, giving rise to scope for both policy learning and comparison of relative success – or failure. Inevitably, as befits a now variegated model, civil servants find themselves serving two masters within what remains, officially at least, a unified civil service. Remarkably little coverage has been afforded to what this means for the continuing legal concept of a unified civil service, an institution that, to date, remains one of the core features of the UK's union and hallmark of its territorial and political integrity and cohesion. Yet, as the Scottish referendum campaign demonstrated most acutely, the practical reality for the civil service under Scottish devolution is changing. For example, enforcement of the Civil Service Code in Scotland, which constitutionally should be UK-wide, has been devolved to the Scottish Government's permanent secretary.

In evidence to the House of Commons Public Administration Select Committee, Mitchell suggested that there had never been a unified civil service:

> We can overstate the extent to which devolution has affected things. That said, yes, I think things have progressed further and, informally, there is a distinct Scottish Civil Service. There always has been, but it is more distinct now than it was in the past.
>
> (cited in Parliament 2015)

Similarly, Paun observed:

> what we have seen is, first of all, that political diversion since 2007 has pulled things apart and, also, the gradual evolutionary change of Civil Services in the respective capitals becoming more systems unto themselves.
>
> (cited in Parliament 2015)

Riddell concluded that 'it is evident already that, in practice, Scotland and Wales are at least more distinct Civil Services' that have, for example, different pay scales. Of the Scottish Government's civil service, he said:

> Scotland has its own reform plan; it is not the same as the one that applies here. The Civil Service has changed an awful lot in Scotland. It is much more outcome directed. There have been a lot of reforms. They, of course, have an integrated rather than departmental Government structure in Scotland. It has changed a lot, but not in the same ways as in England.
>
> (cited in Parliament 2015)

Although the independence referendum of 2014 confirmed Scotland's place within the UK, Riddell believed that there was 'an increasing recognition that there are separate Civil Services within that umbrella' (cited in Parliament 2015). The thorny issue of intergovernmental relations would demand re-examination, which, in turn, throws a spotlight on the working of the civil service within and between the UK and devolved governments. If a unified civil service is a constitutional fiction, however, since civil servants in Scotland are expected to serve the Scottish

Government in the same way as civil servants in Whitehall departments serve the UK government, for the time being, the advantages that flow from having a single Home Civil Service still justify the retention of a single UK civil service.

A further dimension to devolution comes from the UK's membership of the EU and, more importantly, the decision to leave the EU following the 2016 referendum. Inevitably, the UK's secession from the EU heralds a period of considerable uncertainty and unpredictability for the three devolved administrations. The complex system of multi-level governance involved with British membership of the EU is morphing into one in which, although no longer bound by rules forged over forty-seven years, the UK is now politically constituted on a transformed basis from when it acceded. That is, Brexit does not restore the internal status quo ante of 1972. In repatriating powers and functions previously exercised at an EU level, the UK will have to determine an allocation between national and devolved governments. Formally, the UK government has maintained that the powers currently vested with the devolved administrations will remain, with the prospect of additional powers repatriated from Brussels being ascribed in due course. The devolved governments, two of which are opposed to Brexit (Northern Ireland's government being divided on the matter), have countered, contending that any such powers should have been devolved immediately. The period of transition and post-withdrawal has witnessed an inevitable tense negotiation and horse-trading as the devolved governments, eager to consolidate their authority, deploy their considerable powers to maximize their advantage. As the nature of the UK's internal administrative arrangements begins to realign after its departure from the EU, it is the UK civil service that will be tasked with devising ways to allow UK government (central and devolved) to continue to function effectively.

9

Devolution, localism and partnerships

Introduction

At the start of the devolution experiment, local government in the UK was already at a particularly low ebb. As Stoker (1999: 1) observed:

> What happened to British local government during the period of Conservative Government from 1979–1997 was in many respects a brutal illustration of power politics. The funding system was reformed to provide central government with a considerable (and probably unprecedented) level of control over spending. Various functions and responsibilities were stripped away from local authorities or organized in a way that obliged local authorities to work in partnership with other public and private agencies in the carrying out of the functions.

The new Labour government pledged that 'local decision making should be less constrained by central government and also more accountable to local people' (Blair 1998: 20). For the three smaller UK nations, as Bogdanor (2001: 149) observed, devolution meant that 'large powers have been removed from the purview of ministers and Members of Parliament', to become the bailiwick of the newly installed devolved institutions. Hence, while Labour promised a new era in central–local government relations, with a more positive disposition towards local authorities, these relationships would quickly come to be refracted through the new prism of political devolution in each of Scotland, Wales and Northern Ireland. Thus, in creating what has been termed a form of quasi-federalism (Wilson and Game 2011), British asymmetric devolution has provided a further dimension to the differentiated polity outlined by Rhodes over thirty years ago, giving rise to increasingly variegated patterns of local government within each nation (Rhodes 1988).

In both Scotland and Wales, local councils already enjoyed an important status, with key roles in service delivery and accounting for substantial proportions of overall public expenditure. Hence, although relations with the previous Conservative-controlled territorial offices had been strained, each could draw on longstanding links as a prelude to realizing a close partnership with their respective newly devolved governments. In particular, central–local relations within Scotland have long been observed to possess a different character to those within England, being 'closer and more harmonious' (Page 1978), and with interpersonal relations and pragmatism evident (Midwinter and McGarvey 1997; Jeffery 2006). Simply, the scale and proximity of key actors gave interpersonal relations an intimacy neither seen nor likely even possible in England. This meant that the breakdown in relations during the Conservative years never quite reached the depths of that in England (McGarvey 2002). The same can be said of Wales. By contrast, in Northern Ireland, so laden with historical baggage and marginalized was local government in the 'permanent impermanence' of direct rule that relations were always related more to the overarching constitutional question, any change always promised to be a more piecemeal and laboured undertaking, given the political sensitivities involved.

Even before devolution occurred, there had long been concern about its potential to undermine existing local government arrangements (Cole 2006). With Scottish and Welsh ministers and departments assuming responsibility for local authorities, the temptation to intervene and centralize upwards (to the newly devolved bodies in Edinburgh and Cardiff) was real. Indeed, so strained had UK central–local relations become, and so traduced in public discourse the status of local government as an institution following years of bruising conflicts, that there was genuine concern that local government might become, even inadvertently, a loser under any new dispensation. Evidence from overseas gave an additional cause for caution, with the regional governments in Belgium and Spain, for example, 'proving to be centralizers of local government functions and finances' (Jeffery 2006). For several commentators, business more or less as usual appeared likely under devolution, with the inevitable tendency for the higher level (providing most of the funding) to interfere and come into conflict with the lower level (Alexander 1997; Sinclair 1997). As Himsworth (1998: 19) suggested, it 'seems inevitable that the problems of central–local relations will continue [in Scotland] and that they will continue, in most respects, to be fundamentally the same as in England and Wales'. In that respect, devolution appeared initially to not make a lot of difference.

In practice, too, early devolution 'brought little change in the functions of local government' (Birrell 2009: 23). In large measure, the resilience of local government stems from the relative size (accounting for over a third of devolved national expenditure in Scotland and Wales), with councils continuing to possess a wide array of responsibilities. Indeed, they have been key to the implementation strategies of the respective devolved administrations with, in the Scottish case, a 'pivotal role in the delivery of social justice and key policies' (according to McGarvey 2002); in Wales, though Westminster retained formal legislative responsibility in the early years, in practice, the shape, funding and organization of Welsh local government is viewed as a matter for the Welsh Assembly (Chandler 2009: 66) with a legislative onus on ministers to promote local government.

Devolution presented challenges in terms of three existing systems of local government, together with distinct implications for any reform agenda in each case. Certainly, devolution did not remove 'central' audit and inspection, but 'inclusivity' and 'codetermination' became more readily apparent. Hence, despite some early misgivings, the record in Scotland and Wales over the ensuing twenty-plus years indicates that the previous antipathy between local authorities and central government's 'territorial outposts', the Scottish and Welsh Offices, has slowly been replaced by more cordial working relations. Otherwise, reform measures have been concerned chiefly with operational performance and securing value for money (VFM), particularly as the devolved settlement from Whitehall has become more strained during the austerity era, post-2009.

In good measure, the fact that local government had been foremost among the advocates for devolution in both countries undoubtedly ensured that, once devolution had been secured, local authorities had a legitimate stake in making a success of the nascent national political autonomy. Through their respective local government associations, local politicians in Scotland and Wales saw opportunities for rebuilding the status of local government, as well as enjoining with their colleagues in the newly devolved institutions in helping to shape and deliver on their respective policy agendas. That Labour initially dominated at both levels served greatly to cement this new shared enterprise. Additionally, in what are relatively small policy and territorial communities, there is a measure of access afforded to local politicians in Scotland and Wales that their English counterparts can only imagine, while the scale of local authority activity ensured a high measure of interdependence spanning the devolved and local tiers of government. Both levels – and their elected politicians – had clear and vested reasons to make a success of their relationships.

In Northern Ireland, any change in the role and status of local government, still less any substantive alterations, was always subject to the broader pace of political rapprochement and building trust in the new devolved institutions, following the Good Friday (Belfast) Agreement. Its system of local government had been radically reorganized in the early 1970s, as part of a general overhaul of the public administration of the region, a process given added impetus by the onset of 'the Troubles' and calls for reform in public administration to address longstanding grievances around the availability, quality and equitable distribution of public services. The previous system paralleled England and Wales but administrative and financial weaknesses, political corruption in the allocation of public sector jobs and housing, and concerns over the operation of the franchise led to change. The Macrory Report (1970) had envisaged the old Stormont

Parliament as akin to a regional council, to be complemented by a series of single-tier councils for minor services. Although Macrory was overtaken by events, under direct rule, the reorganization that eventuated in 1973 created twenty-six unitary councils with minor powers plus expansion of quangos for services like education and social care (area boards), with housing, water and highways vested in provincial boards or central government departments and agencies. With just 1.9m inhabitants, Northern Ireland had long been accused (perhaps undeservedly) by its own and other politicians, senior administrators and media pundits of being 'over-governed' and 'over-administered'. Alongside a 'democratic deficit', there was a widespread appetite for consolidation (even if the corollary in terms of reductions in public sector jobs and rationalization of service provision was less appreciated) (Carmichael and Knox 2005; Knox and Carmichael 2007).

Structure and functions

Devolution did not imply automatic structural adjustments for local government. Indeed, quite the reverse pertained, for, in both Scotland and Wales, the actions of the previous Conservative government left a legacy that rendered embarking on a further round of restructuring a politically impractical if not impossible proposition. During the 1980s and 1990s, the deteriorating tenor of relations between Whitehall and Great Britain's shire and town halls had culminated in the triumph of a cartographic approach as a panacea for the alleged perceived deficiencies of local government, with the centre exhibiting a growing predilection for unitary local government, as evidenced by the abolition of English metropolitan county government in 1986, and then later, in the work of the Local Government Commission, which had overseen the abolition of a number of two-tier (county/district) arrangements, and their replacement with single-tier (or unitary) 'all-purpose' authorities in England.

With the Conservatives facing increasing electoral pressures in both Scotland and Wales, and the likely prospect of securing control of no major local authority in either nation, both Secretaries of State replicated the drive for unitarism. Hence, in 1992, John Major's Conservative government branded as too remote and expensive the products of earlier reforms in 1974–5. In Scotland, from 1996, the nine regions and fifty-three districts were replaced with thirty-two single-tier authorities (Glasgow City remaining the largest by population, with Clackmannanshire the smallest mainland authority – the three island authorities of Orkney, Shetland and Western Isles being unchanged), see Map 9.1. In Wales, the eight counties and thirty-seven districts were concurrently replaced with a new structure of twenty-two single-tier authorities (Cardiff, the capital city, remaining the largest, with Merthyr Tydfil being the smallest), see Map 9.2. If unintentionally,

Shetland Islands lie approximately 80km N.E of Orkney Islands

SHETLAND ISLANDS

0　　100　　200
kilometres

1. ABERDEEN CITY
2. CLACKMANNANSHIRE
3. WEST DUNBARTONSHIRE
4. INVERCLYDE
5. NORTH AYRSHIRE
6. RENFREWSHIRE
7. EAST RENFREWSHIRE
8. GLASGOW CITY
9. EAST DUNBARTONSHIRE
10. NORTH LANARKSHIRE
11. FALKIRK
12. WEST LOTHIAN
13. CITY OF EDINBURGH
14. MIDLOTHIAN
15. EAST LOTHIAN

ORKNEY ISLANDS

NA H-EILEANAN SIAR

HIGHLAND

MORAY

ABERDEENSHIRE

1

ANGUS

PERTH AND KINROSS

DUNDEE CITY

—— Council Boundary

STIRLING

FIFE

0　　100　　200
kilometres

ARGYLL AND BUTE

2

3　9　11
4　6　8　10　12　13　14　15
7　　　SOUTH
5　LANARKSHIRE

SCOTTISH BORDERS

EAST AYRSHIRE

SOUTH AYRSHIRE

DUMFRIES AND GALLOWAY

ENGLAND

IRELAND　　Northern Ireland

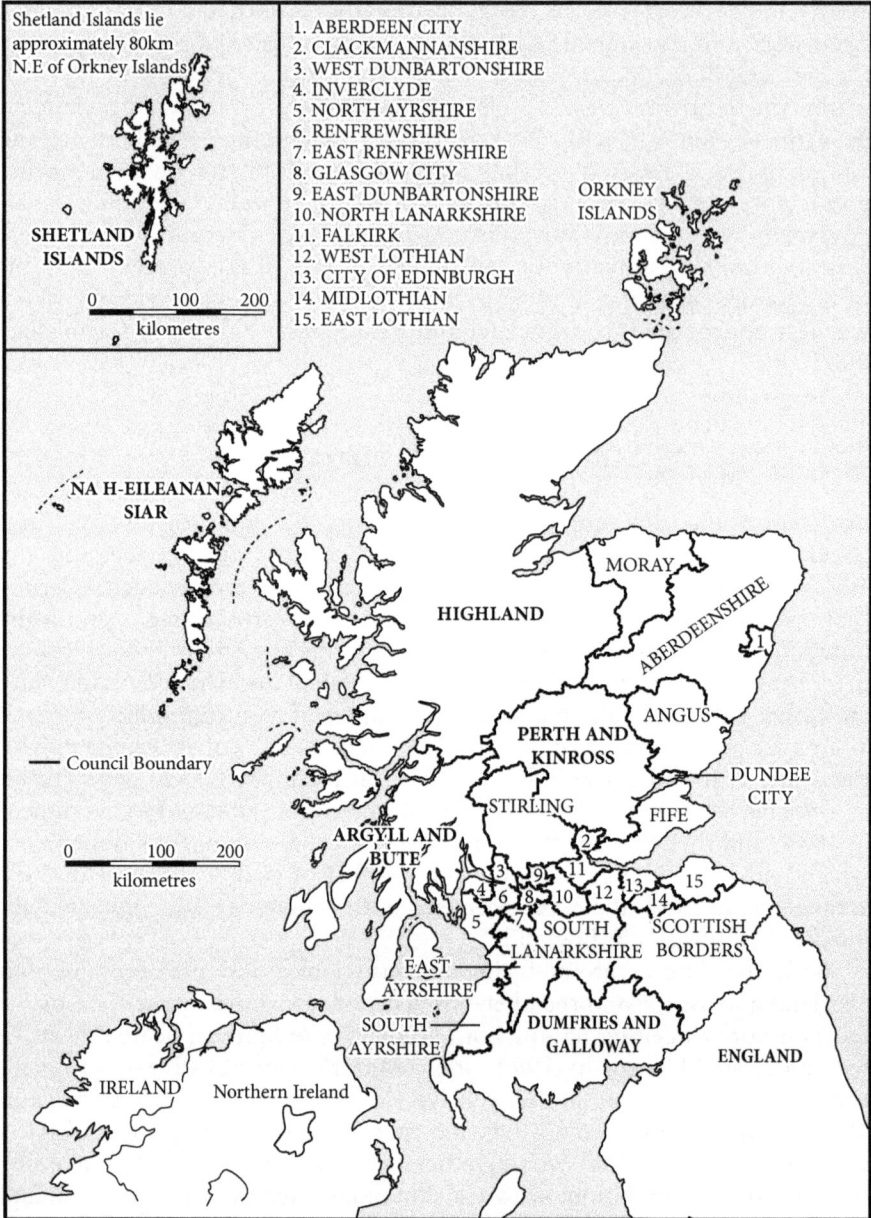

MAP 9.1 *Map of local government in Scotland (1996–present)*
Source: Open Government Licence.

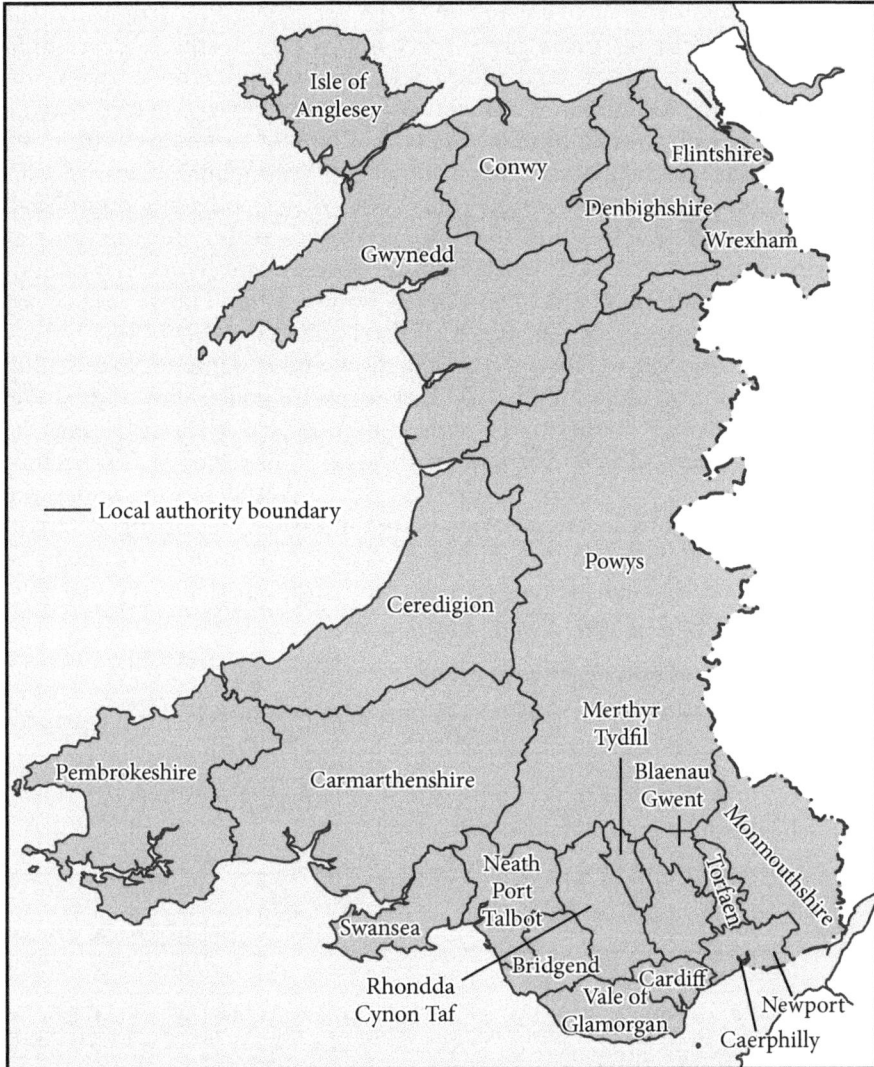

MAP 9.2 *Map of local government in Wales (1996–present)*
Source: Open Government Licence.

the move accentuated the drive for centralizing key public services under a single provider in each country – a process accelerated sharply by Labour's subsequent devolution and the new imperative to develop 'national' approaches in Scotland and Wales. For example, Wales saw rationalization of police and fire services in 1996 into four and three sub-national divisions, respectively. Later, in Scotland, Police Scotland and the Scottish Fire and

Rescue Service were each created in 2013 see Table 9.1. Ironically, the system imposed by a Conservative Party implacably hostile to devolution helped, as it turned out, to make for a smoother transition once devolution became a reality. As Himsworth (1998: 6) noted, a unitary structure 'may be a better basis upon which to make the transition to devolution'. Within the new arrangements, Scotland retained some 1,150 community councils, with Wales possessing some 900 communities, 750 of which having established community councils. Together, these are analogous to but not the same as the parish and town councils in England, representing the lowest tier of non-principal councils. These are non-statutory bodies with no power to tax nor any automatic access to public funds (Wilson and Game 2011: 80).

Whereas the Scottish Government has shown no real interest in pursuing structural reforms (beyond the 2013 changes to police, fire and rescue services), its Welsh counterparts appear preoccupied with revisiting the 1996 arrangements. In 2013, a Commission on Public Service Governance and Delivery was established, chaired by Sir Paul Williams, to undertake a major review into local government organization. Reporting in 2014, the Williams Commission recommended that the number of councils be reduced, albeit through mergers rather than through boundary changes,

TABLE 9.1 *List of local authority functions*

Services	Scotland	Wales	N. Ireland
Education	Y	Y	N
Social care	Y	Y	N
Housing	Y	Y	N
Planning	Y	Y	Y
Libraries	Y	Y	N
Sports, leisure and recreation	Y	Y	Y
Environmental health	Y	Y	Y
Waste collection and disposal	Y	Y	Y
Building control	Y	Y	Y
Roads and footpaths	Y	Y	N
Economic development	Y	Y	Y
Collecting council tax	Y	Y	N
District courts	Y	Y	N
Transport	Y	N	N
Youth services	Y	Y	N
Community planning	Y	Y	Y
Well-being	Y	Y	Y

from twenty-two to ten, eleven or twelve. The savings achieved would, it was contended, recoup any merger costs within two years. Subsequently, the Welsh Government's own proposals involved either an eight or nine authority structure (essentially, the latter would see an additional council in North Wales, otherwise both proposed models were similar) (see Maps 9.3 and 9.4). Interestingly, both models bore a striking resemblance to the upper tier of eight counties that had existed from 1974–96.

However, the plans were scrapped after the 2016 elections to the Welsh Assembly. In announcing that the proposals would be taken 'back to the drawing board', the then first minister Carwyn Jones declared that a new consensus on how to reform local government in Wales would be sought and that the plans for council mergers would also be dropped, unless two or more local authorities themselves instigated such an amalgamation. A Welsh Government White Paper entitled *Reforming Local Government: Resilient and Renewed* was published in January 2017. It proposed the formation of regional bodies to encourage better collaboration between existing local authorities and a possible change in the electoral system from simple plurality or 'first past the post' elections to the single transferable vote (STV) system. The Local Government and Elections (Wales) Act 1921 saw a change to five-yearly terms for local councillors, the voting age reduced from eighteen to sixteen and the ability of individual councils to choose whether to retain the current electoral system or adopt STV. The next local elections were held in 2022. Instead of restructuring exercises, councils were exhorted to cooperate across boundaries in the design, commissioning and/or delivery of joint services, to contain costs and promote greater efficiency. That said, a ten-council model was again promulgated in 2018 (see Map 9.5), for possible introduction in 2022 or 2026 – the upheaval of Covid, this time, thwarting efforts to revisit the matter. The shift in emphasis was concurrent with the establishment of statutory partnerships for each council area, known as Public Service Boards (replacing the Local Service Boards that had existed hitherto). These boards include representatives from other public sector bodies and from the third and community sector. The arrangements were buttressed by the advent of the Partnership Council for Wales (PCfW), created by the Government of Wales Act 1998. The PCfW is designed to foster joint working and cooperation between the Welsh Government and local authorities, providing political accountability and leadership for public service reform and collaboration, while also driving the pace of improvement of public services in Wales. Chaired by the Cabinet Secretary for Finance and Local Government, the PCfW facilitates dialogue between the Welsh Ministers and local politicians on matters affecting local government in Wales, while providing collective political accountability for action to improve the effectiveness and efficiency of public services.

With local government in Northern Ireland being the limiting case of central control, so denuded of powers were local authorities, especially after the 1973 reorganization, that devolution offered a major opportunity

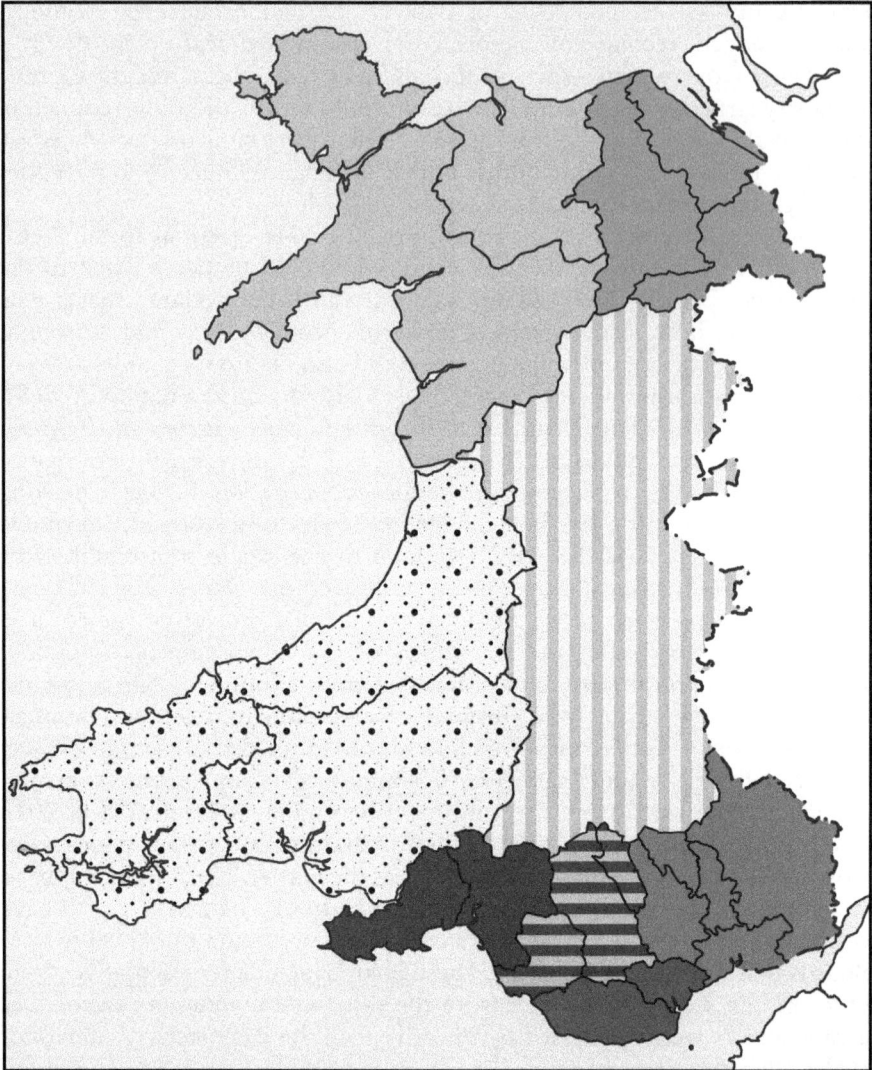

MAP 9.3 *Proposal for eight local authorities models for Wales (2015)*
Source: bbc.co.uk/news/uk-wales-politics-33161855

for fresh thinking about how local government and wider system of public
administration more generally might be reordered to address longstanding
dissatisfaction about democratic accountability, duplication and waste
under the direct rule arrangements. Hence, while the Northern Ireland
Executive eventually initiated a Review of Public Administration (RPA)
in 2002, the fitful nature of devolution (suspended four times between its
1999 and 2003) meant that meaningful progress was always glacial. Mired

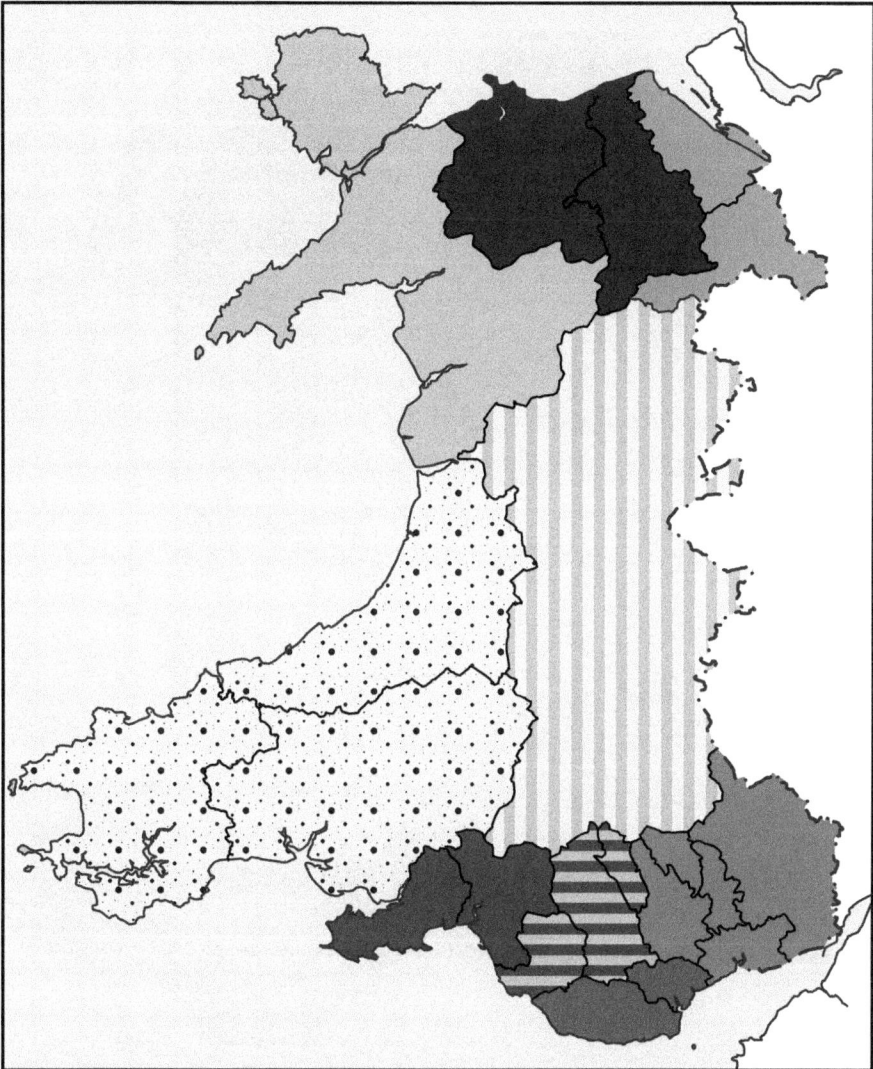

MAP 9.4 *Proposal for nine local authorities models for Wales (2015)*
Source: bbc.co.uk/news/uk-wales-politics-33161855

between the on/off nature of devolution and the eagerness of direct rule ministers to advance the reform agenda in the absence of local actors' ability or willingness to do so, local government found itself consistently the subject of interminable wrangles around familiar questions concerning what functions to be returned to it, together with how many councils to cut (it was widely asserted throughout that twenty-six was too many), and how any new configuration would relate to the devolved settlement.

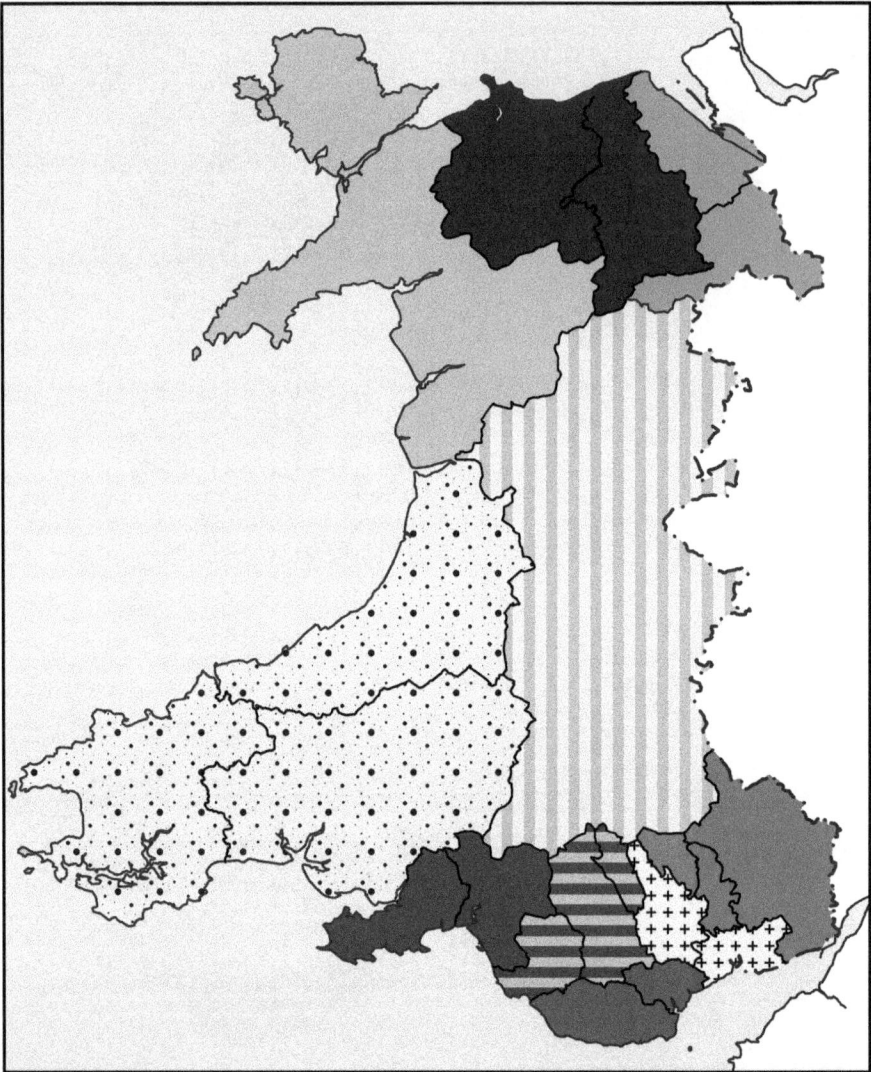

MAP 9.5 *Proposal for ten local authorities model for Wales (2018)*
Source: bbc.co.uk/news/uk-wales-politics-33161855

Eventually, a mix of enhanced powers (spatial planning, conservation, economic development, tourism, urban regeneration, rural affairs, community planning and development, arts and culture, and emergency planning) within a consolidated structure emerged, initially to be achieved through a seven 'super council' model proposed by direct rule ministers in 2005, but eventually an eleven-council model was agreed by a restored devolved Executive in 2009 (the largest council remaining Belfast, the smallest being Fermanagh and Omagh) (see Maps 9.6, 9.7 and 9.8).

MAP 9.6 *Proposed structure of local government in Northern Ireland (2005)*
Source: BBC.

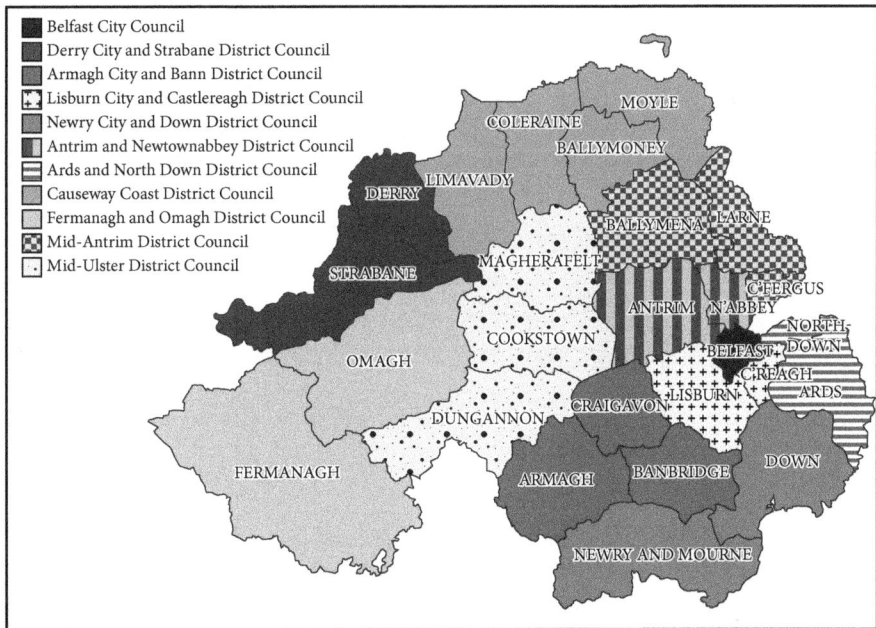

MAP 9.7 *Proposed structure of local government in Northern Ireland (2009)*
Source: BBC.

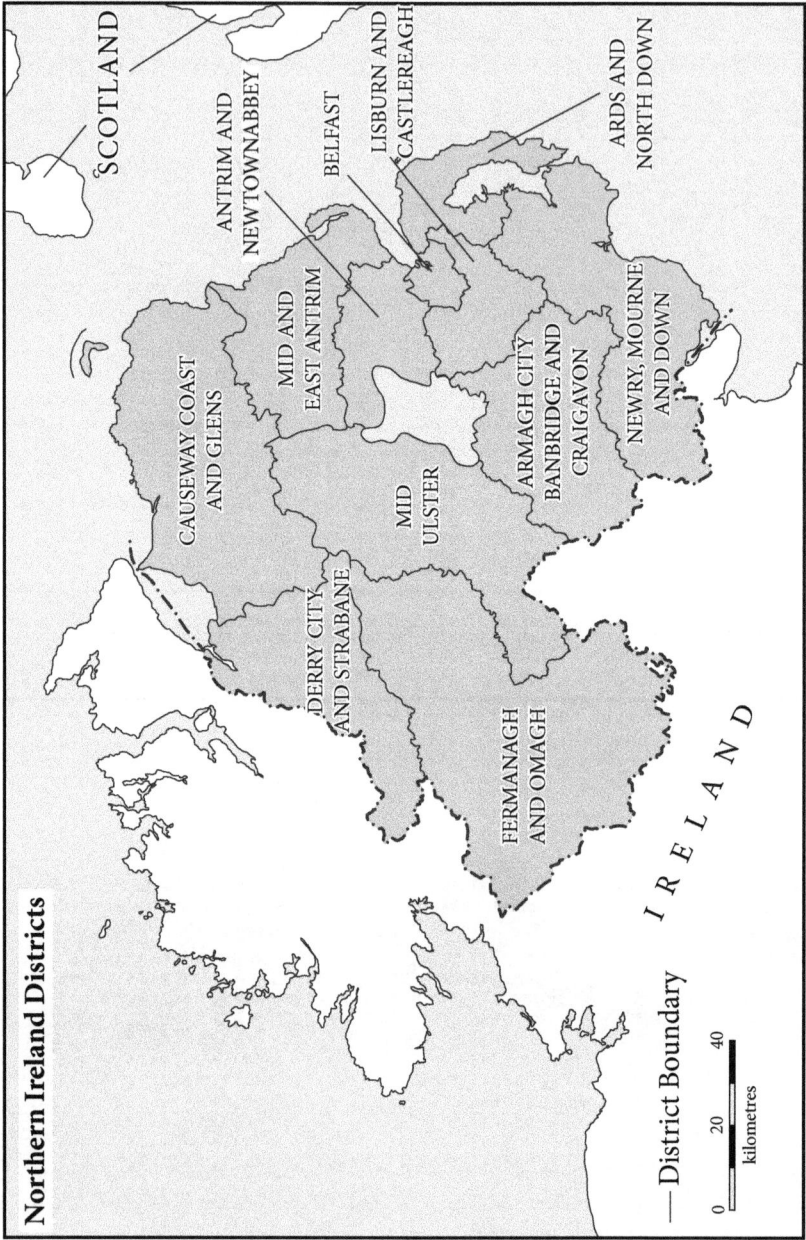

Northern Ireland Districts

SCOTLAND

ANTRIM AND
NEWTOWNABBEY

BELFAST

LISBURN AND
CASTLEREAGH

ARDS AND
NORTH DOWN

CAUSEWAY COAST
AND GLENS

MID AND
EAST ANTRIM

MID
ULSTER

ARMAGH CITY
BANBRIDGE AND
CRAIGAVON

NEWRY, MOURNE
AND DOWN

DERRY CITY
AND STRABANE

FERMANAGH
AND OMAGH

I R E L A N D

—— District Boundary

0   20   40

kilometres

MAP 9.8 *Map of local government in Northern Ireland (since 2015)*
Source: Open Government Licence.

TABLE 9.2 *Local government systems (1 July 2021)*

	Number of councils	Number of councillors	Average population	Number of employees	Community town councils
Scotland	32	1,222	172,406	254,000	1,227
Wales	22	1,257	147,600	140,000	735
N. Ireland	11	462	174,208	10,500	0

An additional consideration was that the inevitably painful process of local government reorganization (and concurrent reform of the extensive mosaic of other non-departmental public bodies) was being attempted by a new devolved government, itself tiptoeing through the process of taking back control from direct rule ministers (Knox and Carmichael 2015). Central–local government relations, therefore, are mediated in a strained regional context of often intermittent devolution. Although a partnership panel exists between central government and local authorities, it is a pale imitation of Welsh and Scottish arrangements, leaving local government in Northern Ireland a poor relation to its counterparts elsewhere.

Modernizing local government and the new localism

When it was elected in 1997, Tony Blair's New Labour government stressed a desire to modernize British local government, repairing the damage it contended had been sustained in central–local government relations during the previous periods of Conservative government. A localist agenda was in vogue that 'expresses the value of devolving power and resources away from central control to local decision-making structures and local communities' (Stoker 2004). The concept of localism has been largely understood with reference to local government in England, given the absence of a regional or intermediate tier of government therein. For the devolved territories, localism has developed along three dimensions: delegation of health delivery down to local community level in Scotland and Wales; a close identification with the role of local government in planning and delivering services at a local level; and smallness. In Northern Ireland's case, localism is largely eclipsed by more dominant values such as streamlining arrangements along with political and pragmatic considerations influencing the eventual structure and functions.

Most prominently, at UK level, while the system of local taxation would remain unaltered (council tax), the previous regime of compulsory competitive tendering (CCT), which dated from the Local Government Planning and Land Act 1980, was speedily replaced by best value (BV), following the Local Government Act 1999. BV became operational in England in April 2000, and was applicable in Wales three months later. In place of the more overtly antipathetical policy towards local government that CCT presented, with its rather narrowly defined focus (loosely, 'the 3Es' of economy, efficiency and effectiveness), BV promised a more inclusive and positive vision for local government, based on 'the 4Cs' – challenge (why and how is a service to be provided), comparison (with a range of performance indicators of other local authorities), consultation (with local citizens), competition (to secure efficient and effective services). In some ways, BV remained 'every bit as centrally prescriptive and potentially more interventionist' (Wilson 2005: 165). Holyrood's Local Government in Scotland Act 2003 extended BV to Scotland. The Beacon Councils Scheme that complemented BV was operational in England but did not apply elsewhere. Officially launched in 1999, the aim was for Beacon Councils 'to serve as pace-setters and centres of excellence'. The scheme ended in 2010 following the change of national government.

The Local Government Act 2000 bestowed powers to local authorities in England and Wales to do 'anything that individuals generally may do' to promote the economic, social and environmental well-being of their area. In turn, the Localism Act 2011 replaced the well-being powers in the Local Government Act 2000 with a general power of competence. While the power extended only to England only, Scottish local authorities have a general 'well-being' power, equivalent to the one in the Local Government Act 2000, a similar power having been introduced in Scotland through the Local Government in Scotland Act 2003. An attempt in the UK House of Commons in 2018 to introduce a general power of competence for Scottish local authorities through an amendment to the Scotland Bill was unsuccessful. In 2021, Welsh Government introduced a general power of competence for its local authorities, broadly reflecting English arrangements with subtle differences. A general power of competence was provided to the new local authorities in Northern Ireland by the Local Government Act (Northern Ireland) 2014. Again, the power largely reflects that available in England.

Outwardly, the rhetoric underpinning central–local government interaction was toned down and, with the relatively benign fiscal environment (until c. 2008), prospects for improved relations looked rosier. Consequently, over the course of three electoral cycles, Labour ushered in further reforms around internal council governance, the provision of services, performance management (including target setting) and the promotion of partnership working with other public agencies as well as the private and community/voluntary sectors. In 2004, Sir Michael Lyons was tasked by the UK government to review local taxation and the funding of local services in England, a remit expanded the following year to consider the future role and function of local government more generally. Perhaps unsurprisingly for a former elected local councillor and three-times local authority chief executive, Lyons was unapologetically pro-local government in his final report; however, he made it explicit that the resolution of the 'wicked issue' of local taxation could only come with a resolution of the broader encompassing question as to the clear role of local government within the British polity (Lyons 2007). Given that that very polity had itself been radically reordered through devolution, the implications within the devolved territories were even more profound. In calling for a new partnership between the centre and localities, Lyons placed a heavy emphasis on the role of local authorities in promoting 'well-being' and 'place shaping', as the lead bodies in their respective localities. In many ways, Lyons' recommendations resonated with the official stance of the government, which was already actively championing the notion of Local Strategic Partnerships (LSPs) established in 2001 across England. A similar vocabulary circulated in Scotland and Wales (albeit with each slowly diverging from England), and later in Northern Ireland, under the rubric of 'community planning' within the Executive's Programme for Government, which saw the role of local councils enhanced (Knox and Carmichael 2015).

In introducing Comprehensive Performance Assessment and LSPs for England and Wales, Labour placed a renewed focus on neighbourhood and community governance. LSPs brought together representatives from the local statutory, voluntary, community and private sectors to address local problems, allocate funding, and discuss strategies and initiatives. They aimed to encourage joint working and community involvement, and prevent 'silo working' (i.e. different agencies that share aims working in isolation), with the general objective of ensuring that resources are better allocated at a local level. LSPs have had an increasingly important role in promoting economic, social and environmental well-being in their area. Well-being would be pursued via Sustainable Community Strategies (SCSs), which set out local priorities, Local Area Agreements (LAAs), which set out agreed priorities between central and local government, and a diverse range of local delivery arrangements. As voluntary partnerships, LSPs were not directly subject to equalities legislation. But their public-sector partners do have legislative obligations to promote equality of opportunity and good community relations.

As part of the LSP paraphernalia, LAAs offered a three-year agreement between central government and a local area working through its LSP. Each contained a set of improvement targets, which local organizations committed to achieving, and a delivery plan setting out what each partner is intending to do to achieve those targets. LAA targets reflected the vision, priorities and challenges set out in the Sustainable Community strategy, which are ten-year vision statements for a given area required by the UK government. LAA targets were chosen in discussion with all partners, and are then negotiated with government departments, working through regional government offices. The government provided a reward grant at the end of three years if LAA targets had been achieved. LAAs were first introduced in 2004/5, starting with twenty pilot areas and extending across the country in three phases. The Local Government and Public Involvement in Health Act 2007 placed LAAs on a statutory footing. All upper-tier local authorities were required to draw up a new LAA for the three-year period 2008/9 to 2010/11. In October 2010, however, as part of its fiscal retrenchment, it was announced that LAAs were to be abolished by the new coalition government.

Labour's approach to local government in England was replicated with not dissimilar approaches in both Scotland and Wales, albeit applied in the context of a generally closer and more cooperative disposition by both devolved governments and their respective local authorities. In Scotland, the equivalents of LSPs are the thirty-two Community Planning Partnerships (CPPs) (one for each council area), covering all those services that come together to take part in community planning. Each CPP is responsible for developing and delivering a plan for its council area. Community planning focuses on where partners' collective efforts and resources can add most value for their local communities, with the emphasis on reducing inequalities. Under the Scottish model, by law, local councils must work with other bodies – public, private and third sector – at local level through CPPs based on local authority areas. In 2011, the *Commission on the Future Delivery of Public Services* report, the Christie Commission, proposed principles for reforming public services in integrating ways, including that of 'empowering individuals and communities that receive public services through involving them in the design and delivery of the services; much more partnership working among and integration between public service providers; prioritization of expenditure on public services which prevent negative outcomes from arising; and, greater efficiency through reducing duplication and sharing services wherever possible' (Christie Commission 2011: vi).

With the Scottish National Party (SNP) in power in Holyrood from 2007, initially as a minority administration and, after 2011, with an overall majority, complemented by a much stronger position across local government, the partnership model of working was further entrenched. Hence, the Community Empowerment (Scotland) Act 2015 established new rights for community bodies and introduced new duties on public authorities, strengthening the voices of communities in the decisions that matter to them. Crucially, the legislation provided a statutory base for community planning. All CPPs published a Local Outcome Improvement Plan (LOIP) for the first time in October 2017, setting out their local priorities. The Improvement Service published an overview of LOIPs in 2018, summarizing them and identifying good practice. Also, Scotland has introduced integrated health and social care partnerships, linking the NHS and local authorities.

In Wales, a series of voluntary Local Service Boards (LSBs) offered a broad equivalent to the English LSPs (Laffin et al. 2002). In 2015, the Well-being of Future Generations (Wales) Act established statutory Public Service Boards (PSBs) to replace the voluntary LSBs in each local authority area. Like their English and Scottish counterparts, the PSBs are charged with improving the economic, social, environmental and cultural well-being by strengthening joint working across all public services in their respective areas, through publication of a Local Well-being Plan. Each PSB carries out an annual review of its plan showing its progress. When producing their assessments of local well-being, PSBs must consult widely. Additionally, the PCfW, comprising MSs and local government representatives, brings the Senedd and local authorities together. The Welsh arrangements are highly formalized within its Statutory Partnership Council. The service delivery agenda gives more scope for closer working relationships between devolved and local government tiers.

The respective local government associations, the Convention of Scottish Local Authorities (COSLA), the Welsh Local Government Association (WLGA), and the Northern Ireland Local Government Association (NILGA), serve to strengthen the partnership in each nation. COSLA was created in 1975 whereas the WLGA, created in 1996, dates only from the inception of the new unitary local government arrangements (Welsh authorities having previously been combined with their English counterparts within the Association of County Councils and Association of District Councils). NILGA only emerged in 2000 following the demise of earlier local authority associations over disputes concerning political balance and representativeness. In short, neither the central command and control approach, nor indeed the perhaps inevitable conflict it sparks, as evident in England, has been replicated (Birrell 2009: 25). Thus, while the level of direct involvement in policy formulation has been small, the scope for participation has been real, and there has been a greater level of openness and accessibility than has been characteristic of the previous territorial offices of state.

In other ways, moreover, evidence of a growing divergence from the UK (in effect, English) 'norm' is accumulating, especially in Scotland. Hence, in Wales, while Labour's electoral hegemony proved resilient, its Scottish counterpart found itself usurped by the SNP as the 'natural party of government', a trend hastened following the recommendations of the McIntosh Commission (1999), which resulted in the Local Governance (Scotland) Act 2004 that adopted a new electoral system (STV) for local government elections from 2007. Wales has moved in a similar way, albeit on a voluntary basis in each council area, since 2021.

The UK Labour government (1997–2010) was an enthusiastic exponent of new models of executive leadership within local authorities, which were commended to councils, involving either a directly elected mayor with a cabinet, a cabinet with a leader or a directly elected mayor with a council manager, following the Local Government Act 2000. English local government proved reluctant to embrace these changes and the least radical proposal was adopted by 95 per cent of English councils. Bluntly, there was little appetite for change. In turn, the coalition government (2010–15) drive for metro mayors in the larger English conurbations had no equivalent in Wales or Scotland. Similar reforms were promoted from 2003 in Scotland. Again, concerned that arrangements were 'often dominated by the party system' (Chandler 2009: 94), McIntosh had advocated a 'rich diversity of different models' in the internal governance of councils. However, the response was even less enthusiastic than in England. No directly elected provosts (a role akin to a mayor in England

and Wales) were instituted, with only five of thirty-two councils opting for the cabinet/leader model, while the rest retained the longstanding committee-based systems. There are no directly elected mayors in Northern Ireland. Offices of mayors in Northern Ireland are purely a ceremonial position. Although Wales is included in the UK legislation, only one Welsh authority, Ceredigion, held a referendum in 2004 on such a proposal – that proposal being defeated by a large majority of voters.

The SNP minority government elected in 2007 signed a concordat with the Convention of Scottish Local Government that removed many of Scottish central government's detailed controls over councils. It also pledged a freeze in council tax rates and greater flexibility in funding arrangements (which endured to 2018). However, austerity left councils struggling to deliver, a situation accentuated by Covid-related pressures (Audit Scotland 2021). In one sense, the concordat signalled an elevated status for central–local government relations, and a concomitant resolve to keep the professional and local government associations closer to the heart of policymaking, certainly than is or indeed could be the case in England (Mair 2016). Progressively, however, SNP ministers have tended to revert to the pattern of their predecessors in centralizing power. Sometimes centralization is borne out of Scottish government frustration that policies are undermined at local level, but at other times it may reflect a 'control-freak' impulse to impose central policies. Whatever the reason, for local government there is little in Scotland's constitutional set-up to prevent centralization happening.

As in England, the large majority of local authority funding in Scotland and Wales comes from central government (i.e. Edinburgh and Cardiff), though in Northern Ireland, reflecting the relatively smaller number of major services at local level, councils are far more reliant on local taxes in relative terms than their counterparts elsewhere in the UK. With less extensive devolution until recently, Wales has seen no serious attempt to change the financial model for local government. Longstanding SNP proposals for local income tax (LIT) to replace council tax in Scotland were not pursued when the party came to power in Holyrood in 2007, ostensibly due to its minority government status in the Scottish Parliament, though, interestingly, they were not resurrected when the SNP achieved an overall majority in 2011. Apart from a switch to capital valuations, Northern Ireland continues with a rating system, though there are obvious parallels with the council tax elsewhere.

Both Scotland and Wales have seen combined public services ombudsmen offices introduced (known as the Standards Commission in Scotland), bringing together parliamentary and health service, local government and housing association ombudsmen (Chandler 2009: 144–6; Wilson and Game 2011: 164). Northern Ireland has seen similar moves. Together with the strong level of scrutiny exercised over local government by the devolved audit bodies, it suggests that oversight generally remains considerable under devolution.

In another key policy development, the UK coalition government's proposals for police and crime commissioners for England and Wales were realized in 2012. In Wales, policing had already been rationalized into four forces (with fire and rescue services having been rationalized into three geographical areas). Following its Westminster victory in 2015, the Conservative government initiated a consultation into proposals that would also bring England's fire services under the control of PCCs. By contrast, in Scotland, following a consultation, the drive for operational efficiency resulted in police forces and fire brigades becoming national services. In Northern Ireland, the Ministry of Justice and Police Authority for Northern Ireland discharge the equivalent role with respect to the Police Service of Northern Ireland, while fire services are also discharged at a regional level, overseen by the Fire and Rescue Service, another NDPB.

Reviving the city regions – City and Growth Deals

Albeit with echoes of the regional agenda that was tried but quietly abandoned by Labour after its 2004 failed referendum attempt in North-East England, the Conservative–Liberal Democrat coalition's agenda for local government possessed a strong sub-regional component, epitomized by the calls for a Northern Powerhouse and a renaissance of its former industrial heartlands, and based heavily on revitalized city regions. The Localism Act 2011 included the Core Cities Amendment, which offered local councils the opportunity to submit proposals on how they planned to promote local economic growth. Successful applicants would then be invited to negotiate 'City Deals' with central government for greater local autonomy over financial and planning matters. Essentially, City and Growth Deals are bespoke arrangements brokered between the Treasury and each recipient City Deal local authority or, more usually, cluster of local authorities. They are designed to promote economic growth and infrastructure while ultimately shifting control of key decisions and allocation of resources away from central government towards local authorities. Generally set for ten-year periods, the deals give local areas specific powers and freedoms to help the region support economic growth, create jobs or invest in local projects, with a number of these deals involving investment in the region of £1 billion through a 'gainshare' funding model. In such deals, 'gainshare' funding is typically provided over twenty or thirty years, subject to five-yearly gateway reviews undertaken by an independent panel focused on delivery, with the city/region having the option to themselves borrow against this delivery-dependent income stream, to translate it into a more intensive growth-focused programme over a typical period of ten years. The central aim is to direct infrastructure spending to projects that boost productivity, employment and economic growth. In respect of the devolved territories, the respective devolved government becomes a third governmental partner, also committing financial resource to each proposal.

Between 2012 and 2014, twenty-six City Deals were agreed. In a one-off deal in August 2014, Glasgow and the Clyde Valley became the first area outside England to agree a deal. In 2016, deals were agreed with Aberdeen, Cardiff and Inverness. The 2016 UK Budget included proposals to begin negotiations with Swansea and Edinburgh while the 2016 Autumn Statement confirmed that the government was working towards deals with Tayside and Stirling. In July 2017, it was confirmed that the UK and Scottish governments had agreed the terms of the Edinburgh and South-East Scotland deal. Currently, there are twelve such deals in Scotland and four in Wales. In Northern Ireland, the 2017 Autumn Budget stated that the government would begin negotiations for a Belfast City Deal, once the Northern Ireland Executive was restored, though the prolonged hiatus at Stormont together with the 'confidence and supply' deal between the DUP and Conservative government meant the Northern Ireland Secretary had to progress matters directly. During a visit by the then Chancellor, an additional City Deal was proposed for Derry and Strabane in 2018, further suggesting that political expediency at Westminster would not allow the local political impasse to impede this important UK-wide initiative. Four City and Growth Deals in Northern Ireland have been approved and are going ahead.

Conclusions

While the constitutional landscape of the UK has been transformed dramatically following devolution, the changes within the systems of local government across the devolved countries have been rather less radical. Initially at UK level after 1997, and then through the respective newly devolved governments, a new language of localism has emerged, stressing partnership, meaningful engagement and more cooperative working relations between central and local government, with central government (first London, then joined by those newly established centres of political power in Edinburgh, Cardiff and, fitfully, Belfast) pledged to greater involvement of local authorities in the decision-making of the devolved territories.

Devolution in Scotland and Wales, less so (to date) in Northern Ireland, has served to build levels of inclusion at local level, providing local communities and their representatives with an enhanced devolved system of political accountability, as Jeffery (2006: 72) adjudged, a project more 'of participation than of policy'. Fifteen years on, that assessment remains accurate. In large measure, the relative strength of the local government sector in Scotland and Wales represents a continuation of a longstanding reality while their newfound influence stems from their enthusiastic support for the creation of the devolved settlements, together with reflecting their criticality in the implementation of the devolved policy agenda. In short, local government is too big to ignore in Scotland and Wales. Reflecting different historical circumstances and a more fragile overarching devolution settlement, local government in Northern Ireland has developed a much slower and less intense relationship with its regional devolved counterpart, with its range of powers and responsibilities remaining correspondingly relatively underdeveloped.

In all three nations, the story can be summarized neatly as a blend of continuity and change. There have been few if any radical departures, rather a case of slow but steady variegation, in keeping with Rhodes' (1997) differentiated polity. While exact parallels with the situation in England have been few, there remains a similarity in the direction of travel in respect of a renewed emphasis on the importance of locality and place, with local authorities at the core of a nexus of agencies charged with improving well-being through 'place-shaping' their localities. Hence, while the nomenclature varies, and with amendments to reflect prevailing conditions, circumstances and preferences in each devolved territory, the same underlying message of partnership and inclusivity resonates across the different countries. What these changes have meant for citizens is less clear. While official statistics indicate that the public sense of well-being has shown some small improvement over recent years (for example: ONS 2017b), it would be speculative to attribute this to the role of local authorities whose straitened fiscal circumstances and resulting reduced services are documented regularly in the media. In other respects, there has been less enthusiasm for the more radical innovations attempted under both Labour- and Conservative-led governments in terms of English local government – traditional ways of doing things have proved difficult to dislodge, with councils in Scotland and Wales being reluctant to embrace internal managerial reorganizations unlike a small number of their English counterparts (notably, around elected mayors). Likewise, the more explicit language of targets and league tables redolent of neo-liberal philosophy has been eschewed in favour of one more in keeping with a traditional social democratic and collectivist conception of the role of government. Moreover, as fiscally 'hard times' since 2009 have placed local authorities on the front line in the austerity agenda, coping with increasingly challenging financial settlements from their respective 'centres' has been a shared preoccupation of councils across the UK. For Northern Ireland, as ever, progress on the wider political process dictates the pace of any meaningful change for local councils. Councils were largely onlookers as its devolved settlement faltered, though determined to 'make the best' of the modest reforms to date, retaining an optimistic outlook none the less.

As devolution becomes longer established across the UK (leaving aside the matter of a second independence vote in Scotland), and assuming fiscal stringency for local authorities relaxes eventually, an emerging challenge will be whether local authorities continue to play any (still less a central) role in public service delivery in their respective countries, given the fundamental strains in the underlying financial basis for local government. Beyond that, will the devolved administrations countenance more radical innovations based on a positive vision for local government in a way that the traditionally centralist British state under both main UK political parties has proved reluctant to embrace?

10

Inter-governmental relations: cooperation and conflict

Introduction

Devolution made forms of inter-governmental relationships inevitable and integral to the UK government. The need for inter-governmental contact and a formal relationship between four different governments was a relatively new dimension to UK governance. The start of devolution had led to a set of agreements between the UK government and the devolved administrations on the principles that underpinned relations between them. The principal formal agreement was a Memorandum of Understanding published in 1999 and subsequently revised. This memorandum was a statement of political intent; it was not a binding agreement and did not create legal obligations (Hazell 2001). All four governments committed themselves to good communication, cooperation, exchange of scientific, technical and policy information and confidentiality. The 2014 version set out more clearly three different overarching concordats: arrangements for EU matters, financial assistance for industry and international relations (Cabinet Office 2014). These were accompanied by a set of sixteen devolution guidance notes. The memorandum also laid out the details for a Joint Ministerial Committee (JMC) as the main mechanism for inter-governmental cooperation.

Joint Ministerial Committee

Apart from the JMC, there were no other formal structures considered or established. In practice, bilateral controls between ministers, departments and more informal links developed. Questions arose about the effectiveness of inter-government relations and a number of inquiries produced recommendations for change. The poor relationship between UK governments and devolved administrations meant radical change was difficult. As a formal body, the JMC consisted of representatives of the four governments who would meet to: discuss non-devolved matters that would impinge on devolved responsibilities; consider treatment of devolved matters in the different parts of the UK; keep arrangements for liaison under review; and consider disputes between the administrations. The membership was the prime minister or a representative as chair, the first ministers of Scotland and Wales, the first and deputy first minister of Northern Ireland, the three Secretaries of State and other ministers. The JMC could meet in plenary, functional and official modes. Its main role for the JMC is as a deliberative and consultative body, not an executive body making decisions.

The JMC has had a shaky history, although it began promisingly with the prime minister in attendance. After a few years it stopped meeting altogether, with no clamour from Scotland or Wales for a meeting. In the early years, the Labour Party was in power in Scotland, Wales and Westminster, and with devolution suspended in Northern Ireland there were few disputes and little need to use the formal inter-governmental structures. The potential of the JMC for resolving disputes between administrations of different political complexions was untested. There was an issue of support and questions were raised about the effectiveness of the JMC machinery. No plenary meetings were held between 2002 and 2008. It appeared that the four administrations were happy to rely on establishing working relations without using the formal structure created. Perceptions changed after the newly elected devolved administrations in 2007, with the SNP particularly enthusiastic to revitalize the JMC. The new Welsh Government welcomed a relaunch based on mutual respect and parity of esteem between the UK government and the devolved administrations. A plenary meeting in 2010 referred to the JMC as the apex of formal relationships between the four governments. The JMC operated with two functioning committees, JMC (Europe) and JMC (Domestic). The latter committee was intended to discuss matters such as poverty but, after 2010, met fairly rarely. JMC (Europe) did meet some four or five times a year, before European Council meetings. To an extent, this was a continuation of a former specialist cabinet committee.

A number of key commissions reported on dissatisfaction with the JMC and inter-governmental relations. The Commission on Scottish Devolution (2009) noted that the JMC had not met as frequently as was originally intended. The Smith Commission on the future of Scottish devolution had identified the issue of weak inter-governmental working and what was needed was the creation of a more productive, robust and visible relationship. In Wales, the Silk report (2014) found some good examples of engagement, but it had received evidence of a lack of consideration for Wales in relation to UK legislation and policy development. There was a general demand from independent commissions for a more institutionalized inter-governmental process. The JMC did not meet annually in plenary form or in domestic format between 2014 and 2016, while JMC (Domestic) had not met since 2013 (McEwan 2017: 673). The Public Administration

Committee of the House of Commons investigated inter-governmental relations. It received evidence from the Scottish Government that there was no real machinery for regular head of government meetings, this being replaced by bilateral discussions. The Welsh Government reported that inter-governmental relations had been underdeveloped in the period 2012–15. The Public Administration Committee urged that the JMC should be at the heart of UK inter-governmental relations but, in practice, bilateralism and informality had become prominent features. It was clear to the Committee that the JMC as it is currently organized was not well equipped to deal with its increasing responsibilities (House of Commons Public Administration and Constitutional Affairs 2016). The House of Lords inquiry into inter-governmental relations in 2015 found that the operation of the JMC was not well received, at least in the eyes of the devolved administration. The plenary JMC meeting of heads of government was seen as ineffective while the domestic sub-committee did not appear to serve a purpose. The JMC (Domestic) sub-committee was particularly criticized as not working in a satisfactory way. Paun and Munro (2015: 6) suggest that the domestic sub-committee had lost its way and should be scrapped. With the devolution settlement becoming increasingly complex, the Lords committee suggested a requirement for a more formal mechanism, advocating putting the inter-governmental framework on a statutory basis. McEwan (2017) drew attention to a preference for bilateral working relations and for informality in inter-governmental relations. The report by Paun and Munro (2015) for the Institute for Government concluded that the JMC was not used in an effective way and that more time and resources should be dedicated to planning and supporting it. The report recommended that the leaders of the four governments should meet in a formal structure annually.

A change in the role of the JMC had occurred when a new formal protocol was introduced to resolve disputes, with a provision in the case of a serious disagreement for any party to refer the matter to the JMC secretariat. There were only four major disputes involving the JMC and all were brought by devolved administrations against the UK government. The four cases all dealt with financial issues. The most serious conflict related to Olympic Games funding in 2012, with all the devolved administrations arguing that there should have been Barnett formula financial consequences arising from this funding in England. This challenged the categorization by the Treasury of the Olympics funding as UK rather than England funding. The dispute was not ended until 2014 when the devolved administrations were given some £30 million, with continuing Treasury intransigence and the JMC failing to resolve the dispute.

A fifth dispute arose in 2017 with the confidence and supply agreement between the Conservative Party and the DUP involving payments from the Treasury to the Northern Ireland Executive and administration. The agreement between the DUP and the Conservative government meant additional financial support to Northern Ireland of £1 billion for two years. The Scottish and Welsh Governments expressed their fundamental disagreement with this, arguing that health, education, infrastructure and deprivation are all devolved matters and should have given rise to the Barnett consequential funding for Scotland and for Wales. The Scottish and Welsh Governments took the view that the action was incompatible with the UK Treasury's Statement of Funding Policy for Devolution. The Scottish Government believed that well-established principles were being disregarded and the Welsh Government saw the rules as being bypassed. Such was the significance attached to the issue that the Scottish and Welsh Governments pursued the formal disputes resolution mechanism through the JMC. The dispute resolution process began in 2017, but the Treasury has the power to determine what is exceptional and outside Barnett.

Although the full JMC had not met since 2013, in October 2016, the prime minister restated a commitment to involve the constituent parts of the UK to develop an approach to the EU withdrawal negotiations. It was agreed to take forward multilateral engagement through a new JMC committee on EU negotiations, to be known as the JMC (EN), to facilitate more detailed discussion and action. The meetings of the JMC (EN) did not meet the suggested bi-monthly timetable but it met four times in 2017 and ten times up to the end of 2018. The meetings were usually attended by the Cabinet Office Minister of State but otherwise resembled JMC plenary meetings, except with no Northern Ireland minister in attendance due to the collapse of the Assembly. Much criticism began to emerge of the functioning of the JMC (EN), as increasingly in practice this special committee was sidetracked, with little influence over the processes in the House of Commons related to the passage of the Withdrawal Bill. The concern of the Scottish and Welsh Governments moved to the issue of the UK government taking powers back from the EU that were actually devolved matters which seemed a threat to devolution. The issue of the UK legislation restricting the devolved governments' powers unilaterally was dealt with by the Scottish and Welsh Governments on a bilateral basis as the JMC (EN) proved ineffective. Overall, the JMC suffered from the perspective that it mattered more to the devolved governments than the UK government (Gallagher 2020: 573). A review of inter-governmental relations, instituted by government, found that the JMC had not fostered efficient collaboration and had lacked clarity of purpose (Dunlop 2017). The JMC (EU) continued to meet, twenty-five times in all, dealing with the transition, the Northern Ireland Protocol and the Internal Market, but was eventually discontinued.

British–Irish Council

The other multi-level structure created to involve all the devolved governments was the British–Irish Council (BIC), established after the Good Friday Agreement. This was a broad east–west representative body providing a forum for the UK and Irish governments, the devolved governments of Scotland, Wales and Northern Ireland together with representatives from the governments of the Isle of Man, Guernsey and Jersey. Its role was defined as a forum to exchange information, discuss, consult and endeavour to reach agreement on cooperation on matters of mutual interest (British-Irish Council 1999). Operationally, it developed tiers of functioning: at summit level; in sectoral level, involving ministers; and at a third level of officials. Originally, there was some scepticism around the interest and commitment of the non-Irish members, especially with the suspension of the Northern Ireland Assembly and Executive from 2002 to 2007. However, the BIC continued to meet, reports were produced by the policy sectoral groups and new agendas developed (Birrell 2012: 221). Clearly, the participants found the sectoral work useful in the exchange of ideas, policy copying, and cooperation in areas such as waste disposal, recognition of driving licences, air routes and anti-drugs policies. Lynch and Hopkins (2010) stated that the BIC had become an important player in governance networks. With Northern Ireland returning in 2007, the number of workstreams increased into areas such as migration, child protection and child poverty. In 2012, a permanent secretariat and administrative headquarters were established in Edinburgh and strengthened the BIC. The work and output of the BIC also continued in 2017–19 in the absence of Northern Ireland ministers, although full ministerial representation returned from 2020. BIC meetings continued dealing with issues such as recovery from Covid-19, languages, early years and the EU–UK relationships.

Quadrilateral meetings

There are other forums outside the formal structures of JMC and BIC for the engagement between of the four administrations. A variety of ministerial quadrilateral meetings exist to discuss specific issues. Quadrilateral meetings of finance ministers have been held since the early years of devolution, to exchange views and inform and learn from each other. This form of meeting was seen as concrete evidence of beneficial working together between the UK Treasury and the devolved administrations. The quadrilateral financial meetings have been used to resolve some technical issues in the context of interpreting the Statement of Funding Policy. It has been argued that there is more interaction at the quadrilateral finance meetings compared to the JMC meetings and that there is a case for this structure continuing as a part of any framework for inter-governmental relations (House of Lords Select Committee on the Constitution 2016: 28). It does not always operate without conflict; in 2020, the three devolved finance ministers demanded a meeting with the Chancellor prior to the first budget of the Boris Johnson administration. There are further examples of quadrilateral meetings, for example, an inter-ministerial group for environment, food and rural affairs, which meets regularly to ensure cooperation and collaboration between the four administrations. Joint statements, critical of the UK government and calling for action, have been made frequently by the three devolved finance ministers, for example, asking for the retention of the addition to Universal Credit during the lockdown and criticizing the shared prosperity fund. If Brexit marked a decline in the significance of quadrilateral meetings, the spread of Covid-19 was to lead to more cooperation and collaboration. This involved meetings between health ministers and chief medical officers. There was close working through a Joint Committee on Vaccination and Immunisation, also close working lockdown arrangements, and also with the Treasury on ensuring extra funding. Quadrilateral meetings also developed on net zero, on climate adaptation and the environment and heating.

Bilateral relationships

Bilateral relationships have always been an attractive way to conduct inter-governmental relations, especially as politicians in the devolved government may identify an advantage in a bilateral meeting. This involves, at the highest level, a meeting between the prime minister and the first minister, essentially with an element of a summit when the UK prime minister meets the Scottish first minister. Other bilateral ministerial meetings may take place. The development of new formal bilateral inter-governmental bodies occurred in Scotland and Wales. This resulted from the devolution in Scotland of tax powers and welfare powers and also in Wales of taxation. The most notable of these was a Joint Exchequer Committee (JEC). This was set up following Scotland having increased responsibility for part of income tax, certain other taxes and borrowing powers introduced in the Scotland Act 2016. A Fiscal Framework Agreement was the background to the JEC. Published in 2016, it went alongside the devolution of tax and welfare powers and dealt mainly with: adjustments to the block grant, revenue forecasting, arrangements for reviewing borrowing, capital borrowing and data sharing. Arrangements for dispute resolution were also included. The JEC covers the implementation, operation and review of the fiscal framework. At meetings of the JEC the Scottish Cabinet Secretary for Finance and the Chief Secretary to the Treasury considered a range of options for adjusting the Scottish block grant in relation to tax and social security. Also considered were methodologies for assigning VAT receipts to the Scottish Government. Relations with the UK HM Customs and Revenue is also overseen by the JEC. The evolution of the JEC may mean this bilateral model will be used to manage interdependences (McEwan 2017: 679). An Intergovernmental Assurance Board also oversaw the implementation of financial provisions.

A Joint Executive Committee (JExC) was established for Wales similar to the bilateral Scottish body. This was linked to the agreement between the Welsh Government and the UK government on the Welsh Government's fiscal framework. This fiscal agreement followed the Wales Act 2014, which provided a legislative framework that devolved new tax and borrowing powers to the National Assembly for Wales, including a Welsh rate of income tax, stamp duty land tax and landfill tax. The agreement covered changes in block grant funding, capital borrowing, budget management tools, treatment of policy spill-over effects and implementation arrangements. The implementation of the agreement would be overseen by a JExC. JExC (Wales) oversaw the work at official level. A Memorandum of Understanding was agreed between the bodies that will perform the duties outlined in the agreement or relating to the new tax powers (Welsh Government 2016). The UK–Wales JExC was attended by Treasury ministers, the Welsh finance minister and the Secretary of State for Wales. Progress on the implementation and operation of the arrangements was reported to the UK Parliament and the National Assembly for Wales through annual reports. A dispute resolution process is set out to apply to all disputes relating to the implementation of the agreement.

The devolution of part of social security to Scotland in the Scotland Act 2016 led to the creation of a bilateral inter-governmental body, a Joint Ministerial Working Group, to provide a forum for discussion and decision-making, to ensure the implementation of welfare- and employment-related aspects. This forum involved UK ministers and Scottish ministers with two co-chairs, the Secretary of State and a Scottish minister. The working group had a range of tasks: to exchange information; to ensure a smooth transition to the new responsibilities to discuss policy and operational practice; to work cooperatively to deliver the transfer of powers and to resolve contentious issues. It was estimated that one quarter of all welfare spending outside the state pension will be devolved. The existence of areas of overlapping responsibilities and coverage across jurisdictions created a clear need for a bilateral inter-governmental mechanism.

Bilateral meetings between ministers grew in scale and tended to be on an ad-hoc basis. The Secretary of State for Business, Energy and Industrial Strategy met the relevant Northern Ireland minister on economic recovery and also met a Scottish Government to discuss heat systems. A Scottish minister also met the UK minister for school standards while the Minister of State for Higher and Further Education met Scottish and Welsh ministers to discuss the effect of Covid on education. The Secretary of State for Levelling Up, Housing and Communities held meetings with Welsh ministers on Freeports, immigration and safety of women (Department for Levelling Up, Housing and Communities 2022b). An annual report on inter-governmental relations for the year provided data on the number of meetings between UK ministers and devolved ministers for the year 2021 described as multilateral meetings (Table 10.1).

TABLE 10.1 *Meetings between UK and devolved governments*

Meetings involving each nation
Scottish Government 210
Welsh Government 256
Northern Ireland Executive 236

Meetings with UK Government only
Scottish Government 94
Welsh Government 106
Northern Ireland Executive 95

Source: Department for Levelling up, Housing and Communities (2022b: 9).

The data indicates the extent of inter-governmental relations at ministerial level as well as broadly indicating a similar amount of contact involving each nation, although Scotland has rather less contact than the other nations, suggesting some difficulty in the relationship.

Inter-governmental departmental cooperation

The majority of inter-governmental cooperation takes place between officials and, at times, ministers in UK government departments and devolved departments. Thus, much inter-governmental cooperation happens below the political radar (Gallagher 2020: 570). Bilateral concordats have been drawn up between Whitehall departments and their counterparts in the devolved administrations and number over forty. Concordats each draw up a set of principles for day-to-day relationships, working together and cooperation. They are not legally binding and they can be regularly updated. A key element in the concordat was communication, to keep each other informed of issues of mutual interest, of policy, of legislation and impact upon each other. The spirit of the concordats was that there would be close interaction. Such interaction tended to mainly involve the policy teams at a working level. Some Whitehall departments, like the Department for Environment, Food and Rural Affairs (DEFRA), had few service responsibilities in the devolved nations, but in DEFRA's case it works closely with the devolved administrations on policy and animal welfare. Built into concordats was a commitment to dispute resolution without referrals to ministers and the JMC and there was also a commitment to confidentiality. The use and experience of inter-governmental cooperation varied between UK and devolved departments, depending on whether a matter was wholly devolved, partly devolved or not devolved. Some UK departments will have a much clearer need for cooperation with devolved departments because of overlaps and close engagement, applying particularly to the Department of Work and Pensions (DWP), as aspects of social security are now devolved, and also to the work of the UK Treasury. Welsh departments also require close cooperation because of the history of integrated legislation and provision. A clear framework was also necessary to provide provision for cooperation between the Department of Health (DH) in Whitehall and its counterpart in Wales on matters affecting the NHS, particularly on cross-border matters. The DWP also had to work closely on issues with its Welsh counterpart. Similarly, the UK Minister of Justice has to work closely with the Welsh administration on non-devolved welfare matters, which are otherwise now devolved in Northern Ireland and Scotland (Paun and Munro 2015: 33).

Extensive guidance has been given to civil servants in Whitehall departments in dealing with the devolved administrations. A set of devolution guidance notes had drawn up original guidelines focusing on such subjects as the circulation of inter-ministerial and inter-departmental correspondence, including the statement that the devolved administrations should not be formal recipients of cabinet committee correspondence unless it had a bearing on their responsibilities. Since 2015, a 'Devolution and You' training programme was initiated to improve the civil servants' knowledge of devolution. The Cabinet Office (2019) published a devolution toolkit to encourage good relationships with the devolved administrations. The toolkit provides advice on how to build relationships, how to decide whether policy impinges on devolved matters, the need to devolution-proof departmental policies and actions, and the need to ascertain the views of the devolved administrations. The UK government has also (2019) published guidance on devolution: for civil servants, based on the principle that understanding how devolution operates in the UK is important for all civil servants. It is also suggested that common values make it easier for civil servants from across the administrations to work together and that regular contact will improve the understanding of devolution.

The UK government did come to the view that the existing inter-governmental machinery was no longer fit for purpose and was in urgent need of reform. Increased interaction was becoming more necessary post-Brexit. This review led to set of recommendations agreed by the UK government and the devolved governments. A number of principles were agreed to underpin inter-governmental relations, including: mutual respect, all governments respecting the rules, increasing accountability and transparency, equal opportunities for all governments, promoting dispute avoidance, and ensuring that processes serve all governments (Cabinet Office and the Department for Levelling Up, Housing and Communities 2022). The new structures and processes would replace the JMC. There would be a focus on ministerial involvement to provide oversight and political accountability. A new three tier structure was proposed for implementation (see Box 10.1).

BOX 10.1 NEW INTER-GOVERNMENTAL STRUCTURE

1   A Council. The Prime Minister and heads of devolved governments.

2   Inter-ministerial Standing Committee. Relevant ministers across portfolios.

3   Inter-ministerial groups. Engagement at official and ministerial level on specific subjects.

4   A standing Inter-governmental Secretariat composed of officials from all governments.

The Council would oversee the strategic direction for inter-governmental relations and deal with dispute resolution, and the Prime Minister would host an annual meeting. The Standing Committee would have matters referred to it from groups. A special Finance Inter-ministerial Standing Committee would replace the existing quadrilateral committee. The special subject groups reflected one to three topics per UK department area (see Box 10.2).

BOX 10.2 EXAMPLES OF INTER-MINISTERIAL GROUPS

- Business and Industry
- Net zero
- Elections
- Culture
- Sports
- Tourism
- Transport
- Trade

Source: Cabinet Office/Department for Levelling up, Housing and Communities (2022: 11).

Much attention was paid to dealing with disputes in the structure. Any government could refer a disagreement to the IGR Secretariat to be classified as a dispute. Another innovation was the requirement for recording and reporting on inter-governmental activity on a regular basis. The first report on the Inter-ministerial Standing Committee meeting in 2022 noted the attendance of the Scottish Deputy First Minister who chaired the session, three parliamentary under-secretaries from the territorial offices, three ministers from the Scottish Government and two each from the Welsh and Northern Ireland Governments. Discussion centred on three items: UK legislative programme, the cost of living and progress with inter-governmental relations (Cabinet Office 2022). The Scottish and Welsh Governments still expressed reservations about the new structures. There were fears that: the final decisions on disputes would rest with the UK government; the reformed system would still not have a legislative basis; the decision-making would rest on an agreed consensus; and that a restatement of the UK funding policy would have been better. The whole process was described as a rebranding exercise and would not deliver a major change in UK government exercise. There was some recognition that there was potential to reduce the role or dominance of the UK government.

Parallel to the establishment of these new structures was another new body with a strong inter-governmental component. The legislation on the UK internal market was accompanied by the formation of a new Office for the Internal Market (OIM). This was designed to provide to provide expertise and independent advice to the UK government and devolved governments through the monitoring the operation of the internal market. The Scottish and Welsh Governments had expressed concern at the UK government overriding devolved powers through the Internal Market Act. In its first report, the OIM paid particular attention to the issue of regularity divergence between the four nations. It identified the areas of the environment, energy, agriculture, animal welfare, food and drink as likely to lead to problems of divergence.

Territorial offices

The three territorial offices had existed before devolution, carrying out a range of administrative and delivery functions. The Scottish Office had existed since 1885, the Northern Ireland Office since 1972 and the Welsh Office since 1964. After devolution, most of the direct functions became the responsibility of the devolved institutions, with only a small department retained in Whitehall and in Edinburgh, Belfast and Cardiff. Two departments were renamed: the Scotland Office and the Wales Office. The territorial offices normally had a minister who was a member of the UK cabinet and a junior minister, plus a spokesperson in the House of Lords. The reconstituted territorial offices took on a new role in facilitating inter-governmental relations between the UK government and the three devolved administrations. Many of the tasks of the three territorial offices are similar. Each Secretary of State and the territorial offices have a key role to act as guardian of the devolution settlement, to maintain the effective working of devolution and strengthen and sustain the operation of devolution. The Secretary of State is the voice for Scotland, Wales and Northern Ireland in the UK cabinet and has specific roles in Parliament. Secretaries of State answer parliamentary questions, make statements and, most importantly, introduce constitutional legislation. The territorial offices are also responsible for making and publishing the official responses to reports from the three territorial committees in the House of Commons and give the UK government response to committee recommendations. The territorial offices also act as a voice for Scotland, Wales and Northern Ireland on a range of matters with Whitehall departments. Each government department has its own devolution team – quite sizeable in some departments – but each department must decide if it has in place adequate mechanisms to facilitate joint working (Dunlop 2017). Also established has been a devolution leaders' network. Despite these developments, there still appears to be a lack of understanding of devolution. The review of Union capability noted that the devolution teams were not close to policy-making (Dunlop 2017: 22). This report called for a greater policy presence of Whitehall departments in Scotland, Wales and Northern Ireland, to involve hubs. This was seen as a means of supporting cooperation and improving governance. Such proposals were met with criticism in Wales and Scotland, whose governments saw them as a challenge to devolution and leading to duplication and conflict (Welsh Government 2021c). At the higher level, there are some arrangements that assist civil service cooperation. There is a weekly meeting of permanent secretaries with those from Scotland and Wales and the head of the Northern Ireland Civil Service. During 2017–18, the Scotland and Wales Offices were renamed as the Offices of the Secretary of States for Scotland and Wales. These changes were viewed by the UK government as appropriate to the increased emphasis on upholding the Union. Obviously, the views of the territorial offices may not accord with the views of the devolved governments, for example, the Scottish Government's and UK government's views on immigration.

Another key role for the Secretaries of State and territorial offices has been to represent and advocate and promote understanding of the UK government policies. They are visible as the UK government voice and focus on communicating the government's message. This takes place in a political context in which the Scottish Secretary of State represents the Conservative Party in Scotland, which has very small representation and support in Scotland and which the SNP government may prefer to ignore. There have been a number of disputes between the Wales Office and the Welsh Government over the division of powers. The confidence and supply agreement between the Conservative Party and the DUP in 2017 produced a more united relationship at Westminster and in Northern Ireland but excluded the other party, Sinn Féin, which was in the suspended Executive. This was, therefore, not an inter-governmental agreement. The Secretaries of State also had further representative roles, on cabinet sub-committees, on the JMC, and on the BIC.

A further common task of the territorial offices is to transfer the Treasury allocations to the devolved administrations. The development of shared functions also highlights the need for collaboration between governments, particularly in the area of the economy and growing investment. The territorial offices and Secretary of State take a major role in introducing non-devolved legislation through the UK Parliament, preparing the bill and background papers and also communicating on legislative consent motions. The devolution settlement means that the territorial offices are responsible for taking direct executive actions on a number of non-devolved matters. This has been particularly important in Northern Ireland in dealing with security matters and victims and legacy issues where consultation with local political and other groups is necessary. The Conservative administration defined the duty of the OSSS to strengthen and sustain the Union and make the London government more visible and accessible. This emphasis on the role of central government also apparent with the publication of the 'UK Government's Plan for Wales' (UK Government 2021), covering investment, infrastructure and energy. The Northern Ireland Secretary of State also took action to bypass blockages in the devolved decision-making by legislating at Westminster on abortion and the Irish language. As part of this commitment to promoting the Union, Whitehall departments were dispersed to new UK government hubs in Scotland, Wales and Northern Ireland. A trade and investment hub was launched in Edinburgh and a cabinet office established in Glasgow (Cabinet Office 2022). These offices were separate from the territorial offices.

Cross-border services

The introduction of devolution produced a new inter-governmental dimension to the provision of services across borders. The provision of services in border areas had, of course, previously existed as an administrative issue in Great Britain prior to devolution. With devolution, issues related to cross-border provision became a matter for inter-governmental contacts. The original Scotland Act 1998 and the Government of Wales Act 1998 made little reference to cross-border matters. It was recognized at the time that a number of quangos had UK-wide responsibilities and it was specified that Scottish ministers should be consulted over appointments. Devolution had more impact on the border between Wales and England, with a large population living in border areas and accustomed to crossing the border to access services. An inquiry by the Wales Affairs Committee (2008) noted 20,000 people resident in England were registered with a GP in Wales and 13,000 people resident in Wales were registered with a GP in England. A protocol was established to cover financial transfers for commissioning and funding hospital care. Health, transport and higher and further education tended to be the main services affected. The Welsh Affairs Committee (2010) reported on the cross-border provision of services. A revised cross-border health protocol and accompanying financial transfers from England to Wales has resolved many of the outstanding disputes with regard to the commissioning and funding of hospital care in England for patients resident in Wales. It stressed the need for awareness of the provision of cross-border specialist services but noted that there was little solid research evidence comparing the performance of the NHS in the devolved administrations. It was reported that any of the special difficulties with further education had been resolved, although some arrangements seemed to focus on the convenience of the providers. There was still some difficulty in students crossing the border to attend colleges for reasons of convenience or special courses. Transport drew more criticisms with concern expressed that there was a lack of acceptance of strategic responsibility for cross-border roads. Also identified was a lack of collaboration between the Whitehall Department of Transport and the Welsh Government to prepare a distinctive ports policy for Wales.

Cross-border working in Ireland is of a different nature, involving mainly cooperation between a devolved government in Northern Ireland but with a bordering sovereign state. The Good Friday Agreement and the introduction of devolution brought a new and more extensive Irish cross-border dimension formally structured through a North–South Ministerial Council. Six statutory cross-border implementation bodies provide a range of fairly minor infrastructure projects. A further six broader policy areas are identified as areas for cooperation: health, education, transport, the environment, agriculture and tourism. The formal bodies of ministerial cooperation have been disrupted by the collapse of devolution.

Inter-governmental relations involving Parliament

No formal procedures were set up to govern a relationship between the devolved governments and the UK Parliament. This did not prevent direct lines of communication at times, particularly relating to the legislative matters and scrutiny matters at Westminster. One aspect of the relationship involves legislative consent motions, which were discussed above (Chapter 4). The other main forms of engagement relate to devolved government contributions to Westminster legislation, usually covering constitutional change in Scotland, Wales or Northern Ireland, and to the activities of the territorial scrutiny committees. The Scottish Affairs Committee, the Welsh Affairs Committee and the Northern Ireland Committee are House of Commons committees, but their modes of operation often draw them into contact with the devolved administrations. It is not just the case that there is a simple boundary around Westminster committees dealing with non-devolved subjects only.

Scottish Affairs Committee

The official role of the Scottish Affairs Committee was to scrutinize the role and actions of the Scotland Office, later the Office of the Secretary of State for Scotland, and examine the wider UK government to assess how politics and legislation have led to a direct impact on Scotland. It also has the power to look at the administration of the Office of the Advocate General for Scotland. Overlaps in powers can put barriers in the way of the Scottish Affairs Committee avoiding the activities of the Scottish Government. In 2019, the committee carried out a major investigation into problem drug use in Scotland (Scottish Affairs Committee 2019). As the Scottish Government is responsible for health delivery, there was also a recommendation from the Scottish Affairs Committee that the Scottish Government should improve its response to the drug problem. An inquiry into the impact of universal credit and the two-child limit on levels of social inequality in Scotland was more clearly within the category of reserved matters. A formal reply to the reports and recommendations is given by the UK government, although often prepared by one Whitehall department. Brexit has given rise to a number of inquiries, for example, on the future of Scottish agriculture post-Brexit, again despite agriculture being a devolved matter.

Ministers from the devolved government have given evidence to the territorial committee, usually in relation to major constitutional legislation such as the Scotland Act 2016, or at inquiries involving the operation of devolution at the committee stage of legislation. Discussions may take place between the UK government in charge of the passage of a bill and Scottish ministers. An amendment to the Scotland Bill 2015 in relation to human rights provision led to the deputy leader of the House of Commons and the Scottish Secretary of State engaging with the devolved administration. When the Scottish Affairs Committee produced a report into the relationship between the UK and Scottish Governments, it reached a conclusion that it was currently unclear what value the Scotland Office adds to the relationship between the UK and Scottish Government (Scottish Affairs Committee 2019). In the early period of devolution, it was suggested that the Scottish Affairs Committee found it difficult to identify areas for investigation and met infrequently (Torrance and Evans 2019). Matters changed with the emergence of major Scottish constitutional and financial legislation. The large number of SNP MPs elected enabled the SNP to take up the chair of the committee and to adopt a wider range of subjects to be investigated.

The terms of reference for the Welsh Affairs Committee were similar to those for the Scottish Affairs Committee, to examine matters within the responsibility of the Secretary of State for Wales excluding relations with the National Assembly for Wales (now Welsh Parliament). In practice, the committee examines policies of the UK government that have an impact on matters, including strategic transport and welfare and the armed forces, which are clearly not devolved. The expansion of Welsh devolved powers did narrow the scope and number of Welsh Affairs Committee inquiries to some three or four per year. The work of the Welsh Affairs Committee in the pre-legislative inquiry on the Wales Bill (2014) has highlighted major problems, generated debates and increased the status of the committee (Cole and Stafford 2015: 9). The Welsh Affairs Committee has taken a flexible approach to interpreting its remit so as to give itself a role to examine the impact of UK government policy in Wales. As well as the mechanics of the devolution settlement, there is liaison between the committee and the National Assembly for Wales (Torrance and Evans 2019: 871), committees through consultations, visits and invitations to appear before each other's committees. House of Commons standing orders were changed to allow the Welsh Affairs Committee to hold joint meetings with Assembly committees. It is also common for the Welsh Government to give written evidence. The Welsh Affairs Committee has used inquiries to make demands of the UK government. A report on City Deals called for more UK government support critical to the growth of such deals in Wales. In 2019, the UK government responded by rejecting the recommendation to devolve air passenger tax to Wales despite supportive evidence from the Welsh Government (Welsh Affairs Committee 2019). An inquiry was also held into the role of the Secretary of State. The Welsh Affairs Committee has worked to create a high profile for itself and produce constructive ideas for the UK government's treatment of Welsh Affairs.

The Northern Ireland Affairs Committee (NIAC) has similar formal functions to the other territorial scrutiny committees, to examine the expenditure, administration and policies of the Northern Ireland Office and associated public bodies. The NIAC also looks at the administration and expenditure, but not the policies, of the Crown Solicitor's Office. When devolution was up and running, the NIAC focused on excepted and reserved powers, i.e. non-transferred powers. There was a special emphasis on justice and policing issues until this changed to a devolved matter, for example, on the police and the prison service. In the lifetime of the last parliament, the most high-profile work conducted by NIAC was an investigation into the on-the-runs cases, which came to the public's attention in 2014. This NIAC inquiry was held in parallel to a UK government inquiry. With devolution suspended between 2017 and 2019, the NIAC has widened its scope to include what were largely devolved matters. A major report was produced on health funding in Northern Ireland (2019), recommending strategic long-term investigation in transformation. In the absence of the Executive and Assembly, in the meantime, it stated measures should be taken to prevent the health system falling behind the rest of the UK. Specific areas suggested as suffering from under-investment were social care, cancer treatment and mental health. Some forty-nine bodies submitted evidence to the inquiry including the Northern Ireland Department of Health. Another major inquiry dealt with problems of devolution and democracy in Northern Ireland, referring to the democratic deficit (Northern Ireland Affairs Committee 2018). Further inquiries in the 2017–19 period were held on education funding, welfare policy and the electricity sector. Brexit has produced a number of reports on the land border between Northern Ireland and Ireland; fisheries and agriculture; the Northern Ireland backstop and the border. A controversial issue was an inquiry into changes to the Renewable Heat Incentive scheme and the misuse of grants. The NIAC was empowered to handle pre-legislative scrutiny but historically has rarely pursued this function (Torrance and Evans 2019: 873). Recommendations from inquiries as in Scotland and Wales required a published response from the UK government; for example, in 2015, a recommendation for public transparency for party donations over £7,500 was rejected by the UK government (Birrell and Gormley-Heenan 2015: 47). With the restoration of devolution, the NIAC returned to its more limited role, focusing on the Northern Ireland Office, and began an inquiry into the implementation of the Stormont House Agreement. Scrutiny became more cross-cutting between devolved and non-devolved areas with the collapse of the Executive.

International relations

While foreign relations and policy remained a reserved matter for the UK government, devolution introduced a perspective concerning the nature of the devolved governments' relationships with foreign countries. Keating (2013) suggests some main reasons for the approach of sub-state governments: a belief that there was an external dimension to everything devolved governments did, that devolved governments wished to establish themselves as something more than administrative units within unitary nation states, and to promote a more favourable image of the territory abroad. The formal Memorandum of Understanding set out principles to underpin the relationship between the UK government and the devolved administrations. Concordats in the memorandum dealt with three issues: the coordination of EU policy, which was a UK government matter; financial assistance to industry; and international relations. It was recognized that aspects of international relationships could touch on the responsibilities of the devolved administrations. The common arrangements covering all three devolved administrations were described (see Box 10.3).

BOX 10.3 ROLE OF DEVOLVED GOVERNMENTS IN INTERNATIONAL RELATIONS

- The exchange of information involving international developments.
- Consultation on involvement in international negotiations relating to devolved matters.
- The implementation of international commitments relating to devolved matters.
- Cooperation over legal proceedings; support on arranging visits.
- The continuing work of the British Council.
- Consultation on trade and investment promotion to avoid duplication.

Within the framework of their responsibilities, it was acknowledged that the devolved administrations might wish to establish offices overseas. The UK government was to take a flexible approach to circumventing some possible constitutional barriers to the devolved administrations' engagement, for example, with international aid. Apart from the concordats, there are no other institutionalized inter-governmental structures or requirements in place.

Scotland had a European and External Relations Committee, which reported on the Scottish Government's international engagement strategy. Scotland placed an emphasis on producing a global trade and investment strategy (Scottish Government 2016) for the period 2016–21, entitled Global Scotland: Trade and Investment Strategy. With economic development powers in the hands of the UK government, Scotland's international investment efforts could put it in competition with other parts of the UK. The result was a compromise under which Invest in Scotland was established as a joint initiative of the Scottish Development Agency and the Scottish Office (Keating 2017). The Scottish Government has the international aim to promote Scotland's reputation as a distinctive global identity and confident of its place in the world. This has been referred to as stepping on to the world's stage, making an impression on the rest of the world and contributing to a responsive international community (Jeffery 2003). For the SNP in government, international relations are part of the political campaign to attain complete independence, and this provided the potential for changes in inter-governmental relations; however, in practice, the main focus remains on UK internal relationships (Cairney 2012a) except for a shift to some proto-diplomacy. Education and culture are two of the fields that are wholly devolved to Scotland. Lynch (2001) saw this paradiplomacy as having a markedly economic focus to attract inward investment and promote exports. There was also an emphasis on Scotland's progressive credentials and contribution to democracy and liberalism (Keating 2017: 183). Scotland did establish a network of international offices to represent its interests. One of the unexpected sides of the devolved administration's involvement in foreign relations has been the development of policies to give assistance to underdeveloped countries. Scotland has developed special programmes for supporting Malawi and a small number of other African countries and South Asia and contributing to the global fight against poverty. Keating (2016: 192) concludes that paradiplomacy as an external expression of devolution is not necessarily conflictual but has been complementary to the diplomacy of the UK. Scotland has developed a global affairs framework which pursues an agenda based on sustainable development goals and continued ties to the EU and its values (Scottish Government 2021c). Scotland also has an External Affairs Department headed up by a government minister.

The contribution of devolution to the promotion of nation building and national identity was clear in Wales. The Welsh Government made an early significant effort to enhance its sub-state diplomatic activity. The most significant attention was paid to international trade and investment and International Business Wales (IBW) was created, combining international efforts to promote inward trade and investment (Wyn Jones and Royles 2012). As in Scotland, the Welsh devolved body and the UK Department of Trade and Industry developed a good working relationship. The formalized agreements contained in the concordats on international relations and financial assistance to industry appeared to promote good collaborative relationships. Wales had produced an international trade strategy and a document on international affairs in general (Welsh Government 2012). The National Assembly for Wales had also a European and External Affairs Committee, which covered all of the Welsh Government's engagement in international affairs, although this committee later merged into a new Constitutional Legal Affairs Committee. For the devolved government in Wales there was a strong incentive to gain recognition as a separate government and political entity. The other main direction of Welsh activity was the promotion of international aid and development. The first focus of the Welsh Government was into countries in sub-Saharan Africa with existing links to Wales. Given international development was a reserved matter, the concept of mutual benefit became central to justifying Welsh devolved actions and expenditure (Wyn Jones and Royles 2012: 260).

The view was expressed that the existing provision on international promotion was patchy and incoherent (National Assembly for Wales 2019b). There was a recommendation for a further five more overseas offices and for developing a special relationship with the United States. With the mixed success of international offices there was further effort required to sell Wales to the world. A study by Elin Royles (2019) suggested that levels of constitutional powers may be limited in their capacity to account for

Welsh sub-state international activity. Varieties in opportunities may exist across different policy domains, reflect historical paths and may continue a role developed by non-governmental quangos. Wales still has opportunities arising from unique cultural and linguistic niches. The Welsh Government (2021a) published a new international relations strategy. This had a commitment to trade and investment and depicted Wales as a globally responsible nation. A Minister of International Relations was appointed and Wales increased its presence in EU countries.

The main focus of inter-governmental relations for the Northern Ireland Executive has been within the framework of Irish cross-border relations (Birrell 2012), with the 1998 Good Friday Agreement leading to the development of new relationships. These relationships, however, were rarely regarded as a matter of foreign relations. The Northern Ireland Act 1998 simply stated that international relations were excepted, i.e. non-devolved matters, and, like Scotland and Wales, were covered by the Memorandum of Understanding and concordats. Differences in the devolution of powers were recognized as giving Northern Ireland ministers responsibilities in observing and implementing the international obligations of the UK. However, the Northern Ireland Executive was slow to develop its own international strategy. A distinct unit was established, albeit with a small budget, although the Northern Ireland Assembly never had a committee with a dedicated brief. Originally, one of the few institutions based abroad, apart from an office in Brussels, was a Northern Ireland Bureau in Washington, which was run directly by the devolved Executive and not by the British Embassy. The production of a document promoting national identity and nation building posed political difficulties in Northern Ireland. There is little enthusiasm among the nationalist or republican parties for promoting Northern Ireland internationally as a distinct or sustainable political entity. Also, in Northern Ireland, cultural attributes often relate to differences between the two communities and can prove to be contentious. Despite this, opportunities were identified as promoting a non-stereotypical vision of Northern Ireland. An international relations strategy in 2014 adopted, as an objective, building on the region's international connections and reputation in the areas of culture, art, sport and entertainment. It is in relation to economic objectives that Northern Ireland appears to converge with the other sub-states and the main strategic aim referred to enhancing international relationships to secure investment, trade, tourism and students. In 2016, the role of the international unit was described as enhancing the international message and developing the beneficial relationships with targeted regions, countries and organizations (Northern Ireland Executive 2016).

In contrast to the Scottish and Welsh Governments, the Northern Ireland Executive did not initiate any international aid policy, indicating an insular approach. An Assembly all-party committee was the only acknowledgement of a possible contribution to assist developing countries. One of the most distinctive features of Northern Ireland's international relations activity has been a focus on the marketing of Northern Ireland as a model of peace-making. Something of a consensus developed that this blueprint could be exported (O'Kane 2010). This contribution to peace building in other parts of the world is not structured in any strategic way but has had an impact in countries such as Iraq and Columbia. The main approach to international relations is dominated by the promotion of trade, foreign investment and tourism rather than any concept of national identity, or other items which are politically divisive. An international strategy has not been revised since 2014 and the main marketing activity is directed by Invest NI.

Conclusions

The operation of inter-governmental relations has been one of the more difficult new requirements of devolution and has proved a difficult aspect to get right. The original main focus on self-government distracted from the need for a suitable system of inter-governmental relations (McEwan 2017: 667). A major initiative was to create a formal structure through the JMC and committees. Political and academic assessments did not judge this institutional initiative successful. A key issue has been the dominant position of the UK government in the structure. This has often led the devolved governments to place more reliance on bilateral inter-governmental relations and informal relationships, especially at senior ministerial level. Unilateral links between governments have proved appealing to devolved governments to pursue their own self-interests and overcome the lack of equity in status in the JMC. It has been suggested that the Welsh Government has been in a weaker position than its counterparts in Scotland and Northern Ireland (McEwan 2017: 684). The formal structure of the JMC experienced a revival encouraged by the SNP and in particular by the creation of a JMC EU negotiations committee, which was an effort to involve the devolved governments in Brexit discussions. However, this did not appear to have much influence on the decisions of the UK government. A further question arose over the focus of the JMC on dispute resolution while rather lacking the powers to achieve this. Gallagher (2020: 581) suggested that the existing architecture of inter-governmental relations was not fit for purpose. Outside the JMC, there were successful examples of quadrilateral ministerial meetings on matters such as finance and also new initiatives in bilateral departments. A series of major political developments has placed pressure on building good inter-governmental relations: the Scottish referendum, Brexit, austerity and the extension of devolved powers in Wales and Scotland producing more jagged edges with the delineation of functions. The growing intervention strategies by the UK government, intervening on devolved subjects, has further damaged inter-governmental relations.

As an aspect of devolution, inter-governmental relationship is not just a mechanism for consultation and collaboration but should be seen as vital to the nature of UK governance, which includes devolution. It is important to agree at least upon a set of coherent and joined-up principles to govern inter-governmental relations between the four governments. It is another question whether this should be accompanied by agreed legislation and institutions to manage inter-governmental relations within the union. The issue of inter-governmental relations has not really been a major issue for UK governments, with the devolved governments more engaged. However, there were a number of factors that present something of a barrier to strong inter-governmental mechanisms, particularly the absence of a written constitution and the principle of parliamentary sovereignty (McEwen et al. 2012: 332) and other constitutional conventions. On the other hand, there are factors that encourage close cooperation: the civil service ethos, common interests, professional bodies, policy and research bodies and the role of judicial decisions. Action to reform inter-governmental relations has been initiated. A new review has been undertaken jointly by the four governments. One of its main recommendations proposed a new UK Intergovernmental Council, replacing the JMC. In response, the UK government has proposed a Union Strategy Committee, chaired by the prime minister as a cabinet committee, a civil service interchange scheme and a new position of new Permanent Secretary to the Union. These proposals were not well received by the Scottish and Welsh Governments and producing respected and smooth working arrangements still seems difficult.

Calls for the reform of the system led to the formulation and implementation of a new three tier structure. This may inspire a commitment to improving relations and working between the four governments. The third tier of inter-departmental cooperation is based on a more developed and more coherent structure. There are still some likely obstacles to the new structure repairing the existing weakness in inter-governmental relations. Doubts still exist about the UK government's commitment to the structure and to equality of status between the four governments. Questions can be raised about the attendance of the Prime Minister at tier one meetings. A major focus of the reformed structure is on dispute resolution, but agreement on what type of issues should be resolved is unclear. Devolved governments or the UK government may prefer to use the Supreme Court if appropriate, or two governments may still prefer to use bilateral negotiations instead of the formal structures. The political context of sharp policy divisions and attitudes between the four government leaders may mean continuing difficulties in inter-governmental relations.

11

Conclusions

Assessing the development of devolution, especially in the last decade, has become a more complex task than may have been envisaged a few years ago. The key aspects that form the basis of this evaluation are presented as: the public and political acceptance of devolution; the growth of devolved powers; the scope and embeddedness of the devolved institutions in the systems of governance; the nature and efficacy of inter-governmental relations between the devolved nations and the UK government; and policy differences and achievements. Party political developments in the UK, Brexit, along with the impact of austerity, Covid-19, and the cost-of-living crisis had major implications for governance. Continuing political divisions in Scotland and Northern Ireland has raised questions about the future trends in devolution. Subsequently, the UK government has developed a major strategy to promote the Union and intervene more directly with devolved matters.

Public and political perceptions of devolution

Public acceptance of devolution in the three devolved nations has become well-established. Despite the growth in significance of the option of independence for Scotland, public trust in devolution in Scotland has remained high. Support for devolution in Wales has grown substantially since its level at the time of the initial referendum. Successive opinion polls in Northern Ireland have found that devolution remains the most popular option compared to any alternative forms of governance. Covid-19 led to an increasing awareness of the nature and significance of devolution throughout the UK as the devolved governments took on their devolved responsibilities for health, a process that increased the status of devolved ministers. While UK government support for devolution remains official policy, this has to be set against the UK government asserting strong support for the Union, following on from Brexit. This has been seen in the renaming of the Scotland and Wales offices, the opening of more Whitehall department offices in the devolved nations, more direct UK Treasury funding of projects in the devolved nations, with cabinet meetings being held in Scotland and the UK government overriding devolved powers. A major trend likely to impact upon future attitudes in devolved governance is linked to the rising importance of identity politics and nationalisms, which include Scottish nationalism, Welsh nationalism, Irish nationalism, Northern Irish unionism and English nationalism.

Growth of devolved powers

The strength and scale of devolution has been largely measured in terms of the growth of devolved powers. There has been a continuing process of growth in devolved capacity, including some major developments. Wales moved to having full legislative devolution, bringing it into line with Scotland and Northern Ireland. Law and justice powers were devolved to Northern Ireland. Important fiscal powers over income tax were devolved to Scotland and Wales and there was a new partial devolution of social security/welfare benefits, to Scotland. The scope of devolution was also extended by a number of innovative policies, for example, a smoking ban and charges for plastic bags. A degree of policy copying was associated with such measures and responses to austerity. Responses to Covid also produced policy differences in advisory structures, public guidance, strategies, legal requirements, as well as policy coordination, and cooperation and policy copying. The exercise of powers was constrained by the Treasury allocations through the Barnett formula, which has continued throughout devolution and produces pressure for convergence in some policy areas. Pressure for convergence increased with UK-based measures and funding to deal with Covid and through City Deals and levelling-up measures, and the Internal Market Act. Replacement EU funding also appears likely to remove some financial capacity from the devolved administrations as well as promoting convergence. The emergence of initiatives to increase devolved fiscal responsibility and accountability has the potential to enhance policy capacity building. This has been led to date by Scotland, with Wales following and Northern Ireland being encouraged to follow. It is still not possible to identify a common trajectory of gradual increase in devolved powers. There are a number of influences. At any time, the existing inherited practices may be preferred. There is the possibility of major political upheavals, such as an independence vote in a Scottish referendum, or political upheavals in Northern Ireland involving a collapse of the Executive or the consequences of a border poll. Decisions may have to be made on the acceptance or rejection of policy copying. There has been increasing dispute over devolved powers because of overlapping powers, conflict between powers, and confusion over the division of powers. The UK government has chosen to increasingly exercise sovereign power to set aside existing devolved powers or legislate on devolved matters or pass legislation impacting to some degree on devolved matters, refusing to devolve powers repatriated from the EU, or delivering funding to be spent on projects that fall under devolved matters.

Efficacy of devolved institutions

The centre of the devolved institutions is the Scottish Parliament, the Northern Ireland Assembly and Senedd Cymru, formerly the National Assembly for Wales. As new bodies in Scotland and Wales, they have established themselves as the centre of government and decision-making and, also as a centre of civic and political participation. One of the earlier expectations of devolution was that it would lead to a more participative form of democracy with more transparent responsibility to the community. The extent to which this has been achieved is debatable but, in all three jurisdictions, the legislatures have proved very accessible to the public. This has operated through the subject committee systems, which can carry out detailed scrutiny and consultation processes, the relative ease of access to ministers and members by lobbying groups, and by the public petitions system in Scotland and Wales. All three elected bodies had an extensive committee system with scrutiny and legislative functions and a strong public accounts body following Westminster practice. Some hopes that the committees would evolve as the driving force of devolution, increasing public accountability, have not really materialized. While doing useful work, committees have found a lot of time undertaken by legislative scrutiny rather than policy and delivery monitoring work. The power to initiate legislation and oversee quangos has been little used. Senedd Cymru has a problem with low numbers to serve on committees and Northern Ireland committees have shown little independence from the Executive and have periodically ceased to operate.

A major expectation in 1999 was that the governments might display diversity and not be composed of a single party. While Northern Ireland had a statutory form of power-sharing for the Executive, an element of proportional representation electoral practice was introduced in the other nations to boost the likelihood of a coalition or partnership government. Importantly, though, this did little to stop the largely dominant role of the SNP in Scotland and Labour in Wales. Similar hopes that at least a spirit of power-sharing or less adversarial approach would predominate in the devolved Parliament and Assemblies rarely, in practice, materialized. While Northern Ireland was able to proceed with an independent devolved civil service, the reliance of Scotland and Wales on the UK civil service has not, as feared, operated as a major drawback for the Scottish and Welsh Governments. The UK Home Civil Service has adapted well to serving the governments in Scotland and Wales. Relationships between the devolved governments and local government systems have generally worked smoothly. More difficulty was expected in the relationship with the large quango or public bodies sector, with original talk of a bonfire of quangos, but this approach calmed down. The existing structures of local councils and quangos developed working relationships with the devolved administration with limited conflict, although disputes over finance, controls and powers have arisen at times.

Inter-governmental relations

The last decade has seen a less than viable and beneficial system of inter-governmental relations. The major statutory system set up in 1999, the Joint Ministerial Committee (JMC), proved less than workable. An attempt to revitalize it, promoted by the Scottish Government, met with limited success. Generally, the devolved governments preferred to use bilateral meetings to discuss problems with devolution or possible conflicts. The JMC structure was revised and used as a vehicle for involving the UK government and the devolved governments in the early stage of negotiations on withdrawal from the EU. Brexit clearly put a strain on inter-governmental relations, especially given the proportion of remain votes in Scotland and Northern Ireland. Scotland and Wales found the JMC special negotiations mechanism breaking down and ineffective in giving them a say. JMC arrangements for dispute resolution also seemed unsatisfactory when the Scottish and Welsh Governments objected to the confidence and supply agreement between the Conservative Party and the DUP. When difficulties arose concerning the repatriation of EU powers, the UK government appeared to wish to bypass the devolved governments. While inter-governmental relations have normally involved ministers of each jurisdiction in formal bodies such as JMC and BIC, devolved ministers may also seek meetings with UK ministers and or the Secretaries of State. The DUP in Northern Ireland has frequently sought individual meetings with the prime minister rather than participate in meetings involving the whole Northern Ireland Executive.

Another major dispute accompanied the passing of the UK Internal Market Act 2020, which sought to establish common frameworks to guarantee businesses access across the UK with common standards. This drew hostility from the Scottish and Welsh Governments, which saw it as undermining devolution. The UK government proceeded on a unilateral basis despite criticisms that this would impose restrictions on the exercise of devolved powers and also threaten policy innovation. As part of the divergent EU Withdrawal Agreement, a Northern Ireland Protocol had been agreed with the EU to maintain Northern Ireland in alignment with EU laws, in order to prevent a hard border on the island of Ireland. This threatened the relationship of Ulster's unionist parties with the UK government, and it meant the Northern Ireland Executive was divided. A further divisive consequence of Brexit was that the UK government proposed to replace EU funding through payments of subsidies and introduce a UK Prosperity Fund to replace EU structural funds. This fund will operate through a single UK-wide framework administered by the UK government with a limited role for devolved administrations – seen by Scotland and Wales as interfering with devolution matters and hindering economic development. Responses to Covid-19 saw strong elements of collaboration between governments, with devolved ministers attending COBRA meetings and quadrilateral meetings and agreement on the application of Coronavirus Act 2020 and the vaccine programme. However, as each government determined its own lockdown arrangements, advisory structures, joint meetings and close working began to cease. Overall, the experience of Brexit and Covid-19 led to an acceptance of the need for inter-governmental meetings to be put on a stronger and confidence-building basis.

Policy divergence

Early assessments of the policy achievements of devolution tended to focus on the social policy outcomes as this appeared to constitute the major part of devolved powers. To an extent this has remained the case. Health has remained the major area for expenditure in all three nations, with public health and social care also receiving much attention. Devolution has also seen measures to tackle Covid tailored to each jurisdiction's needs. Scotland had an extensive structure of formal committees giving expert advice on Covid-19, Wales also had a number of these multi-disciplinary committees, but Northern Ireland had none. Scotland and Northern Ireland have pursued as a priority the integration of health and social care. At the same time, major difficulties remain with the structure of acute care and waiting lists, mental health and the reform of social care. Taking on more responsibility for social security and tackling poverty has been an objective of the devolved administrations. Education has been an area of policy divergence and there have been concerns expressed about the achievements in devolved education policy and practice. Economic achievements and indicators in the devolved countries do not provide clear evidence that there has been major impact by the devolved governments. This has to be understood in the context of the responsibilities of the UK government for the overall economic and fiscal policy and for international trade. It is difficult for the devolved administrations to take radical decisions impacting on economic policy.

The devolved governments have each adopted the use of statistical performance indicators to monitor how governments are providing services and making such information available to the public. The use of such approaches differs between the three administrations. Increasing devolved capacity has been an important principle and trend in Scotland, towards devolution max, despite the continuing overall goal of the SNP for an independent Scotland. Wales has been cautious about using more powers and has been mainly concerned with what is seen as an inappropriately lengthy set of matters reserved to Westminster. The proposition that Northern Ireland should increase devolved capacity has attracted little support, with the continuance of volatility in the devolved structures. The rise of the Northern Ireland Alliance Party has increased calls for a fundamental reform of the system of power-sharing. A qualified voluntary coalition has been suggested as a viable alternative to the current system of a mandatory coalition. The fallout from the Northern Ireland Protocol meant policy issues such as health, education and infrastructure were relegated to secondary issues. The future of devolution remains uncertain with the independence debate ongoing in Scotland, the ever-present threats to devolution in Northern Ireland with a major party withdrawing from the Executive, and Wales working to develop devolution further but frustrated at the UK government's treatment of and lack of respect for devolution.

The future of devolution

Devolution in the UK was introduced for several reasons, foremost among them a desire in Westminster to neutralize the incipient nationalist threat to the Union, especially in Scotland. The re-establishment of a devolved settlement on revised consociational terms in Northern Ireland was integral to transforming a delicate and protracted peace process to a new post-conflict dispensation there. For Wales, initially at least, devolution was an experiment greeted with, at worst, suspicion and, at best, indifference, with little enthusiasm, as demonstrated by the narrow vote on a relatively low turnout in favour of its introduction. In England, overwhelming in population and influence relative to the other parts of the UK, devolution has for much of the time been a distraction, indeed an occasional irritant, and generally it is a place which seemingly does not lend itself readily to a regionalized apparatus of government more redolent of federal states. Consequently, while doubtless variegated, even messy, asymmetrical arrangements for the territorial governance and management of all four constituent parts of the UK in large measure reflect the fact that administratively neat solutions of a one size fits all nature are ill suited to the widely divergent needs, aspirations and circumstances of each entity, each of which, for the time being at least, display a continued preference to maintain the common bonds of political union.

All that said, save for those relatively few observers who regarded the whole enterprise as embarking on a slippery slope towards more bureaucracy (and politicians), costlier government, added rancour, division and possible secession by one or more constituent parts of the UK, the notion that devolution might coincide with, or even fuel, the fissiparous tendencies of separatism culminating with the dissolution of the Union and break-up of the UK, was regarded as fanciful. Tam Dalyell's characterization of devolution as putting Scotland on a motorway to independence with no exits remains to be vindicated. And yet, now, after almost a quarter of a century, widespread speculation on 'the future of the UK' is commonplace. The fragmentation and disintegration of what has hitherto been one of the most stable and political unions in the world is now accorded serious credence and is a greater possibility than ever before. Successive crises in Northern Ireland, with other simmering resentments in both Wales and England, simply compound the sense of foreboding in terms of what lies ahead in terms of public service delivery, political stability, governmental structures and constitutional futures, to say nothing of notions of 'national unity'. Observers could easily be forgiven in concluding that devolution as an experiment has failed.

If there is a crisis of devolution, then it is most immediate and acute in the case of Scotland. The rise of the SNP to become 'the natural party of government' in Scotland, together with its seemingly unassailable hegemony in terms of dominating Scottish representation at Westminster, was accompanied by a bruising two-year electoral campaign pursuant to a highly divisive referendum on independence in 2014. The relative narrowness of the referendum outcome in favour of Scotland remaining within the UK heavily whetted the appetite among separatists for 'one more heave'. With the UK-wide Brexit referendum less than two years later presaging British secession from the EU, the tensions in the British political union were subject to even stronger centrifugal force, as the voters of Scotland (and Northern Ireland) diverged from their English and Welsh neighbours. Brexit, together with its aftermath and continuing Conservative dominance of the UK national political scene, helped nourish renewed calls for a second independence referendum in Scotland on the grounds that there had been a material change in circumstances which warranted revisiting the matter, much earlier than the 'once in a generation' timescale otherwise understood to be a more plausible expectation. For the time being, the Scottish electorate is highly polarized – while the recorded levels of support for separation have yet to scale heights sufficient to make independence more certain, the case for the Union continues to be under pressure. That the UK endures, refracted through a political accommodation built around a 'home rule' settlement with a powerful devolved Parliament, owes as much to public misgivings around separation and fear of the unknown, as it does to warmth and enthusiasm for continued membership in a 'voluntary Union'. Self-rule in Scotland has, arguably, more or less reached its maximum extent – the new contested ground is now on matters of shared rule, that is, matters to be mediated by both London and Edinburgh.

For Northern Ireland, where the atavistic fears and instincts of a divided population had been largely quiescent in the protective institutional framework of, and safeguards afforded by, the Belfast Good Friday Agreement, old enmities and divisions rarely disappear altogether, quickly resurfacing at the behest of events, circumstances and some ill-chosen interventions by politicians and others with more sinister motivations and corresponding actions. The political touchpaper of dormant mutual suspicions and antagonisms was always highly flammable and easily reignited. Hence, together with fundamental disagreements over a host of domestic policy matters that had already resulted in sporadic devolution for much of the earlier period after the Belfast Agreement, Brexit rekindled a fresh political crisis, serving as a ready accelerant to keep the fires burning, and resulting in further suspensions of the devolved institutions. With the long-term shift of demographics and electoral opinion over time, involving the end of a Unionist majority, triumph of Sinn Féin as largest party for the first time, and emergence of a vibrant 'third pillar' of community voting in the form of a rejuvenated Alliance Party at Stormont, Northern Ireland has become a place of multiple minorities and identities supplanting the old bi-confessional, bi-national-cum-ethnic divide. Even if devolution can be restored, therefore, there is growing pressure among nationalist and republicans for a border poll on Irish unification which, while unlikely to be granted in the near term (and with little immediate enthusiasm among the political elite in the Republic of Ireland), has now sparked renewed speculation over Northern Ireland's long-term constitutional status within the UK. Consequently, calls have grown for a re-examination and review of the operation of the devolved institutions and indeed of the wider constitutional architecture for the territorial governance of the British-Irish archipelago. Whatever proposals emerge, it appears that Northern Ireland will remain sui generis, a special case of parity with particularity.

In Wales, where devolution was so vehemently opposed in the 1979 referendum and in which voters only narrowly endorsed its introduction in 1997, developments have been no less pronounced, albeit devoid of the wider scrutiny which, perhaps inevitably, focuses more acutely on the respective experiences of Scotland and Northern Ireland. Nonetheless, something of a quiet revolution has been underway in politics and governance within Wales. While Labour has reasserted its electoral hegemony, certainly in terms of Westminster representation, its continued domination of the devolved government through successive elections has been accompanied by a decisive shift in its approach as well as wider public attitudes. From initial suspicion bordering on hostility to passionate embrace, the Welsh electorate has demonstrated a growing attachment to the rapidly maturing institutions of the devolved settlement in Wales, as demonstrated both in the strength of support for the bolstering of powers of the Assembly (later Parliament) in the 2011 Referendum as well as the growing calls for independence. Though clamouring for independence, for now anyway, is very much a minority pastime in Wales, the Welsh experience, particularly post-Covid, has been one characterized by a fervent belief in the positive achievements that devolution confers. Moreover, under Labour's aegis, Wales has displayed an enthusiasm for devolution alongside a reaffirmation of the benefits of the remaining within the UK. That said, the case for Wales in the Union is not without criticism of the national UK government and its penchant for displays of assertive or muscular unionism which have been held to marginalize, bypass or even flagrantly ignore the devolved institutions, whether over Brexit, Covid or indeed related matters of finance and the role, distribution and capacity of public expenditure to advance well-being. While all too often eclipsed by the greater salience of Scottish and Northern Irish political circumstances, it is clear that Wales has assumed a higher profile – and louder voice – in pan-UK discourse and is no longer prepared to be seen as a constitutional afterthought.

For England, devolution has been a process at which it has been accorded 'observer status' for much of the period since great experiment was launched. The seismic developments leading to devolved institutions in Belfast, Cardiff and Edinburgh arouse a mix of curiosity, indifference, mild resentment or even occasional hostility, not least in terms of the impact of the 'other countries' on the national UK political landscape. These sentiments become heightened especially during periods of minority Westminster government or when the interests of 'the Celtic fringe' are perceived to be injurious to notions of the national (i.e. English) interests. Innovations such as English Votes for English Laws proved, in the end, to be a form of parliamentary novelty that lacked credibility, still less sufficient forethought as to their operationalization and impact. Constituting five-sixths of the UK population, it is inevitable that such an imbalance in the respective size and influence of England with respect to the other three entities of the UK causes some friction, bordering on indignation, among the parties involved. However, to cast the story as one of 'England versus the rest' is to grossly oversimplify matters. Trite and indeed pejorative contentions about 'Perfidious Albion' imply a unity of view, purpose or interest in England that ignores what has become a highly complex and contested political space within that country and which underplay the deep and profound issues, passions and grievances which are no less valid or real for being evident in England as distinct from Scotland, Wales or Northern Ireland. While beyond the scope of our book, it is clear that 'the English question' remains to be answered (if it can be resolved at all) in terms of how England both relates to its fellow parts of the UK but also, and as crucial, to itself. Thus far, beyond some limited examples of administrative devolution, devolution writ large has largely bypassed England, with the failure to launch regional assemblies in the early 2000s seemingly leaving the idea of political devolution stillborn in an English context. Instead, a modest revival of local authority powers based around a curious mix of combined authorities, metro mayors, and city and growth deals appears to be preferred way of devolving power in England, albeit accompanied by a heavy and sustained dose of fiscal retrenchment that serves to emasculate much of local government's practical ability to exercise its recently acquired powers of general competence. The approach may prove its worth in the fullness of time though the fundamental question of the nature of centre-periphery relations in England remains thorny, and answers that command consensus, even more elusive. Nonetheless, England will be indispensable to how the UK's wider territorial governance evolves.

Predictions that political devolution might herald the beginning of the end of the UK – or at least serve as a midwife in its dissolution – are, for now, somewhat wide of the mark. The UK's political union has proved remarkably resilient despite the many pressures to which it has been and remains subjected (including several self-inflicted 'home goals' that serve to undermine its continuity and appeal to the four component parts of which it is comprised). However, for the UK to continue in existence as a political entity, the devolved settlement must evolve, perhaps radically so. No end of examples and possible alternatives can be observed elsewhere among the world's liberal democracies as to how things might be done differently. Space means that comparative analysis with overseas is beyond the scope of this book. Suffice to say, however, that any territorial governance arrangement, and the inter-governmental and political relationships therein, warrant periodic review and refreshment in the light of experience. Sound public administration and good government demand no less. Hence, to some extent, the process of evolution is both natural and desirable, even if there were no existential threat to the Union.

That such jeopardy *is* a credible prospect in the British case demands that those tasked with maintenance of the Union and territorial integrity of the UK conduct their affairs and take appropriate steps accordingly. While no one can guarantee that such an approach might stave off 'the inevitable', cosmetic measures, still less masterly inactivity or indifference by Westminster and Whitehall, will surely exacerbate tensions, stoke disaffection and hasten pressure for secession. Much will depend on the outcome of future General Elections and the political colour of the next administration in London. However, whoever prevails in those contests, a measure of taking stock is timely, along with an assessment of outcomes, deficiencies, achievements and disappointments. Some reconsideration of the purpose and aim of devolution must be warranted. It is fanciful to expect complete consensus to emerge, given the diametrically opposed aspirations of Unionists and separatists, but pragmatism and the needs of the public for whom government at all levels and politicians of all opinions are there to serve, mean it ought to be possible to secure improvements in the working of devolution and the outcomes it facilitates. Hence, tangible reforms around the esteem, role, powers and finance of the devolved institutions, together with a thoroughgoing overhaul of the inter-governmental arrangements between them and London, will be indispensable elements in efforts to make the territorial architecture of the UK more robust, sustainable and fit for the future.

REFERENCES

Alexander, A. (1997), 'Scotland's Parliament and Scottish Local Government: Conditions for a Stable Relationship', *Scottish Affairs*, 19: 22–8.

All Wales Convention (2009), *All Wales Convention Report*. Available online: www.allwalesconvention.org (accessed 21 September 2021).

Anderson, P. (2016), 'The 2016 Scottish Parliament Election: A Nationalist Minority, a Conservative Comeback and a Labour Collapse', *Regional and Federal Studies*, 26 (4): 555–68.

Andrews, L. (2015), 'How Welsh Public Services Benefit from Cross-UK Evidence Exchange', *Institute for Government*, 27 November. Available online: https://www.instituteforgovernment.org.uk/blog/how-welsh-public-services-benefit-cross-uk-evidence-exchange (accessed 25 September 2021).

Armstrong, H. (2015), *Wales, Current Devolution Proposal 2014–15, Standard Note SN/PC/07066*, London: House of Commons Library.

Armstrong, H. and Bowers, P. (2015), *Scotland: Devolution Proposals 2014–15, Standard Note SN/PC/06987*, London: House of Commons Library.

Arter, D. (2006), 'From "Spectral Democracy" to "Inclusive Democracy"? The Peripatetic Committees as Linkage', *Regional and Federal Studies*, 16 (3): 239–62.

Audit Scotland (2021), 'An Overview of Local Government in Scotland 2021'. Available online: www.audit-Scotland.gov.uk/about/ac (accessed 21 September 2021).

Awan-Scully, R. (2018), *The End of British Party Politics*, Hull: Biteback Publishing.

Ayres, S. and Stafford, I. (2014), 'Managing Complexity and Uncertainty in Regional Governance Networks: A Critical Analysis of State Rescaling in England', *Regional Studies*, 48 (1): 219–36.

Ayres, S., Flinders, M. and Sandford, M. (2018), 'Territory, Power and Statecraft: Understanding English Devolution', *Regional Studies*, 52 (6): 853–64.

Basta, K. and Henderson, A. (2021), 'Multinationalism, Constitutional Asymmetry and COVID: UK Responses to the Pandemic', *Nationalism and Ethnic Politics*, 27 (3): 293–310.

Beecham, J. (2006), *Beyond Boundaries: Citizen-centred Local Services for Wales*. Available online: http://www.wales.nhs.uk/sitesplus/documents/829/WAG%20-%20Beyond%20Boundaries%20%28Beecham%20Review%29%202006.PDF (accessed 25 September 2021).

Bevin, G. (2014), *The Impacts of Asymmetric Devolution on Health Care in the Four Countries of the UK*, London: The Health Foundation, The Nuffield Trust.

Birrell, D. (1978) 'The Mechanics of Devolution: Northern Ireland Experience and the Scotland and Wales Bills', *Political Quarterly*, 49 (3): 304–21.

Birrell, D. (2009), *The Impact of Devolution on Social Policy*, Bristol: Policy Press.

Birrell, D. (2010), 'Devolution and Approaches to Social Policy', in G. Lodge and K. Schmuecker (eds), *Devolution in Practice 2010*, 125–40, Newcastle upon Tyne: Institute for Public Policy Research.

Birrell, D. (2012), *Comparing Devolved Government*, Basingstoke: Palgrave Macmillan.

Birrell, D. and Gormley-Heenan, C. (2015), *Multi-Level Governance and Northern Ireland*, Basingstoke: Palgrave.

Birrell, D. and Gray, A.M. (2017), *Delivering Social Welfare*, Bristol: Policy Press.

Birrell, D. and Heenan, D. (2017), 'The Continuing Volatility of Devolution in Northern Ireland: The Shadow of Direct Rule', *The Political Quarterly*, 88 (3): 473–89.

Birrell, D. and Heenan, D. (2020), 'The Confidence and Supply Agreement between the Conservative Party and the Democratic Unionist Party: Implications for the Barnett Formula and Intergovernmental Relations in the UK', *Parliamentary Affairs*, 73 (3): 586–602.

Blair, T. (1998), *Leading the Way: A New Vision for Local Government*, London: Institute of Public Policy Research.

Bochel, C. (2012), 'Petitions: Different Dimensions of Voice and Influence in the Scottish Parliament and the National Assembly for Wales', *Social Policy and Administration*, 46 (2): 142–60.

Bochel, H. and Powell, M. (2016) *The Coalition Government and Social Policy: Restructuring the Welfare State*, Bristol: Bristol Policy Press.

Bogdanor, V. (1999), *Devolution in the United Kingdom*, Oxford: Oxford University Press.

Bogdanor, V. (2001), *Devolution in the United Kingdom*, Oxford: Oxford University Press.

Bort, E. (2012). 'Annals of the Parish: The Year at Holyrood, 2010–11', *Scottish Affairs*, 78 (Winter): 37–85.

Bowers, P. (2012), *Scotland Bill: Amendments in the House of Lords, SN/PC/06302*, London: House of Commons Library.

Bowers, P. (2016), *Wales Bill 2016–17, Briefing Paper No. 07617*, London: House of Commons Library.

Bradbury, J. (2008a), 'Devolution in Wales: An Unfolding Process', in J. Bradbury (ed.), *Devolution, Regionalism and Regional Development: The UK Experience*, 44–66, London: Routledge.

Bradbury, J. (ed.) (2008b), *Devolution, Regionalism and Regional Development*, London: Routledge.

Bradbury, J. and Mitchell, J. (2005), 'Devolution Between Governance and Territorial Politics', *Parliamentary Affairs*, 58 (2): 287–302.

Bradley, A. and Ewing, K. (2007), *Constitutional and Administrative Law*, 14th edn, London: Longman.

Bratberg, Ø. (2009), 'Institutional Resilience Meets Critical Junctures: (Re)allocation of Power in British Parties Post-devolution', *Publius*, 40 (1): 59–81.

Brien, P. (2016), *Public Expenditure by Country and Region, Briefing Paper 04033*, London: House of Commons Library. Available online: https://researchbriefings. files.pa0rliament.uk/documents/SN04033/SN04033.pdf (accessed 25 September 2021).

Brien, P. (2018), *UK Funding from the EU, Briefing Paper 7847*, London: House of Commons Library.

Brien, P. (2019), *The European Investment Bank, Briefing Paper 08145*, London: House of Commons Library.

Brien, P. (2020), *Public Spending by Country and Region, Research Briefing*, London: House of Commons Library.

British-Irish Council (1999), Joint Communique, Summit Meeting. Available online: https://www.britishirishcouncil.org/sites/default/files/communiqu%C3%A9s/1%20-%20Inaugural%20Summit%20-%20London%20-%2017%20Dec%201999.pdf

Brown, G., Harper, B. and Pidgeon, C. (2013), *Update on Fiscal Devolution and Devolved Funding, Research Paper NIAR 903-12*, Belfast: NI Assembly Research and Information Service.

Burnham, J. and Horton, S. (2013), *Public Management in the United Kingdom*, Basingstoke: Palgrave Macmillan.

Cabinet Office (2012), *Devolution, Memorandum of Understanding and Supplementary Agreements*. Available online: https://www.gov.uk/government/publications/devolution-memorandum-of-understanding-and-supplementary-agreement (accessed 1 July 2021).

Cabinet Office (2014), *Memorandum of Understanding: UK and Devolved Governments*. Available online: https://assets.publishing.service.gov.uk/government/uploads/system/uploads/attachment_data/file/316157/MoU_between_the_UK_and_the_Devolved_Administrations.pdf (accessed 1 July 2021).

Cabinet Office (2019), *Devolution Guidance for Civil Servants*. Available online: https://www.gov.uk/government/publications/devolution-guidance-for-civil-servants/devolution-guidance-for-civil-servants (accessed 1 July 2021).

Cabinet Office (2022) *Communiques from the Inter-ministerial Standing Committee*. Available online: https://www.gov.uk/government/publications/communiques-from-the-interministerial-standing-committee/interministerial-standing-committee-communique-29-june-2022 (accessed 1 August 2022).

Cabinet Office and the Department of Levelling-up, Housing and Communities (2022). Review of Intergovernmental Relations.

Cairney, P. (2006), 'The Analysis of Scottish Parliament Committee Influence: Beyond Capacity and Structure in Comparing West European Decisions', *European Journal of Political Research*, 45: 181–208.

Cairney, P. (2007), Using Devolution to Set the Agenda? Venue Shift and the Smoking Ban in Scotland', *The British Journal of Politics and International Relations*, 9 (1): 73–89.

Cairney, P. (2011), *The Scottish Political System Since Devolution: From New Politics to the New Scottish Government*, Exeter: Imprint Academic.

Cairney, P. (2012a), 'Intergovernmental Relations in Scotland. What was the SNP Effect?' *Journal of Politics and International Relations*, 14 (2): 231–49.

Cairney, P. (2012b), *Understanding Public Policy: Theories and Issues*, Basingstoke: Palgrave.

Cairns, A. (2016), *The Devolution of Power to Wales*, Speech by Secretary of State for Wales. Available online: https://www.gov.uk/government/speeches/the-devolution-of-power-to-wales (accessed 25 September 2021).

Cameron, E. (2008) 'The Politics of the Union in the Age of Unionism', in T.M. Devine (ed.), *Scotland and the Union*, 123–9, Edinburgh: Edinburgh University Press.

Carmichael, P. (1992), 'Is Scotland Different? Local Government Policy under Mrs. Thatcher', *Local Government Policy Making*, 18 (5): 25–32.

Carmichael, P. and Knox, C. (2005), 'The Reform of Public Administration in Northern Ireland: From Principles to Practice', *Political Studies*, 53 (4): 772–92.

Chandler, J. (2009), *Local Government Today*, Manchester: Manchester University Press.

Christie Commission (2011), *Commission on the Future Delivery of Public Services*, Edinburgh: Scottish Government.

Cole, A. (2006), *Beyond Devolution and Decentralisation*, Manchester: Manchester University Press.

Cole, A. (2012), 'Serving the Nation: Devolution and the Civil Service in Wales', *British Journal of Politics and International Relations*, 14 (3): 458–76.

Cole, A. and Stafford, I. (2015), *Devolution and Governance: Wales Between Capacity and Constraint*, Basingstoke: Palgrave.

Cole, A., Jones, B. and Storer, A. (2003), 'Inside the National assembly for Wales: The Welsh Civil Service under Devolution', *The Political Quarterly*, 74: 223–32.

Commission on Devolution in Wales (2012), *Part I: Empowerment and Responsibility: Financial Powers to Strengthen Wales*. Available online: https://webarchive.nationalarchives.gov.uk/ukgwa/20140605075122/http:/commissionondevolutioninwales.independent.gov.uk/files/2013/01/English-WEB-main-report1.pdf (accessed 25 September 2021).

Commission on Devolution in Wales ('Silk Commission') (2012), *Empowerment and Responsibility: Financial Powers to Strengthen Wales*, Cardiff: Commission on Devolution in Wales.

Commission on Devolution in Wales (2014), *Part II, Empowerment and Responsibility: Legislative Powers to Strengthen Wales*. Available online: https://www.gov.uk/government/publications/empowerment-and-responsibility-legislative-powers-to-strengthen-wales (accessed 25 September 2021).

Commission on Justice in Wales (2019), *Report*. Available online: https://gov.wales/commission-justice-wales-report (accessed 10 February 2022).

Commission on Parliamentary Reform (2017) *Commission on Parliamentary Reform. 2017*. Report on the Scottish Parliament. Available online: https://www.parliament.scot/parliamentarybusiness/CurrentCommittees/108084.aspx (accessed 1 July 2021).

Commission on Public Service, Governance and Delivery (2014), *Full Report*. Available online: https://gov.wales/sites/default/files/publications/2019-01/commission-public-service-governance-delivery-full-report.pdf (accessed 25 July 2014).

Commission on Scottish Devolution (2009), *Serving Scotland Better: Scotland and the United Kingdom in the 21st Century*. Available online: https://www.qmul.ac.uk/law/maccormick/media/maccormick/timeline/15_06_09_calman.pdf (accessed 25 September 2021).

Convery, A. (2016), *The Territorial Conservative Party: Devolution and Party Change in Scotland and Wales*, Manchester: Manchester University Press.

Cowie, G. (2018), *Legislative Consent and the European Union (Withdrawal) Bill (2017–2019)*, *Research Briefing*, London: House of Commons Library.

Cowie, G. (2018), *Legislative Consent and the European Union (Withdrawal) Bill (2017–2019)*, *Research Briefing*, London: House of Commons Library.

Cunningham, M. (2001), *British Government Policy in Northern Ireland 1969–2000*, Manchester: Manchester University Press.

Curtice, J. (2001), 'Hopes Dashed and Fears Assuaged', in A. Trench (ed.), *The State of the Nations 2001*, Exeter: Impact Academic.

Curtice, J. (2009), 'Devolution, the SNP and the Electorate', in G. Hassan (ed.), *The Modern SNP: From Protest to Power*, 55–68, Edinburgh: Edinburgh University Press.

Curtice, J. (2010), 'Policy Divergence: Recognising Difference or Generating Resentment?' in J. Adams and P. Robinson (eds), *Devolution in Practice: Public Policy Differences*, London: Institute for Public Policy Research.

Curtice, J. (2020), 'High Noon for the Union?' *IPPR Progressive Review*, 27 (3): 223–34.

Cutts, D. and Russell, A. (2015), 'From Coalition to Catastrophe: The Electoral Meltdown of the Liberal Democrats', *Parliamentary Affairs*, 68 (suppl. 1): 70–87.

Danson, M., MacLeod, G. and Mooney, G. (2012), 'Devolution and the Shifting Political Economic Geographies of the United Kingdom', *Environment and Planning C: Government and Policy*, 30: 1–9.

Davies, D.H. (1983), *The Welsh Nationalist Party 1925–1945: A Call to Nationhood*, New York: St Martin's Press.

Davies, J. (1994), *A History of Wales*, New York: Penguin.

Deacon, R. (2006), *Devolution in Britain Today*, Manchester: Manchester University Press.

Denters, B. and Rose, L.E. (eds) (2005), *Comparing Local Governance*, Basingstoke: Palgrave.

Denver, D. (2011), 'Another "historic moment": The Scottish Parliament Elections 2011', *Scottish Affairs*, 76 (Summer): 33–50.

Department for Levelling Up, Housing and Communities (2022a), Levelling-up the UK. Available online: https://www.gov.uk/government/publications/levelling-up-the-united-kingdom (accessed 1 August 2022).

Department for Levelling-Up, Housing and Communities (2022b), Intergovernmental Relations Annual Report 2021. Available online: https://www.gov.uk/government/publications/intergovernmental-relations-review-annual-report-for-2021 (accessed 1 August 2022).

Devine, T.M. (2008), 'The Challenge of Nationalism', in T.M. Devine (ed.), *Scotland and the Union: 1707–2007*, 143–56, Edinburgh: Edinburgh University Press.

Devine, T.M. (2017), *Independence or Union: Scotland's Past and Scotland's Present*, London: Penguin.

Drakeford, M. (2021), Oral evidence to House of Lords Constitution Committee.

Driver, S. and Martell, L. (2002), *Blair's Britain*, Cambridge: Cambridge University Press.

Dunlop, Lord (2017), *Review of UK Government Union Capability*. Available online: https://assets.publishing.service.gov.uk/government/uploads/system/uploads/attachment_data/file/972987/Lord_Dunlop_s_review_into_UK_Government_Union_Capability.pdf (accessed 10 February 2022).

Eggins, B. (2015), *History and Hope: The Alliance Party in Northern Ireland*, Dublin: The History Press.

Electoral Reform Society (2010), *The UK General Election: In-depth*. Available online: http://www.electoral-reform.org.uk/images/dynamicImages/file4e3ff1393b87a.pdf (accessed 25 September 2021).

Elias, A. (2021), 'Election 2021: What to Look Out For in Wales', *The Conversation*, 5 May. Available online: https://theconversation.com/elections-2021-what-to-look-out-for-in-wales-160322 (accessed 25 September 2021).

Enderlein, H., Walti, S. and Zürn, M. (2010), *Handbook on Multi-level Governance*, Cheltenham: Edward Elgar.

Ethrington, E. and Jones, M. (2016), 'Agreeing to Austerity: Does Signing Up to Devolution Challenge the Northern Powerhouse?', *Policy blog*, 17 November. Available online: http://blog.policy.manchester.ac.uk/posts/2016/11/agreeing-to-austerity-does-signing-up-to-devolution-challenge-the-northern-powerhouse/ (accessed 25 September 2021).

Evan, J. and Tonge, J. (2012), 'From Abstentionism to Enthusiasm: Sinn Féin, Nationalist Electors and Support for Devolved Power-sharing in Northern Ireland', *Irish Political Studies*, 28 (1): 39–57.

Evans, A.B. (2015), 'The Squeezed Middle? The Liberal Democrats in Wales and Scotland: A Post-Coalition Reassessment', *Scottish Affairs*, 24 (2): 163–86.

Exworthy, M., Powell, M. and Mannion, E. (eds) (2016), *Evaluating the Coalition's Health Reforms*, Bristol: Policy Press.

Farrington, C. (2001), 'Ulster Unionist Political Divisions in the Late Twentieth Century', *Irish Political Studies*, 16 (1): 49–71.

Farry, S. (2019), 'Alliance's Success is No Fluke – We Have Changed Northern Irish Politics for Good', *New Statesman*, 16 December.

Finlay, R.J. (2008), 'Thatcherism and the Union', in T.M. Devine (ed.), *Scotland and the Union 1707–2007*, Edinburgh: Edinburgh University Press.

Fleming, S. and Osborne, S. (2019) 'The Dynamics of Co-production in the Context of Social Care Personalisation: Testing Theory and Practice in a Scottish Context', *Journal of Social Policy*, 48 (4): 671–97.

Foley, B. (2013), *Scotland and the United Kingdom*, Edinburgh: British Academy Policy Centre 9000, Royal Society of Edinburgh.

Foster, H. (2015), 'The Effectiveness of the Public Accounts Committee in Northern Ireland', *Public Money and Management*, 35 (6): 401–8.

Frain, A. (2019), 'The Scottish Parliament: The UK's Most Fractious Political Scene', *Politics Home*, 29 August. Available online: https://www.politicshome.com/thehouse/article/the-scottish-parliament-the-uks-most-fractious-political-scene (accessed 25 September 2021).

Full Fact (2014), *Is Wales Getting the Best Deal Out of the EU?* Available online: https://fullfact.org/europe/wales-getting-best-deal-out-eu/ (accessed 1 July 2021).

Fyfe, G. and Johnston, K. (2016), 'Gender and Equality in Scotland: Mind the Gap', in D. McTavish (ed.), *Politics in Scotland*, Edinburgh: Edinburgh University Press.

Gallagher, J. (2016), 'Making the Case for Union: Exactly Why Are We Better Together?', in A. McHarg, T. Mullen, A. Page and N. Walker (eds), *The Scottish Independence Referendum*, 127–52, Oxford: Oxford University Press.

Gallagher, J. (2020), 'Intergovernmental Relations: Two Decades of Co-operation, Competition, and Constitutional Change', in M. Keating (ed.), *The Oxford Handbook of Scottish Politics*, 565–83, Oxford: Oxford University Press.

Gamble, A. (2006), 'The Constitutional Revolution in the United Kingdom', *Publius: The Journal of Federalism*, 36 (1): 19–35.

Gash, T., Randall, J. and Sims, S. (2014), *Achieving Political Decentralisation*, London: Institute for Government.

Gordon, T. (2021), 'SNP Ministers Lose Landmark Cases on Extent of Holyrood's Powers', *The Herald*, 6 October. Available online: https://www.heraldscotland.com/politics/19628046.snp-ministers-lose-landmark-cases-extent-holyroods-powers/ (accessed 23 October 2021).

Gray, A.M. and Birrell, E. (2013), 'The Structures of the NHS in Northern Ireland: Divergence, Policy Copying and Policy Deficiency', *Public Policy and Administration*, 28 (3): 274–89.

Greer, S.L. (2004), *Territorial Politics and Health Policy: UK Health Policy in Comparative Perspective*, Manchester: Manchester University Press.

Greer, S.L. (2016), 'Devolution and Health in the UK: Policy and its Lessons since 1998', *British Medical Bulletin*, 118 (1): 16–24.

Greer, S., Jarman, H. and Azorsky, A. (2015), 'Devolution and the Civil Service: A Biographical Study', *Public Policy and Administration*, 30 (1): 31–50.

Greer, S.L., Wilson, I. and Donnelly, P.D. (2016), 'The Wages of Continuity: Health Policy under the SNP', *Scottish Affairs*, 25 (1): 28–44.

Griffiths, S., Kippin, H. and Stoker, G. (eds) (2013), *Public Services: A New Reform Agenda*, London: Bloomsbury.

Guarneros-Meza, V., Downe, J., Entwistle, T. and Martin, S. (2014), 'Putting the Citizen at the Centre? Assembling Local Government Policy in Wales', *Local Government Studies*, 40 (1): 64–81.

Hadfield, B. (2001), 'Seeing It Through? The Multifaceted Implementation of the Belfast Agreement', in R. Wilford (ed.), *Aspects of the Belfast Agreement*, 84–106, Oxford: Oxford University Press.

Hallwood, P. and McDonald, R. (2016), 'Corks on a Beach? Finding a Hard Budget Constraint for the Scottish Government', in D. McTavish (ed.), *Politics in Scotland*, 91–107, Abingdon: Routledge.

Ham, C., Heenan, D., Longlay, M. and Steel, D.R. (2013), *Integrated Care in Northern Ireland, Scotland, England and Wales, Lessons for England*, London: The King's Fund.

Hammond, E. (2015), *Devo Why? Devo How?* London:: Centre for Public Scrutiny.

Harvey, M. (2020), 'Devolution', in *The Oxford Handbook of Scottish Politics*, 370–85, Oxford: Oxford University Press.

Hassan, G. (2009), 'The Making of the Modern SNP: From Protest to Power', in G. Hassan (ed.), *The Modern SNP: From Protest to Power*, 1–18, Edinburgh: Edinburgh University Press.

Hassan, G. and Shaw, E. (2012), *The Strange Death of Labour Scotland*, Edinburgh: Edinburgh University Press.

Hayward, K. (2020), 'The 2019 General Election in Northern Ireland: The Rise of the Centre Ground?', *The Political Quarterly*, 91 (1): 49–55.

Hazell, R. (2000), 'Intergovernmental Relations', in R. Hazel (ed.), in *The State of the Nations*, 149–82, Exeter: Imprint Academic.

Hazell, R.(2001), 'Intergovernmental Relations: Whitehall Rules?' in R. Hazel (ed.), *The State and the Nations*, 149–82, Thorverton: Imprint Academic.

Hazell, R. (2015), *Devolution and the Future of the Union*, London: UCL Constitution Unit. Available online: https://www.ucl.ac.uk/constitution-unit/sites/constitution-unit/files/4fd7c881.pdf (accessed 10 September 2020).

Hazell, R. and Morris, B. (1999), 'Growing Apart', *Public Service Magazine* (May).

Hazell, R. and R. Rawlings (eds) (2005), *Devolution, Law Making and the Constitution*, 71–111, Exeter: Imprint Academic.

Heald, D. (2020), 'The Politics of Scotland's Public Finances', in M. Keating (ed.), *The Oxford Handbook of Scottish Politics*, 512–42, Oxford: Oxford University Press.

Heald, D. and McLeod, A. (2005), 'Revenue Raising by UK Devolved Administrations Within the Context of an Evidence-based Financial System', *Regional and Federal Studies*, 39 (4): 306–12.

Heath, O. and Goodwin, M. (2017), 'The 2017 General Election, Brexit and the Return to Two-Party Politics: An Aggregate Level Analysis of the Result', *The Political Quarterly*, 88 (3): 345–58.

Heenan, D. and Birrell, D. (2018), 'Between Devolution and Direct Rule: Implications of a Political Vacuum in Northern Ireland', *The Political Quarterly*, 89 (2): 306–12.

Hellowell, M. and Pollock, A. (2009), 'Non-Profit Distribution: The Scottish Approach to Private Finance in Public Services', *Social Policy and Society*, 8 (3): 405–18.

Henderson, A. and Mitchell, J. (2018), 'Referendums as Critical Junctures? Scottish Voting in British Elections', *Parliamentary Affairs*, 71 (1): 109–24.

Hennessey, T., Braniff, M., McAuley, J.W., Tonge, J. and Whiting, S.A. (2019), *The Ulster Unionist Party: Country Before Party?* Oxford: Oxford University Press.

Henry, A., Malik, A. and Aydın-Aitchison, A. (2019), 'Local Governance in the New Police Scotland: Renegotiating Power, Recognition and Responsiveness', *European Journal of Criminology*, 16 (5): 573–91.

Hepburn, E., Keating, M. and McEwen, N. (2021), *Scotland's New Choice: Independence after Brexit*, Edinburgh: Centre on Constitutional Change.

Himsworth, C. (1998), 'New Devolution: New Dangers for Local Government', *Scottish Affairs*, 24: 6–28.

HM Government (2015a), *Powers for a Purpose: Towards a Lasting Devolution Settlement for Wales, Cm 9020*, London: Her Majesty's Stationery Office.

HM Government (2015b), *Scotland in the United Kingdom: An Enduring Settlement*, London: Her Majesty's Stationery Office.

HM Government (2019), '*Devolution Guidance for Civil Servants*. Available online: https://www.gov.uk/government/publications/devolution-guidance-for-civil-servants/devolution-guidance-for-civil-servants (accessed 10 September 2020).

HM Government/Welsh Government (2016), *The Agreement between the Welsh Government and the UK Government on the Welsh Government's Fiscal Framework*. Available online: https://gov.wales/sites/default/files/publications/2018-11/agreement-on-welsh-government-fiscal-framework.pdf (accessed 25 September 2021).

HM Revenue and Customs (2013), Air Passenger Duty (APD) Devolution of Rates to Northern Ireland. Available online: https://assets.publishing.service.gov.uk/government/uploads/system/uploads/attachment_data/file/192078/apd_ni_210212.pdf (accessed 1 July 2021).

HM Treasury (2006), 'Chancellor Sets Out St Andrews Agreement Funding
    Package for Northern Ireland', Press Release, 1 November. Available online:
    https://cain.ulster.ac.uk/issues/politics/docs/pmo/gb011106.htm (accessed
    25 September 2021).
HM Treasury (2007) Review of VAT Policy in Northern Ireland (Varney Review).
    Available online: https://data.parliament.uk/DepositedPapers/Files/DEP2008-
    1140/DEP2008-1140.pdf (accessed 1 July 2021).
HM Treasury/Wales Office (2013), *Empowerment and Responsibility: Devolving
    Financial Powers to Wales*. Available online: https://assets.publishing.service.
    gov.uk/government/uploads/system/uploads/attachment_data/file/259359/
    empowerment_and_responsibility_181113.pdf (accessed 25 September 2021).
HM Treasury (2015), *Statement of Funding Policy: Funding the Scottish
    Parliament, National Assembly for Wales and Northern Ireland Assembly*.
    Available online: https://assets.publishing.service.gov.uk/government/uploads/
    system/uploads/attachment_data/file/479717/statement_of_funding_2015_print.
    pdf (accessed 25 September 2021).
HM Treasury (2018), 'Private Finance Initiatives (PFI) and Private Finance 2
    (PF2): Budget 2018 Brief', Press Release, 29 October. Available online: https://
    www.gov.uk/government/publications/private-finance-initiative-pfi-and-private-
    finance-2-pf2-budget-2018-brief (accessed 25 September 2021).
HM Treasury (2020), *HM Treasury and Regional Analysis: November 2020*.
    Available online: https://www.gov.uk-statistics.
HM Treasury (2021a), *Country and Regional Analysis November 2018*. Available
    online: https://assets.publishing.service.gov.uk/government/uploads/system/
    uploads/attachment_data/file/759560/Country_and_Regional_Analysis_
    November_2018_rvsd.pdf (accessed 25 September 2021).
HM Treasury (2021b), Statement of Funding Policy. Funding the Scottish
    Government, Welsh Government and Northern Ireland Executive 9th edition.
HM Treasury (2021c), Levelling-up Fund. Available online: https://assets.
    publishing.service.gov.uk/government/uploads/system/uploads/attachment_data/
    file/966138/Levelling_Up_prospectus.pdf (accessed 1 July 2021).
Holtham, G. (2009), *Final Report: Fairness and Accountability: A New Funding
    Settlement for Wales*, Cardiff: Independent Commission on Funding and
    Finance for Wales.
Hooghe, L. and Marks, G. (2003) 'Unravelling the Central State, but How? Types
    of Multi-level Governance', *American Political Science Review*, 97 (2): 233–43.
Hooghe, L. and Marks, G. (2010), 'Types of Multi-level Governance', in
    H. Enderlein, S. Walti and M. Zurn (eds), *Handbook of Multi-level Governance*,
    17–32, Cheltenham: Edward Elgar.
Hooghe, L. and Marks, G. (2016) *Community, Scale and Regional Governance:
    A Postfunctionalist Theory of Governance*, Vol. II, Oxford: Oxford University
    Press.
Housden, P. (2014), 'This Is Us: A Perspective on Public Services in Scotland',
    Public Policy and Administration, 29 (1): 64–74.
House of Commons Communities and Local Government Committee (2016)
    *Devolution; The Next Five Years and Beyond, First Report of Session 2015–16
    HC 369*, London: The Stationary Office.
House of Commons Justice Committee (2009), *Devolution: A Decade On, Hc 529*,
    London: The Stationery Office.

House of Commons Library (2011), *Scotland Bill Research Paper 11/06*, London: House of Commons.

House of Commons Library (2021), *The UK Shared Prosperity Fund*, London: House of Commons.

House of Commons Public Accounts Committee (2018), *Private Finance Initiatives*, Conclusions. Available online: https://publications.parliament.uk/pa/cm201719/cmselect/cmpubacc/894/89405.htm (accessed 25 September 2021).

House of Commons Public Accounts Committee (2019), *Funding for Scotland, Wales and Northern Ireland*. Available online: https://publications.parliament.uk/pa/cm201719/cmselect/cmpubacc/1751/175102.htm (accessed 25 September 2021).

House of Commons Public Administration and Constitutional Affairs Committee (2016*), The Funding of the Union Part Two: Intro-instructional relations in the UK. HC834*, London: House of Commons.

House of Commons Treasury Committee (2011), *Private Finance Initiatives*. Available online: https://publications.parliament.uk/pa/cm201012/cmselect/cmtreasy/1146/1146.pdf (accessed 25 September 2021).

House of Lords (2009), *The Barnett Formula, HL Paper 139*, London: The Stationery Office.

House of Lords Constitutional Committee (2015) *Inter-governmental Relations in the United Kingdom HL-146*. Available online: https://publications.parliament.uk/pa/ld201415/ldselect/ldconst/146/146.pdf (accessed 1 July 2021).

House of Lords Select Committee on the Constitution (2016), *The Union and Devolution*, HL Paper 149. Available online: https://publications.parliament.uk/pa/ld201516/ldselect/ldconst/149/149.pdf (accessed 25 September 2021).

House of Lords Select Committee on the Constitution (2018), European Union (Withdrawal Bill).

House of Lords Select Committee on the Constitution (2022), *Respect and Co-operation: Building a Stronger Union for the 21st Century*, HC 142, London: House of Lords.

Hudson, N. (2022), *The UK Shared Prosperity Fund: Competing Claims*. May 17th Scottish Parliament. Available online: https://spice-spotlight.scot/2022/05/17/the-uk-shared-prosperity-fund-competing-claims (accessed 1 August 2022).

Hunt, J. and Minto, R. (2017), 'Between Intergovernmental Relations and Paradiplomacy: Wales and the Brexit of the Regions', *British Journal of Politics and International Relations*, 19 (4): 647–62.

Hunt, J. and Phylip, H. (2018) *Partners no More Scotland Wales and the Withdrawal Bill in the House of Lords. UK in a Changing Europe*. Available online: https://ukandeu.ac.uk/partners-no-more-scotland-wales-and-the-withdrawal-bill-in-the-house-of-lords/ (accessed 1 July 2021).

Ifan, G. and Sion, C. (2019a), *Devolving Welfare: How Well Would Wales fare?*, Wales Fiscal Analysis. Available online: https://www.cardiff.ac.uk/__data/assets/pdf_file/0010/1476352/devolving_welfare_final2.pdf (accessed 25 September 2021).

Ifan, G. and Sion, C. (2019b), *Cut to the Bone? An Analysis of Local Government Finances in Wales, 2009–10 to 2017–18 and the Outlook to 2023–24*, Cardiff: Wales Governance Centre, Cardiff University. Available online: https://www.cardiff.ac.uk/__data/assets/pdf_file/0009/1432719/local_government_finance_report_jan19_final.pdf (accessed 29 July 2021).

Ilott, O. (2016), *The Civil Service in the Devolved Nations*, Institute for Government, 14 June. Available online https://www.instituteforgovernment.org.uk/blog/civil-service-devolved-nations (accessed 10 September 2020).

Independent Commission on Funding and Finance for Wales (2009), *Funding Devolved Government in Wales: Barnett and Beyond (Holdham Commission)*, Cardiff: Independent Commission on Funding and Finance for Wales.

Independent Fiscal Commission for Northern Ireland (2021), *Final Report – More Fiscal Devolution for Northern Ireland?* Available online: https://www.fiscalcommissionni.org/evidence/fcni-interim-report-more-fiscal-devolution-northern-ireland (accessed 10 February 2022).

Institute for Government (2018), Sewel Convention. Available online: https://www.instituteforgovernment.org.uk/explainers/sewel-convention (accessed 1 July 2021).

Institute for Government (2020a), 'Location of the Civil Service'. Available online: https://www.instituteforgovernment.org.uk/explainers/location-of-civil-service (accessed 10 September 2020).

Institute for Government (2020b), *Co-ordination and Divergence: Devolution and Coronavirus*, London: Institute for Government.

Institute for Government (2021), *Electoral Systems across the UK*, London: Institute for Government. Available online: https://www.instituteforgovernment.org.uk/explainers/electoral-systems-uk (accessed 12 September 2020).

Jarman, H. and Greer, S.L. (2015), 'The Big Bang: Health and Social Care Reforms under the Coalition', in M. Beech and S. Lee (eds), *The Conservative-Liberal Coalition: Examining the Cameron-Clegg Government*, 55–67, Basingstoke: Palgrave Macmillan.

Jeffery, C. (2002), 'Uniformity and Diversity in Policy Provision: Insights from the US, Germany and Canada', in J. Adams and P. Robinson (eds), *Devolution in Practice: Public Policy Differences Within the UK*, 176–97,London: Institute for Public Policy Research and the Economic Social Research Council.

Jeffery, C. (2006), 'Devolution and Local Government', *Publius: The Journal of Federalism*, 36 (1): 57–73.

Jeffery, C. (2007), 'The Unfinished Business of Devolution', *Public Policy and Administration*, 22 (1): 92–108.

Jeffery, C. (2009), 'Devolution in the United Kingdom: Problems of a Piecemeal Approach to Constitutional Change', *Publius: The Journal of Federalism*, 39 (2): 289–314.

Jeffery, C. and Palmer, R. (2003), 'Stepping Sofely onto the International Stage: The External Relations of Scotland and Wales', in Hrbek, R. (ed.), *External Relations of Regions in Europe and the World*, 159–70, Baden-Baden: Nomos Verlag.

Jeffery, C. and Wincott, D. (2006), 'Devolution in the United Kingdom: Statehood and Citizenship in Transition', *The Journal of Federalism*, 36 (1): 3–18.

Johns, R. (2021), 'As You Were: The Scottish Parliament Election of 2021', *The Political Quarterly*, 92 (3): 493–9.

Johnston, J. (2009), 'The Legislative Process: The Parliament in Practice', in C. Jeffrey and J. Mitchell, *The Scottish Parliament 1999–2009: The First Decade*, 29–36, London: Hansard Society.

Jones, E., Richards, M. and Thomas, A. (2016), *The Wales Bill: Reserved Matters and their Effect on the Assembly's Legislative Competence, Legal and Research Briefing*, Cardiff: National Assembly for Wales Research Service.

Jones, T. and Lister, S. (2019), 'Localism and Police Governance in England & Wales: Exploring continuity and change', *European Journal of Criminology*, 16 (5): 552–572.

Judge, D. (2005), *Political Institutions in the United Kingdom*, Oxford: Oxford University Press.

Kay, A. (2003), 'Evaluating Devolution in Wales', *Political Studies*, 51 (1): 51–66.

Keating, M. (2002), 'Devolution and Public Policy in the United Kingdom: Divergence or Convergence?' in J. Adams and P. Robinson (eds), *Devolution in Practice*, London: Institute for Public Policy Research.

Keating, M. (2005), *The Government of Scotland: Public Policy Making after Devolution*, Edinburgh: Edinburgh University Press.

Keating, M. (2010), *The Government of Scotland: Public Policy Making after Devolution*, Edinburgh: Edinburgh University Press.

Keating, M. (2013), *Rescaling the European State. The Making of Territory and the Rise of the Meso*, Oxford: Oxford University Press.

Keating, M. (2017), *A Wealthier, Fairer Scotland: The Political Economy of Constitutional Change*, Edinburgh: Edinburgh University Press.

Keep, M. (2020), *Country and Regional Public Sector Finances*, London: House of Commons Library.

Kennedy, S. (2015), *Further Devolution of Powers to Scotland: Devolved Benefits and Additional Discretionary Payments, Standard Note SN07107*, London: House of Commons Library.

Kennedy, S., McInnes, R., Bellis, A., O'Donnell, M. and Steele, S. (2019), *Devolution of Welfare*, London: House of Commons Library.

Kenny, M. (2022), *Relations between the UK and Devolved Governments*. Bennett Institute for Public Policy. Available online: https://www.bennettinstitute.cam. ac.uk/blog/uk-and-devolved-governments (accessed 1 August 2022).

Kenny, M. and Sheldon, J. (2020), *How Covid-19 is Exposing Unresolved Issues about How England is Governed*, London: The British Academy.

Kilbrandon, Lord (1973), *Royal Commission on the Constitution, Vol. 1, Cmnd 5460*, London: HMSO.

Knox, C. and Carmichael, P. (2007), '"Bureau Shuffling": The Review of Public Administration in Northern Ireland', *Public Administration*, 84 (4): 941–65.

Knox, C. and Carmichael, P. (2015), 'Local Government Reform: Community Planning and the Quality of Life in Northern Ireland', *Administration*, 63 (2): 31–58.

Laffin, M. and Shaw, E. (2007), 'British Devolution and the Labour Party: How a National Party Adapts to Devolution', *British Journal of Politics and International Relations*, 9 (1): 55–72.

Laffin, M., Taylor, G. and Thomas, A. (2002), *A New Partnership?: The National Assembly for Wales and Local Government*, York: Joseph Rowntree Foundation.

Law, A. (2012), 'Between Autonomy and Dependency: State and Nation in Devolved Scotland', in G. Mooney and C. Scott (eds), *Social Justice and Social Policy in Scotland*, 25–42, Bristol: Policy Press.

Lewis, H. (2019), 'Why Nationalists Fail: The Welsh independence Movement Lags Far Behind the Scottish Version. Why?' *The Atlantic*, 11 December. Available online: https://www.theatlantic.com/international/archive/2019/12/uk-election-wales-scotland-independence/603283/ (accessed 25 September 2021).

Local Government Association (2015), *English Devolution: Local Solutions for a Successful Nation*, London: Local Government Association.

Lodge, G. and Schmuecker, K. (eds) (2010), *Devolution in Practice*, London: Institute for Public Policy.

Lodge, G. and Trench, A. (2014), 'More Devolution Would Benefit and Improve the Whole of the United Kingdom', *Democratic Audit Blog*, 18 March.

Lowndes, V. and Pratchett, L. (2012), 'Local Governance under the Coalition Government: Austerity, Localism and the "big society"', *Local Government Studies*, 38: 21–40.

Lundberg, T.C. (2007), *Proportional Representation and the Constituency Role in Britain*, Basingstoke: Palgrave Macmillan.

Lynch, P. (2001), *Scottish Government and Politics: An Introduction*, Edinburgh: Edinburgh University Press.

Lynch, P. and Hopkins, S. (2010) 'The British-Irish Council: Progress Frustrated', *Regional Studies*, 35 (8): 753–8.

Lynch, P. and McAngus, C. (2012), 'A Sign of Things to Come? The Collapse of the Liberal Democrats at the Scottish Election 2011', PSA Paper.

Lyons, M. (2007), *Lyons Inquiry into Local Government: Place Shaping: A Shared Ambition for the Future of Local Government*, London: The Stationery Office.

Mackay, C. (2009), 'The SNP and the Scottish Parliament: The Start of a New Sang?' in G. Hassan (ed), *The Modern SNP: From Protest to Power*, 79–92, Edinburgh: Edinburgh University Press.

MacKinnon, D. (2015), 'Devolution, State Restructuring and Policy Divergence in the UK', *The Geographical Journal*, 181 (1): 47–56.

Mackley, A. and McInnes, R. (2020), *Social Security Powers in the UK*, *Research Briefing*, 9 November. Available online: https://commonslibrary.parliament.uk/research-briefings/cbp-9048/ (accessed 25 September 2021).

Madgwick, P. and Rose, R. (eds) (1982), *The Territorial Dimension in United Kingdom Politics*, Basingstoke: Macmillan.

Mair, C. (2016), 'Scottish Local Government: Past, Present and Futures', in D. McTavish (ed.), *Politics in Scotland*, 108–22, Abingdon: Routledge.

Making Laws for Wales. Available online: https://senedd.wales/how-we-work/our-role/making-laws/ (accessed 1 August 2022).

McAllister, L. (2001) *Plaid Cymru: The Emergence of a Political Party*, Bridgend: Poetry Wales Press.

McAngus, C. (2015), 'Party Elites and the Search for Credibility: Plaid Cymru and the SNP as New Parties of Government', *British Journal of Politics and International Relations*, 18 (3): 634–49.

McAteer, M. and Bennett, M. (2005), 'Devolution and Local Government: Evidence from Scotland', *Local Government Studies*, 31 (3): 285–306.

McConnell, A. (2006), 'Centre-Local Government Relations in Scotland', *International Review of Administrative Sciences*, 72 (1): 73–84.

McEwen, N. (2002), 'State Welfare Nationalism: The Territorial Impact of Welfare State Development in Scotland', *Regional and Federal Studies*, 12 (1): 65–90.

McEwen, N. (2017), 'Still Better Together? Purpose and Power in Inter-governmental Councils in the UK', *Regional and Federal Studies*, 27 (5): 667–90.

McEwen, N. and Parry, R. (2005), 'Devolution and the Preservation of the United Kingdom Welfare State', in N. McEwen and L. Moreno (eds), *The Territorial Politics of Welfare*, Ch. 2, London: Routledge.

McEwen, N., Kenny, M., Sheldon, J. and Swan, C. (2020), 'Intergovernmental Relations in the UK: Time for a Radical Overhaul?', *Political Quarterly*, 91 (3): 632–40.

McEwen, N., Swendon, W. and Bolleyer, N. (2012), 'Inter-governmental Relations in the UK: Continuity in a Time of Change?' *British Journal of Politics and International Relations*, 14 (2): 323–42.

McGarvey, N. (2002), 'Intergovernmental Relations in Scotland Post-devolution', *Local Government Studies*, 28 (3): 29–48.

McGarvey, N. (2003), 'Intergovernmental Relations in Scotland Post-devolution', in P. Carmichael and A. Midwinter (eds), *Regulating Local Government: Emerging Patterns of Central Control*, 29–48, London: Frank Cass.

McGarvey, N. (2012), 'Expectations, Assumptions and Realities: Scottish Local Government Post-Devolution', *BJPIR*, 14 (1): 153–74.

McGarvey, N. (2020), 'Local Government', in M. Keating (ed.), *The Oxford Handbook of Scottish Politics*, 544–64, Oxford: Oxford University Press. DOI: 10.1093/oxfordhb/9780198825098.013.2.

McGarvey, N. and Cairney, P. (2008), *Scottish Politics: An Introduction*, Basingstoke: Palgrave Macmillan.

McGlinchey, M. (2019), 'Does Moderation Pay in a Consociational Democracy? The Marginalisation of the SDLP in the North of Ireland', *Swiss Political Science Review*, 25 (4): 426–49.

McHarg, A. (2015), 'The Constitutional Implications of the Rise of the SNP', *LSE Constitution UK blog*. Available online: http://eprints.lse.ac.uk/63239/1/democraticaudit.com-The%20constitutional%20implications%20of%20the%20rise%20of%20the%20SNP.pdf (accessed 25 September 2021).

McHarg, A., and Mitchell, J. (2017). 'Brexit and Scotland', *The British Journal of Politics and International Relations*, 19(3): 512–26.

McHarg, A., Mullen, T., Page, A. and Walker, N. (eds) (2016), *The Scottish Independence Referendum*, Oxford: Oxford University Press.

McIntosh, N. (1999), *Commission on Local Government and the Scottish Parliament*, Edinburgh: Scottish Executive.

McKeever, G. (2016), *Social Security Devolution: Northern Ireland and Scotland*, Briefing Paper. Available online: https://archive2021.parliament.scot/S5_Social_Security/Inquiries/112._McKeever_Professor_Grainne.pdf (accessed 25 September 2021).

McKenna, H. (2015), *Devolution: What it Means for Health and Social Care in England*, London: The King's Fund.

McTavish, D. (2016), 'Political Parties in Scotland', in D. McTavish (ed.), *Politics in Scotland*, 59–90, Abington: Routledge.

Midwinter, A. (2006), 'The Barnett Formula and its Critics Revisited, Evidence from the Post Devolution Period', *Scottish Affairs*, 55: 64–86.

Midwinter, A. and McGarvey, N. (1997), 'The Reformed System of Local Government Finance in Scotland', *Policy and Politics*, 25 (2): 143–52.

Mitchell, J. (2009), *Devolution in the UK*, Manchester: Manchester University Press.

Mitchell, J. (2014), *The Scottish Question*, Oxford: Oxford University Press.

Mitchell, J. (2015), 'Sea Change in Scotland', *Parliamentary Affairs*, 68 ((Suppl. 1): 88–100.

Mitchell, J. and Henderson, A. (2020), 'Elections and Electoral Systems', in M. Keating (ed.), *The Oxford Handbook of Scottish Politics*, 203–19, Oxford: Oxford University Press.

Mitchell, J., Bennie, L. and Johns, J. (2012), *The Scottish National Party: Transition to Power*, Oxford: Oxford University Press.

Mitchell, J., Johns, R. and Bennie, L. (2009), 'Who are the SNP Members?' in G. Hassan (ed), *The Modern SNP: From Protest to Power*, 68–78, Edinburgh: Edinburgh University Press.

Moon, D.S. (2013), 'Rhetoric and Policy Learning: On Rhodri Morgan's "Clear Red Water" and "Made in Wales" Health Policies', *Public Policy and Administration*, 28 (3): 306–23.

Moon, D. and Evans, T. (2017), 'Welsh Devolution and the Problem of Legislative Competence', *British Politics*, 12 (3): 335–60.

Mooney, G. and Scott, G. (2012), 'Devolution, Social Justice and Social Policy: The Scottish Context', in G. Mooney and G. Scott (eds), *Social Justice and Social Policy in Scotland*, 1–24, Bristol: Policy Press.

Mooney, G. and Williams, C. (2006), 'Forging "new ways of life"? Social Policy and Nation Building in Devolved Scotland and Wales', *Critical Social Policy*, 26 (3): 608–29.

Mooney, G., Scott, G. and Williams, C. (2006), 'Rethinking Social Policy Through Devolution', *Critical Social Policy*, 26 (3): 483–97.

Morphet, M. (2022), *The Impact of Covid-19 on Devolution,* Recentralising the British State beyond Brexit? Bristol: Bristol University Press.

Moss, N. and Jones, E. (2017), *Research Briefing: The European Union (Withdrawal) Bill: An Introductory Guide*, Cardiff: National Assembly for Wales, Research Services.

Mullen, T. (2016), 'Devolution of Social Security', *Edinburgh Law Review*, 20 (3): 382–8.

Mullen, T. and Hunt, J. (2019), 'Review of Implications of Brexit-Related UK Legislation for Devolved Competence', Scottish Parliament Paper. Available online: https://archive2021.parliament.scot/S5_Finance/General%20 Documents/201908_Paper_by_Prof_Tom_Mullen_and_Prof_Jo_Hunt.pdf (accessed 1 July 2021).

Murphy, M. (2009), 'Pragmatic Politics: The Ulster Unionist Party and the European Union', *Irish Political Studies*, 24 (4): 589–602.

Murphy, M.C. and Evershed, J. (2019), 'Between the Devil and the DUP: The Democratic Unionist Party and the Politics of Brexit', *British Politics*, 15: 456–77.

National Assembly for Wales (2004), *Report of the Richard Commission, Commission on the Powers and Electoral Arrangements of the National Assembly for Wales*, Cardiff: National Assembly for Wales.

National Assembly for Wales (2011), *The Road to the Independent Commission on devolution in Wales, Paper No. 11/052*, Cardiff: National Assembly for Wales Research Service.

National Assembly for Wales (2018), 'Wales in the World: An Inquiry into the Welsh Government's Approach to External Affairs'. Available online: www.business.senedd/wales (accessed 25 September 2021).

National Assembly for Wales (2019), 'Legislation (Wales) Act 2019 – Explanatory Notes'. Available online: https://www.legislation.gov.uk/anaw/2019/4/notes/division/3/2/16 (accessed 25 September 2021).

National Assembly for Wales (2021), *Economy, Infrastructure and Skllls Committee Fifth Legacy Report*. Available online: https://senedd.wales/committees/economy-infrastructure-and-skills-committee-fifth-senedd/ (accessed 1 July 2021).

National Assembly for Wales, Assessment Commission (2016), *A Platform for Strength: The Legacy Report of the National Assembly for Wales Commission*. Available online: https://business.senedd.wales/documents/s49421/Legacy%20Report%202011-2016.pdf (accessed 25 September 2021).

National Assembly for Wales, Constitutional and Legislative Affairs Committee (2016), *Report on the UK Government's Wales Bill*. Available online: https://senedd.wales/laid%20documents/cr-ld10771/cr-ld10771-e.pdf (accessed 25 September 2021).

National Audit Office (2019), *Investigation into Devolved Funding, HC 1990*. Available online: https://www.nao.org.uk/wp-content/uploads/2019/02/Investigation-into-devolved-funding.pdf (accessed 25 September 2021).

National Audit Office (2021), *Administration of Scottish Income Tax 2019–20, HC 1074*. Available online: https://www.nao.org.uk/wp-content/uploads/2021/01/Administration-of-Scottish-income-tax-2019-20-.pdf (accessed 25 September 2021).

Nichol, A. (2013), 'The Capacity of the Civil Service in Wales', in J. Osmond and S. Upton (eds), *A Stable, Sustainable Settlement for Wales*, 30–42, Cardiff: UK Changing Union Partnership.

Northern Ireland Affairs Committee (2018), *Devolution and Democracy in Northern Ireland – Dealing with the Deficit*. Available online: https://publications.parliament.uk/pa/cm201719/cmselect/cmniaf/613/61302.htm (accessed 1 July 2021).

Northern Ireland Assembly (2013), *Report of the Committee Group Review of the Committee System of the Northern Ireland Assembly, October 2013, NIA 135/11–15*. Available online: http://www.niassembly.gov.uk/assembly-business/committees/report-of-the-committee-review-group-review-of-the-committee-system-of-the-northern-ireland-assembly-october-2013/ (accessed 25 September 2021).

Northern Ireland Assembly (2014), *The Barnett Formula: Update 2014*, Belfast: NI Assembly Research and Information Service.

Northern Ireland Assembly (2016), *Public Accounts Committee, Legacy Report 2011–16*, Belfast: NI Assembly.

Northern Ireland Assembly Committee for Finance and Personnel (2015), *Report on the Review of the Operation of the Barnett Formula*, Belfast: NIA.

Northern Ireland Office (1998), *The Agreement*, Belfast: Northern Ireland Office.

Northern Ireland Office (2010) *Hillsborough Castle Agreement*, February 2010. Available online: https://www.gov.uk/government/publications/hillsborough-castle-agreement (accessed 1 July 2021).

Northern Ireland Office (2018) *The Belfast Agreement: Agreement Reached at the Multi-party talks on Northern Ireland*. April 1998. Available online: https://assets.publishing.service.gov.uk/government/uploads/system/uploads/attachment_data/file/1034123/The_Belfast_Agreement_An_Agreement_Reached_at_the_Multi-Party_Talks_on_Northern_Ireland.pdf (accessed 1 July 2021).

Northern Ireland Office (2019), *Annual Reports and Accounts 2018–19. HC 52*, London: Stationery Office.

Northern Ireland Office (2020), *New Decade, New Approach*, Belfast: Northern Ireland Office.

Nyatanga, D. (2020), 'Welsh Independence: Can Brexit Awaken the Sleeping Dragon?', *LSE blog*, 4 June. Available online: https://blogs.lse.ac.uk/brexit/2020/06/04/welsh-independence-can-brexit-awaken-the-sleeping-dragon/ (accessed 25 September 2021).

O'Brien, P. and Pike, A. (2015), 'City Deals, Decentralisation and the Governance of Local Infrastructure Funding and Financing in the UK', *National Institute Economic Review*, 233: R14–R26.

O'Kane, E. (2010), 'Learning from Northern Ireland? The Uses and Abuses of the Irish Model', *British Journal of Politics and International Relations*, 12 (3): 239–56.

Office of the First Minister and Deputy First Minister (OFMDFM) (2010), *Departmental Spending Plans 2010–11*. Available online: http://www.niassembly.gov.uk/assembly-business/official-report/committee-minutes-of-evidence/session-2009-2010/february-2010/revised-departmental-spending-plans-2010-11/ (accessed 25 September 2021).

Office of the Secretary of State for Scotland (2015), *Scotland in the United Kingdom. An Enduring Settlement*, CM 8990, London: Stationery Office.

Office of the Secretary of State for Scotland (Scotland Office) (2018), *Annual Report and Accounts 2018–19, HC 2360*, London: House of Commons.

Office of the Secretary of State for Wales (Wales Office) (2019), *Annual Report and Accounts 2019–2020, HC 566*, London: House of Commons.

Oliver, D. (2003), *Constitutional Reform in the United Kingdom*, Oxford: Oxford University Press.

ONS (2017), *Personal Well-being in the UK: January to December 2017: Estimates of Personal Well-being in the UK, with Analysis by Country*. Available online: https://www.ons.gov.uk/peoplepopulationandcommunity/wellbeing/bulletins/measuringnationalwellbeing/januarytodecember2017 (accessed 1 July 2021).

ONS (2018), *Civil Service Statistics*. Available online: https://www.ons.gov.uk/employmentandlabourmarket/peopleinwork/publicsectorpersonnel/bulletins/civilservicestatistics/2018 (accessed 10 September 2020).

ONS (2019), *Country and Regional Public Sector Finances: Financial Years Ending 2019*. Available online: https://www.ons.gov.uk/economy/governmentpublicsectorandtaxes/publicsectorfinance/articles/countryandregionalpublicsectorfinances/financialyearending2019 (accessed 1 July 2021).

Oung, C. (2020), 'Social Care across the Four Countries of the UK: What Can We Learn?', *Nuffield Trust*, 18 March. Available online: https://www.nuffieldtrust.org.uk/news-item/social-care-across-the-four-countries-of-the-uk-what-can-we-learn (accessed 25 September 2021).

Oung, C., Curry, N. and Schlepper, L. (2020), 'Who Organises and Funds Social Care?' *Nuffield Trust*, 18 March. Available online: https://www.nuffieldtrust.org.uk/news-item/who-organises-and-funds-social-care (accessed 25 September 2021).

Oung, C., Schlepper, L. and Curry, N. (2020) "What Steps Are Currently Being Taken to Reform Social Care?' *Nuffield Trust*, 18 March 2020. Available online: https://www.nuffieldtrust.org.uk/news-item/what-steps-are-currently-being-taken-to-reform-social-care (accessed 25 September 2021).

Page, A. (2016), 'The Referendum Debate: The Democratic Deficit and the Governance of Scotland', in A. McHarg, T. Mullen, A. Page and N. Walker (eds), *The Scottish Independence Referendum*, Ch. 12, Oxford: Oxford University Press.

Page, E. (1978), 'Why Should Central-Local Relations in Scotland Be Different to Those in England?', *Public Administration Bulletin*, 28: 51–72.

Palmer, R. (2008), *Devolution, Asymmetry and Europe: Multi-Level Governance in the United Kingdom*, Brussels: P.I.E. Peter Lang.

Parliament (2015), *Lessons for Civil Service Impartiality from the Scottish Independence Referendum – Public Administration – 2 Serving Two Masters: A Unified Civil Service*. Available online: https://publications.parliament.uk/pa/cm201415/cmselect/cmpubadm/111/11105.htm (accessed 10 September 2020).

Parliament (2016), *The Future of the Union, Part Two: Inter-institutional Relations in the UK – 4 The Civil Service, Post-devolution*. Available online: https://publications.parliament.uk/pa/cm201617/cmselect/cmpubadm/839/83907.htm (accessed 10 September 2020).

Parry, R. (1982), 'The Centralisation of the Scottish Office: An Administrative History', paper to the Political Studies Association annual conference, April.

Parry, R. (2007), 'Social Security under Devolution in the United Kingdom', in J. V. Langendonck (ed.), *The Right to Social Security*, 109–19, Antwerp: Intersentia.

Parry, R. (2012a), 'What Can UK Public Administration Learn from the Devolved Nations?', *Public Policy and Administration*, 27 (3): 248–64.

Parry, R. (2012b), 'The Civil Service and Intergovernmental Relations in the Post-Devolution UK', *British Journal of Politics and International Relations*, 14 (2): 285–302.

Parry, R. (2016), 'Civil Service and Machinery of Government', in D. McTavish (ed.), *Politics in Scotland*, 123–39, London: Routledge.

Parry, R. (2020a), 'The Civil Service and Government Structures', in M. Keating (ed.), *The Oxford Handbook of Scottish Politics*, 386–404, Oxford: Oxford University Press.

Parry, R. (2020b), *Under the Spotlight: The Civil Service in the Scottish Devolved System*, Edinburgh: Centre on Constitutional Change, University of Edinburgh.

Paun, A. and McCrory, S. (2019), *Has Devolution Worked? The First 20 Years*, London: Institute for Government.

Paun, A. and Munro, R. (2015), *Governing in an Ever Looser Union: How the Four Governments of the UK Co-Operate, Negotiate and Compete*, London: Institute of Government. Available online: http://www.instituteforgovernment.org.uk/publications/governing-ever-looser-union (accessed 25 September 2021).

Paun, A., Bishop, T.K., Valsamidis, L. and de Costa, A. (2019), *Ministers Reflect on Devolution*, London: Institute for Government. Available online: https://www.instituteforgovernment.org.uk/publications/ministers-reflect-devolution (accessed 10 September 2020).

Paun, A., Cheung, A. and Nicholson, E. (2021), *Funding Devolution: The Barnett Formula in Theory and Practice*, London: Institute for Government.

Paun, A., Cheung, A. and Valsamidis, L. (2019), *Devolution at 20*, London: Institute for Government.

Paun, A., Rutter, J. and Nicholl, A. (2016), *Devolution as a Policy Laboratory: Evidence Sharing and Learning between the UK's Four Governments*, London: Alliance for Useful Evidence/Institute for Government. Available online: https://

www.instituteforgovernment.org.uk/publications/devolution-policy-laboratory (accessed 25 September 2021).

Paun, A., Sargeant, J. and Nicholson, E. (2020), 'Sewel Convention', *Institute for Government*, 8 December. Available online: https://www.instituteforgovernment. org.uk/explainers/sewel-convention (accessed 25 September 2021).

Pearce, N. (2011), 'The Decline of the Conservative Party in Scotland Has More to do with its Own Failings than the Rise of the SNP', *LSE blog*, 7 September. Available online: https://blogs.lse.ac.uk/politicsandpolicy/decline-scottish-conservative-party/ (accessed 25 September 2021).

Pemberton, S. (2016), 'Statecraft, Scalecraft and Local Government Reorganisation in Wales', *Environment and Planning C: Government and Policy*, 34 (7): 1306–23.

Pemberton, S. and Lloyd, G. (2008), 'Devolution, Community Planning and Institutional Decongestion', *Local Government Studies*, 34 (4): 437–51.

Phillips, D. (2015), *Health Spending Protected by More in England, But Social Services Spending Protected More in Wales*, Institute for Fiscal Studies. Available online: https://ifs.org.uk/publications/7591 (accessed 25 September 2021).

Pidgeon, C. (2010), *Methods of Budgeting*. NIA Research Paper, 06/10. Belfast: NIA.

Political and Constitutional Reform Committee (2015), *The Funding of Devolution after the Scottish Referendum, HC 700*, London: The Stationery Office.

PricewaterhouseCoopers (2013), *Fiscal Powers: A Review of the Fiscal Powers of the Northern Ireland Assembly*, Belfast: NICVA Centre for Economic Empowerment.

Prosser, P. (2003), *Development of a Welsh Public Service*, Cardiff: Institute for Welsh Affairs.

Qvortrup, M. (2016), 'Scotland and British Constitutional Reform: "Oops, I did it again!" Cameron and the Britney Spears Model of Constitutional Reform', in D. McTavish (ed.), *Politics in Scotland*, 229–42, London: Routledge.

Ralston, R. and Smith, K. (2017), 'Congruence and Incoherence: Public Health Governance and Policy in a Devolved UK', in M. Bevir and J. Waring, *Decentring Health Policy: Learning from British Experiences in Healthcare Governance*, 148–67, London: Routledge.

Randall, J. and Casebourne, J. (2016) *Making Devolution Deals Work*, London: Institute for Government.

Rawlings, R. (2005), 'Law Making in a Virtual Parliament: The Welsh Experience', in R. Hazell and R. Rawlings (eds), *Devolution, Law Making and the Constitution*, 71–111, Exeter: Imprint Academic.

Rawlings, R. (2015), 'Riders on the Storm: Wales, the Union, and Territorial Constitutional Crisis', *Journal of Law and Society*, 42 (4): 471–98.

Requejo, F. (2005), *Multinational Federalism and Value Pluralism*, London: Routledge.

Rhodes, R.A.W. (1988), *Beyond Westminster and Whitehall: The Sub-Central Governments of Britain*, London: Routledge.

Rhodes, R.A.W. (1997), *Understanding Governance*, Buckingham: Open University Press.

Rhodes, R. (2001), 'Unitary States', in N. Smelser and P.E. Baltes (eds), *International Encyclopaedia of the Social and Behavioural Sciences*, 15968–71, Oxford: Pergamon.

Rhodes, R., Carmichael, P., McMillan, J. and Massey, A. (2003), *Decentralizing the Civil Service: From Unitary State to Differentiated Polity in the United Kingdom*, Buckingham: Open University Press.

Richard Commission (2004) *Report of the Commission on the Powers and Electoral Arrangements of the National Assembly for Wales*, SN/PC/3018, London House of Commons.

Rose, R. (1971), *Governing without Consensus*, Boston: Beacon Press.

Rowe, M. (2017), 'Does Brexit Spell the End for the Unified British Civil Service?', *Civil Service World*, 1 December. Available online: https://www.civilserviceworld.com/in-depth/article/does-brexit-spell-the-end-for-the-unified-british-civil-service (accessed 10 September 2020).

Roy, E. (2011), *The Barnett Formula and the Changing Face of Devolution Funding*, Cardiff: NAfW.

Royles, E. (2019), 'Charting a Course for Welsh International Relations', *Politics and Policy*, April 2019. Available online: https://www.iwa.wales/agenda/2019/04/charting-a-course-for-welsh-international-relations/

Rummery, K. (2016), 'Social Policy in a Devolved Scotland: Different, Fairer?', in D. McTavish (ed.), *Politics in Scotland*, Ch. 8, Edinburgh: Edinburgh University Press.

Ryan, C. (1999), 'Growing Apart', *Public Service Magazine*, May: 19.

Rycroft, P. and Barnes, R. (2015), 'Devolution and You', at Civil Service Live 2015, Manchester. Available online: https://civilservice.blog.gov.uk/2015/07/29/devolution-and-you/ (accessed 10 September 2020).

Rycroft, P. and Barnes, R. (2016), 'Getting to Grips with the Devolution Challenge', *Civil Service Blog*, 2 May. Available online: https://civilservice.blog.gov.uk/2016/02/05/getting-to-grips-with-the-devolution-challenge/ (accessed 10 September 2020).

Sandford, M. (2015), *Scotland Bill 2015–16 Briefing Paper 7205*, London: House of Commons Library.

Sandford, M. and Hetherington, P. (2005), 'The Regions at the Crossroads: The Future for Sub-National Government in England', in A. Trench (ed.), *The Dynamics of Devolution: The State of the Nations 2005*, 91–113. Exeter: Imprint Academic.Sandfr

Sandry, A. (2011), *Plaid Cymru: An Ideological Analysis*, Cardiff: Welsh Academic Press.

Sargeant, J., Atkins, G. and Benoit, G. (2020), *Co-ordination and Divergence: Devolution and Coronavirus*, London: Institute for Government.

Sargeant, J. and Jack, M. (2021), *The United Kingdom Internal Market Act 2020*, London Institute for Government. Available online: https://www.instituteforgovernment.org.uk/sites/default/files/publications/uk-internal-market.pdf (accessed 1 July 2021).

Scotfact (2018), *Key Facts 2018*. Available online: www.scotfact.com/keyfacts (accessed 1 July 2021).

Scotland Office (2009), *Scotland's Future in the United Kingdom*, Cm 7738, London: The Stationery Office.

Scotland Office (2010), *Strengthening Scotland's Future*, Cm 7973, London: The Stationery Office.

Scott, G. and Mooney, G. (2009), 'Poverty and Social Justice in the Devolved Scotland: Neoliberalism Meets Social Democracy', *Social Policy & Society*, 9: 379–89.

Scottish Affairs Committee (2015), *The Implementation of the Smith Agreement, HC 835*, London: House of Commons.

Scottish Affairs Committee (2019), *The Relationship Between the UK and the Scottish Government, HC 1586*. Available online: https://publications.parliament.uk/pa/cm201719/cmselect/cmscotaf/2532/253202.htm (accessed 25 September 2021).

Scottish Executive (2007), *Choosing Scotland's Future: A National Conversation*, Edinburgh: Scottish Executive.

Scottish Government (2008), *Equally Well: Report of the Ministerial Task Force on Health Inequalities*, Edinburgh: Scottish Government.

Scottish Government (2009), *Your Scotland, Your Voice: A National Conversation*, Edinburgh: Scottish Government.

Scottish Government (2016), *Global Scotland: Trade and Investment 2016–21*. Available online: https://www.gov.scot/publications/global-scotland-scotlands-trade-investment-strategy-2016-2021/ (accessed 1 July 2021).

Scottish Government (2018) *Scottish Income Tax: 2019–2020*. Available online: https://www.gov.scot/publications/scottish-income-tax-2019-2020/ (accessed 1 July 2021).

Scottish Government (2021a), *A Fairer, Greener Scotland: The Programme for Government for 2021 to 2026*. Available online: https://www.gov.scot/publications/fairer-greener-scotland-programme-government-2021-22/ (accessed 10 February 2022).

Scottish Government (2021b), *The Brexit Referendum 5 Years On. Summary of Impact to Date*. Available online: https://www.gov.scot/binaries/content/documents/govscot/publications/research-and-analysis/2021/06/brexit-vote-5-years-know-far/documents/brexit-referendum-5-years-summary-impacts-date-information-note-scottish-government/brexit-referendum-5-years-summary-impacts-date-information-note-scottish-government/govscot%3Adocument/brexit-referendum-5-years-summary-impacts-date-information-note-scottish-government.pdf (accessed 25 September 2021).

Scottish Government (2021c), *After Brexit: The UK Internal Market Act and Devolution*, Edinburgh: Constitution and Cabinet Directorate.

Scottish Government (2021d), *The Brexit Vote, 5 Years On – What Do We Know So Far?* Available online: https://www.gov.scot/publications/brexit-vote-5-years-know-far/ (accessed 1 July 2021).

Scottish Parliament (2015), *The Impact of EU Membership In Scotland*, Scottish Parliament Information Service. Available online: https://archive2021.parliament.scot/S4_EuropeanandExternalRelationsCommittee/General%20Documents/SB_15-71_The_impact_of_EU_membership_in_Scotland.pdf (accessed 1 July 2021).

Scottish Parliament (2017), *Commission on Parliamentary Reform*. Available online: www.parliamentaryreform.scot (accessed 25 September 2021).

Scottish Parliament (2019), *Legislative and Public Bodies Act, Consent Memorandums and Motions Statistics*. Available online: www.parliament.scot/parliamentarybusiness/Bills/19023.aspx (accessed 25 September 2021).

Scottish Parliament, Equality and Human Rights Committee (2018), Getting Rights Right, Human Rights and the Scottish Parliament. Available online: https://digitalpublications.parliament.scot/Committees/Report/EHRiC/2018/11/26/Getting-Rights-Right–Human-Rights-and-the-Scottish-Parliament-3 (accessed 1 July 2021).

Scottish Parliament Health and Sport Committee (2019), https://archive2021.
parliament.scot/parliamentarybusiness/currentcommittees/105069.aspx
(accessed 15 February 2020).

Scottish Parliament Information Centre (2021), *Consent Processes in the Scottish Parliament*. Available online: https://www.parliament.scot/-/media/files/spice/
factsheets/parliamentary-business/consent-processes-in-the-scottish-parliament-
14-april-2021.pdf (accessed 10 February 2022).

Scottish Parliament Public Petitions Committee (2021a), *Session 5 Legacy Report*.
Available online: https://digitalpublications.parliament.scot/Committees/
Report/PPC/2021/3/25/8f0da8f6-422c-41c7-bc0c-f7272f4ab73c (accessed
10 February 2022).

Scottish Parliament Public Petitions Committee (2021b), *Annual Report 2020–
2021*. Available online: https://digitalpublications.parliament.scot/Committees/
Report/PPC/2021/3/25/102b34db-b469-4277-b9c9-7381ab47b68c (accessed
10 February 2020).

Seely, A. (2012), *Devolution of Tax Powers to the Scottish Parliament, SNO 5984*,
London: House of Commons Library.

Seely, A. (2018) *Corporation Tax in Northern Ireland*, Research Briefing, London:
House of Commons Library.

Seely, A. and Keep, M. (2016), *Devolution of Financial Powers to the Scottish
Parliament: Recent Developments*, Briefing Paper, London: House of Commons
Library.

Select Committee on the Constitution (2015), *Scotland Bill, HL Paper 59*, London:
House of Lords.

Senedd Research (2021), *Legislative Consent in the Sixth Senedd: The Story So Far*,
Cardiff: Welsh Parliament.

Senedd Wales (2020), *Internal Market Bill Imposes UK Will on Wales*. Available
online: https://senedd.wales/senedd-now/news/internal-market-bill-imposes-uk-
government-s-will-on-wales-and-favours-the-interests-of-england/

Senedd Wales (2022), *The Shared Prosperity and Levelling-up Funds. What's the
Latest?* Available online: https://research.senedd.wales/research-articles/the-
shared-prosperity-and-levelling-up-funds-what-s-the-latest/

Senedd Wales (Petitions Committee) (2021), *Fifth Senedd Legacy Report*. Available
online: https://senedd.wales/media/eccmngfv/cr-ld14319-e.pdf (accessed
10 February 2022).

Shaw, E. (2019), 'The Labour Party since Devolution', *Centre on
Constitutional Change blog*, 29 October. Available online: https://www.
centreonconstitutionalchange.ac.uk/news-and-opinion/labour-party-devolution
(accessed 25 September 2021).

Shaw, J. and MacKinnon, D. (2011), 'Moving On with Filling In? Some Thoughts
on State Restructuring after Devolution', *Area*, 43 (1): 23–30.

Shortridge, J. (2009), 'Debate: Ten Years of Devolution', *Public Money and
Management*, 29 (3): 142–3.

Shortridge, J. (2010), 'New Development: The Evolution of Welsh Devolution',
Public Money and Management, 30 (2): 87–90.

Simpkins, F. (2018), 'Challenging Theresa May's Vision of Brexit Britain: Ruth
Davidson and the 2017 UK General Election', *Observatoire de la société
britannique*, 2 (1): 141–60.

Simpson, M. (2017), 'The Social Union after the Coalition: Devolution Divergence and Convergence', *Journal of Social Policy*, 46 (2): 251–68.

Simpson, M., McKeever, G. and Gray, A.M. (2017), *Social Security Systems Based on Dignity and Respect*, Equality and Human Rights Commission Scotland. Available online: https://www.equalityhumanrights.com/sites/default/files/social_security_systems_based_on_dignity_and_respect.pdf (accessed 25 September 2021).

Sinclair, D. (1997), 'Local Government and a Scottish Parliament', *Scottish Affairs*, 19: 14–21.

Smith, D. and Wistrich, E. (2014), *Devolution and Localism in England*, Farnham: Ashgate.

Smith, K. and Hellowell, M. (2012), Beyond Rhetorical Differences: A Cohesive Account of Post-devolution Developments in UK Health Policy', *Social Policy and Administration*, 46 (2): 178–98.

Smith, L. (2014), *Report of the Smith Commission for Further Devolution of Powers to the Scottish Parliament*. Available online: https://www.smith-commission.scot/wp-content/uploads/2014/11/The_Smith_Commission_Report-1.pdf (accessed 20 June 2015).

Smyth, C. (2016) Stormont's Petition of Concern Used 115 Times in Five Years, *The Detail*, 29 September. Available online: https://www.thedetail.tv/articles/stormont-s-petition-of-concern-used-115-times-in-five-years (accessed 1 July 2021).

Somerville, S. MSP (2019), 'Devolution of Benefits', Ministerial Statement, 28 February. Edinburgh: Scottish Government.

Stewart, J. (2004), *Taking Stock: Scottish Social Welfare After Devolution*, Bristol: Policy Press.

Stoker, G. (1999), *The New Management of British Local Governance*, Basingstoke: Macmillan.

Stoker, G. (2004), *Transforming Local Governance from Thatcherism to New Labour*, Basingstoke: Palgrave Macmillan.

Stoker, G. and Wilson, D. (eds) (2004), *British Local Government into the 21st Century*, Basingstoke: Palgrave.

Sullivan, W. (2019), 'Is There Proportional Representation in Scotland?', *Electoral Reform Society blog*, 5 September. Available online: https://www.electoral-reform.org.uk/is-there-proportional-representation-in-scotland/ (accessed 25 September 2021).

Tabor, D. and Stockley, L. (2018), 'Personal Well-being in the UK: January to December 2017', Office for National Statistics. Available online: https://www.ons.gov.uk/peoplepopulationandcommunity/wellbeing/bulletins/measuringnationalwellbeing/januarytodecember2017 (accessed 25 September 2021).

Taylor-Collins, E. and Bristow, D. (2020), *Administering Social Security in Wales: Evidence on Potential Reforms*, Cardiff: Wales Centre for Public Policy.

Tetlow, G. and Cheung, A. (2021), *The Fiscal Position of Scotland, Wales and Northern Ireland*, London: Institute for Government.

Thomas, A. (2011a), *The Road to the Independent Commission on Devolution in Wales*, Research Paper 11/066, Cardiff: National Assembly for Wales.

Thomas, A. (2011b), *The Silk Commission, National Assembly for Wales, Research Paper 11/066*, Cardiff: National Assembly for Wales.

Thomas, A. and Roberts, O. (2013), *Assembly Committee Structures, Research Paper*, Cardiff: National Assembly for Wales.

Tierney, S. (2009), 'Federalism in a Unitary State: A Paradox too Far', *Regional and Federal Studies*, 19 (2): 237–53.

Timmons, N. (2013), *The Four UK Health Systems*, London: The King's Fund.

Tomaney, J. (2000), 'The Regional Governance of England', in R. Hazell (ed.), *The State and the Nations, The First Year of Devolution in the United Kingdom*, 117–44, Exeter: Imprint Academic.

Tonge, J. (2005), *The New Northern Irish Politics*, Basingstoke: Palgrave Macmillan.

Tonge, J. (2017), 'Supplying Confidence or Trouble the Deal between the DUP and the Conservative Party', *The Political Quarterly*, 88 (3): 412–16.

Tonge, J. (2020), 'Beyond Unionism versus Nationalism: The Rise of the Alliance Party in Northern Ireland', *The Political Quarterly*, 91 (2): 461–6.

Tonge, J. and Evans, J. (2020), 'Northern Ireland: From the Centre to the Margins', *Parliamentary Affairs*, 73 (Suppl. 1): 172–88.

Tonge, J., Braniff, M., Hennessey, T., McAuley, J.W. and Whiting, S. (2014), *The Democratic Unionist Party: From Protest to Power*, Oxford: Oxford University Press.

Tonge, J. (2022), 'Voting into Void? The 2022 Northern Ireland Assembly Election', *The Political Quarterly*, 93 (3): 523–9.

Torrance, D. (2018), *A Process, Not an Event: Devolution in Wales 1998–2018*, Briefing Paper No. 08318, London: House of Commons Library.

Torrance, D. (2020), *Internal Market Bill? Reactions from Scottish and Welsh Governments*, London: House of Commons Library.

Torrance, D. (2022), *Intergovernmental Relations in the United Kingdom*, Research Briefing, London: House of Commons Library.

Torrance, D. and Evans, A. (2019), 'The Territorial Select Committees, 40 Years On', *Parliamentary Affairs*, 72: 860–78.

Torrance, D. and Johnson, J. (2021), *Northern Ireland Elections and Petitions of Concern 2020–21*, London: House of Commons Library.

Trench, A. (2015), 'Devolution: The Basics', *Devolution Matters blog*, February. Available online: https://devolutionmatters.wordpress.com/devolution-the-basics/ (accessed 25 September 2021).

UK Government (2019), *Devolution: Guidance for Civil Servants*. Available online: https://www.gov.uk/government/publications/devolution-guidance-for-civil-servants/devolution-guidance-for-civil-servants (accessed 10 September 2020).

UK Government (2021), *UK Government's Plan for Wales 2021*. Available online: https://www.gov.uk/government/publications/uk-governments-plan-for-wales-2021 (accessed 1 July 2021).

UK Government (2022), *Income Tax in Wales*. Available online: https://www.gov.uk/welsh-income-tax (accessed 1 August 2022).

UK Government /Irish Government ((1998), *The Agreement*, London and Belfast: UK and Irish Government.

UK Government (Scottish Government) (2016), *The Agreement between the Scottish Government and the United Kingdom (2016)*. Available online: https://www.gov.uk/government/publications/the-agreement-between-the-scottish-government-and-the-united-kingdom-government-on-the-scottish-governments-fiscal-framework (accessed 25 September 2021).

Wade, S. (2016), *Rules and Arrangements Governing All-Party Groups in the Northern Ireland Assembly and other UK Parliaments/Assemblies, Briefing Paper 16/17, NIAR 362–16*, Belfast: Northern Ireland Assembly.

Wales Audit Office (2015), *A Picture of Public Services.* Available online: https://cardiff.moderngov.co.uk/documents/s9893/6.1d%20App%201%20-%20WAO%20Picture%20of%20Public%20Services.pdf (accessed 1 July 2021).

Wales Office (2005), *Better Governance for Wales, Cm 6582*, Norwich: The Stationery Office.

Wales Office/UK Government (2012), *UK Government's Evidence to the Commission on Devolution in Wales*, Part II, Cardiff: Cardiff University.

Wallace, J. (2019), *Wellbeing and Devolution: Reframing the Role of Government in Scotland, Wales and Northern Ireland*, Basingstoke: Palgrave Macmillan.

Wane, K., Berry, K., Kidner, C. and Georghiou, N. (2016), *New Social Security Powers, Scottish Parliament Information Centre 16/45*, Edinburgh: Scottish Parliament.

Ward, M. (2020), *City Deals, Briefing Paper*, No 715C, London: House of Commons Library.

Welsh Affairs Committee (2010), *Cross Border Provision of Public Services in Wales, Follow-up Government Response HC419*, SSSLondon: House of Commons.

Welsh Affairs Committee (2016), *Welsh Affairs Committee 1st Special Report. Pre-Legislative Scrutiny of the Draft Wales Bill: Government Response to the Committee's 1st Report of Session 2015–16*, Cardiff.

Welsh Affairs Committee (2019), *Devolution of Air Passenger Duty to Wales: Government Response to the Committee's Fifth Report, HC 2634*, London: House of Commons.

Welsh Agenda (2021), *Will the Internal Market Act Block Wales' Ability to Make its Own Decisions?* Cardiff: Institute of Welsh Affairs.

Welsh Assembly Government (2007), *Communities First Guidance 2007*, Cardiff: Welsh Assembly Government.

Welsh Assembly Government (2014), *White Paper – Reforming Local Government*, Cardiff: Welsh Assembly Government.

Wales Audit Office (2015), *A Picture of Public Services.* Cardiff. Available online: https://cardiff.moderngov.co.uk/documents/s9893/6.1d%20App%201%20-%20WAO%20Picture%20of%20Public%20Services.pdf (accessed 1 July 2021).

Welsh Governance Centre (2017), *Fair Funding for Taxing Times? Assessing the Fiscal Framework Agreement*, Cardiff: Cardiff University.

Welsh Government (2012), *International Affairs: Public Diplomacy Issues and International Relationships*, Cardiff: Welsh Government.

Welsh Government (2014), *Commission on Public Service Governance and Delivery Summary Report*, Cardiff: Welsh Government (January). Available online: https://gov.wales/sites/default/files/publications/2019-01/commission-public-service-governance-delivery-summary-report.pdf (accessed 10 September 2020).

Welsh Government (2016), *Government and Laws in Wales Draft Bill, Explanatory Summary*, Cardiff: Government of Wales.

Welsh Government (2017a), 'Formal Dispute Resolution Underway Over Fair Share of Barnett Consequentials from UK Government's DUP Deal'. Available online: https://gov.wales/formal-dispute-resolution-process-underway-over-fair-share-barnett-consequentials-uk-governments (accessed 1 July 2021).

Welsh Government (2017b), 'Joint Minister from First Minster of Wales and Scotland in Reaction to the EU Withdrawal Bill'. Available online: https://gov.wales/joint-statement-first-ministers-wales-and-scotland-reaction-eu-withdrawal-bill (accessed 1 July 2021).

Welsh Government (2019), *Terms of Reference: Joint Executive Committee*. Available online: https://gov.wales/workforce-partnership-council-joint-executive-committee/terms-of-reference (accessed 25 September 2021).

Welsh Government (2021a), *Reforming our Union: Shared Governance in the UK*. June. Available online: https://gov.wales/reforming-our-union-shared-governance-in-the-uk-2nd-edition (accessed 1 July 2021).

Welsh Government (2021b), *Draft Budget 2022–2023*. Available online: https://gov.wales/draft-budget-2022-2023

Welsh Government (2021c), *Wales Act 2014*, part 2 (Finance) Annual Report 2021, Cardiff: Welsh Government.

Welsh Government (2021d), Ministers Call for an End to Bypassing of Devolved Governments. Available online: https://gov.wales/ministers-call-for-an-end-to-bypassing-of-devolved-governments

Welsh Government Committee (2016), *Pre-legislative Scrutiny of the Draft Wales Bill, Cm 9144*, London: House of Commons.

Whiting, M. (2018), 'Moderation without Change: The Strategic Transformation of Sinn Féin and the IRA in Northern Ireland', *Government and Opposition*, 53(2): 288–311.

Wilson, D. (2005), 'The United Kingdom', in B. Denters and L.E. Rose (eds), *Comparing Local Governance*, 155–73, Basingstoke: Palgrave.

Wilson, D. and Game, C. (2011), *Local Government in the United Kingdom*, 5th ed., Basingstoke: Palgrave Macmillan.

Wollmann, H. (2012), 'Local Government Reforms in (Seven) European Countries: Between Convergent and Divergent, Conflicting and Complementary Developments', *Local Government*, 38 (1): 41–70.

Woodhouse, J. (2020), *Alcohol: Minimum Pricing, Briefing Paper*, House of Commons Library. Available online: https://commonslibrary.parliament.uk/research-briefings/sn05021/ (accessed 25 September 2021).

Wyn Jones, R. and Hazell, R. (2015), *Delivering a Reserved Power Model of Devolution for Wales*, Cardiff: Welsh Governance Centre at Cardiff University.

Wyn Jones, R. and Royles, E. (2012), 'Wales in the World. Intergovernmental Relations and Sub-State Diplomacy', *The British Journal of Politics and International Relations*, 14 (2): 250–69.

Wyn Jones, R. and Scully, R. (2008), 'Welsh Devolution: The End of the Beginning, and the Beginning of …?', in A. Trench (ed.), *The State of the Nations*, 57–85, Exeter: Imprint Academic.

Wyn Jones, R. and Scully, R. (2012), *Wales Says Yes. Devolution and the 2011 Welsh Referendum*. Cardiff: University of Wales.

Zolle, N. (2016), *Implications of Brexit on Public Services in Wales*, Cardiff: Wales Public Services. Available online: http://sites.cardiff.ac.uk/walespublicservices2025/files/2016/05/Brexit-WPS-2025-Final.pdf (accessed 1 July 2021).

INDEX